KMH

EMPOWERMENT DAILY DEVOTIONAL

By

Gilbert Samba/Kingdom Media House

ISBN (Paperback): 978-164633436-0

Published by:

KINGDOM MEDIA HOUSE

For further information, address to:

KINGDOM MEDIA HOUSE

Buea, South West Region, Cameroon

Tel?WhatsApp: +8613885060470/+237679709707

Email: sebaskema@outlook.com

To order copies of this book, contact via social media at:
favorsamba@gmail.com
Tel./WhatsApp: +1 (301) 232-8092
On Facebook: https://www.facebook.com/evangelist.gilbert.3

Scripture quotations are from the Holy Bible and indicated within the text.

Cover Design by: POSTERITY DESIGN, BUEA CMR, +237674082871

CONTENT

DEDICATION

This book is dedicated first and foremost to the Holy Spirit who inspired me with the truths therein for the last two years.

To my wife and kids for their constant support and encouragement throughout this tedious process.

I also want to dedicate this book to my mentor Rev. Nkwelle Godlove and my sons and daughters in the Lord who kept reminding me to put down these daily Facebook posts into a book form.

To my mother, brothers and sisters, in-laws, advisers, instructors, for their support and to TJC for providing me with study materials.

This book is equally dedicated to my godmother late Deaconess Takweni Christine and late Mrs. B. Antoinette, who always gave me good counsel and I know even now you are still praying for me standing with the cloud of witnesses.

RECOMMENDATIONS

I assure you who picked up a copy of this devotional that you will not be disappointed in the content. It is well written, with captivating topics that draw you in to soak in the body of educational material and sound biblically based advice. This devotional will leave most of us more informed; yet to some of us, it will be the deliverance you never knew you needed. I believe as you dwell in the pages of this book, the Lord will do a new work in your life and leave you better and more encouraged at the end of your reading.

The topics are diverse and also relevant to the challenges of this generation. The style is simple yet compelling as Evangelist Gilbert proclaims with boldness the Word of God to his readers and challenges them to rise from passivity and be as wise and noble as the Berean Christians who were not gullible but valued their gift of salvation enough to ensure that what they received from Apostle Paul was written in the Word of God by searching the scriptures for themselves (Acts 17:11).

This is concisely written but well measured to help you jumpstart your day as you soar through the year.

Gloria Ngwendson
First Lady, The Apostolic church
West Saint Paul, MN

The Christian faith is an ongoing process similar to an athlete running a race. We must prepare ourselves by learning to trust and obey the Lord without which we will not be able to face and overcome the obstacles of life which confront us daily. That is why I recommend this exceptional devotional by Evangelist Gilbert Samba. It will help you to start your day ready for any challenge or onslaught of our adversary the devil.

Rev. Innocent Anye
Senior Pastor, The Apostolic Church USA Filed
Dallas Texas

Praise God and hello to everyone reading this divinely inspired timely devotionals. The Spirit of The Lord God Almighty in Evangelist Gilbert

Samba has led him to put on paper a life giving series of daily devotionals that will change the life of any person. While there are numerous ways that reading the Bible brings us closer to God and benefits us daily, here is an opportunity through the great work in this devotional to keep you and I in the very secret place of the Most High, serving as a reminder to stay therein on a daily basis. In this devotionals you find topics like: CONSISTENCY IS THE SECRET OF ACHIEVERS, GOD HATES FLYMSY EXCUSES. Praise God indeed this ministers to me deeply. Get this devotional, you get a seasoned prophetic word for each day of the year prepared and ready for you with respect to your busy schedule.

Rev. John Sama M.Div.
Senior Pastor Glorious Times Ministries
Maryland USA

These revelation and expository gospel truths and guides are the best way to start a day. Be it a minister challenged by what the day holds for him/her and their flock, or a young Christian forging their way through the new life they are called into, you will find life-changing encouragement, edification, and if need be, a rebuke from every one of these daily detailed, yet easy to read devotionals. The combination of questions and instructional nuggets are uplifting spiritual guides to building Christian character beyond the walls of the church into the daily activities in the community and the crowd of onlookers in the world. This inspiring and encouraging devotional explains the importance of living with love, how to set the tone for the day, and how to resist the temptation of giving-up. The reader is encouraged to read the daily Scripture as they search for hopeful spiritual truths, strength, comfort, and power with a little lesson of how the verse applies to their daily life. They are inspirational compilations written as if Jesus is speaking to you as He accompanies you through even the most challenging of your day, yet still be a blessing to those you come in contact with.

Jeannette Awasum
First Lady Omega Gospel Mission
Maryland USA

“These are very inspiring and lively words that give believers the balanced truth from the ancient landmarks of the Scriptures. So much is happening in Christianity today that the Evangelist has addressed so well with some red-hot uncompromising gospel truth. A skillful combination of motivation, truth, and wisdom is well displayed here for a victorious daily walk with Jesus. The illustrations and examples communicated here are real day-to-day scenarios every Christian must understand how to deal with. This is a life transforming material."

Samuel G. Musong PhD.

In every generation, God choses from the called, a few voices to preserve and improve the inheritance of that generation. This Daily Devotional is a package in time to empower this generation and give Hope to the next generation.

Apostle Mark Fundoh
Senior Pastor, GLIC
President, TACNAM.

INTRODUCTION

If you will pay attention to the times we are living in, then you will agree with me that we are living in the last days. This is the epoch which Paul told Timothy will come when men will not put up with sound doctrine but will gather for themselves teachers to say what their itching ears want to hear (2 Tim 4:3). The church of God ought to be a place for sound doctrine and divine direction for life. Sadly enough, it is not the case in our time. There is so much pollution and falsehood that leaves those with a genuine hunger for God starving for the pure milk of God's Word.

It is in this light that Empowerment Daily Devotional was born. The book is a compilation of daily post on my Facebook page for a period of two years. It aimed at shining the light of God's Word and exposing the lies of the devil. The darkness of deception threatens the light of God's truth and unless we boldly proclaim His message without fear or compromise, we will see the enemy devour God's precious people. Personal knowledge of God's Word is the only way the present day believer can thrive in these last days. Like the Bereans, you must make a conscious and deliberate effort to study God's Word for yourself. This is not the time when you solely depend on the preacher on Sunday morning to feed you with enough Word to carry you through the week till you meet again the next Sunday.

This devotional, being intercessory in nature will compel you to talk to God daily and intercede for others through its daily prayer points. The expository nature of the passages will give you in-depth knowledge into God's Word. "The word of God is like a lion, when it is being attacked, just loose the lion and let it fight for itself." (Christopher Ash). That is exactly the style in these devotionals: the Word is allowed to speak for itself. Before you step out each day, empower yourself and be fully armed with truth that cannot be compromised. Failure to do this will make us vulnerable in the hands of the devil and he will strike us down with the arrows of falsehood.

Findings have revealed that what kills most people during a crash is not even the impact of the accident; it is their fear. Most people die as a result of shock even the actual impact occurs. Fear will kill you even before what you fear actually reaches you. A closer look at humanity will tell you that fear lingers around every person rich or poor, young or old, black or white. Job in his wealth and affluence had a shadow of fear following him everywhere he went. He was rich so he feared to lose his wealth. He had children who were healthy and doing well but he feared he might one day lose those kids to some tragic occurrence. Though Job shared these thoughts with no one, they lived with him every second of his life until the day that what he feared actually came upon him.

What the enemy really wants to instill in you is the spirit of fear. He knows that a person controlled by fear cannot achieve much in life. On the other hand, God wants you to conquer fear and that's why the words "fear not" appears about 365 times in the bible. God wants you to live up to the fullness of your potentials and the only that is possible is by you conquering your fear. Instead of being afraid of a situation, God wants you to pray about it. When the time came in the life of Jesus when the fear of death gripped him, instead of bowing to fear and escaping the cross, Jesus went to God in prayer and was strengthened.

If you let fear get into you because of that medical report, what you fear may come your way. If you fear that you might fail in that exam, then what you fear may come your way. If you fear you may never get married, get a job or get that breakthrough, then what you fear may come upon you.

Job had allowed fear to grow in him and in the end Bible records Job saying "what I feared has come upon me." Job 3:25. Fear is a spirit and you must rebuke that spirit out of your life. Job 3:25. "What I feared has come upon me; what I dreaded has happened to me."

PRAYER

Heavenly Father, I thank you for this new year you have granted me the privilege to see and I know that there are many things you want me to accomplish this year, therefore Lord I pray that nothing, not even fear will stop me from accomplishing those things in Jesus name, Amen.

Father, I declare that any spirit of fear living in me, from today I rebuke you and I command you to take your hands off my life and my family. We conquer every fear in Jesus' name, Amen.

NOTES ....

....

....

....

Jesus gives the following parable teaching us that there is no extend God's love will not go to save even a single soul. *"Or suppose a woman has ten silver coins and loses one. Does she not light a lamp, sweep the house and search carefully until she finds it? And when she finds it, she calls her friends and neighbors together and says, 'Rejoice with me; I have found my lost coin.' In the same way, I tell you, there is rejoicing in the presence of the angels of God over one sinner who repents." Luke 15: 8-10.*

The love of God towards us is so deep that heaven will invest all her resources to see that one single soul is saved. If God had any option other than Jesus by which He could redeem the world back to Himself, He would have used it. But God sent his only begotten son to come and die in our place to pay the penalty for our sins so that you and I can stand before God blameless. Jesus in the above verses makes us know that heaven cares so much about you as an individual. God wants you to enjoy the beauty of His presence when He fathers you. The heart of God is "broken" so to say when one of His children turns their back on Him. God is so displeased that He will do everything to get you back to himself. And when he does, he throws a party in heaven to celebrate your return to the Lord.

As you begin this year, don't let anyone make you feel that your sins are too many for God to care about you. It is time you stop walking farther away from God and start walking back to God because He has been coming after. Heaven wants to rejoice today because of your new commitment to walk with God and the determination to pick up from where you had walked away.

PRAYER

Dear Heavenly Father, I come to you this asking that you will forgive me for the moments I wondered away from you. Thank you, Lord, for not giving up on me.
Lord, I receive this day the grace to be fully committed to you and walk with you every single day of my life. I come against any form of distraction that may want to take me away from you in Jesus' name. Amen.

NOTES ....

....

....

....

....

....

....

....

....

....

In the early days when Jesus started His ministry, He began to call men to follow Him. A few left everything they were doing and followed Jesus. But others gave so many reasons why they could not follow him. One said he was willing to come but needed to go bury his father first. Another said he needed to go wave his family good-bye. Looking at the above excuses, one can agree with them that they needed to go carry out those functions. But our Lord Jesus responded differently. His response to both can be summarized to mean just one thing: "I don't delight in flimsy excuses."

The truth is, there WILL ALWAYS BE A REASON WHY you CANNOT carry out a task at a given time. And in as much as your excuses may sound convincing, in God's sight it is considered flimsy because when you truly have the willingness to do it, there will always be a way to do it. It is important to keep your job, but that's not enough reason to take you away from God. It is important to attend to the needs of your kids, but that should not sway you from God. It's important to earn good grades in school, but you must create time to fellowship with God.

Luke 9:59-62

"He said to another man, "Follow me." But the man replied, "Lord, first let me go and bury my father." Jesus said to him, "Let the dead bury their own dead, but you go and proclaim the kingdom of God." Still another said, "I will follow you, Lord; but first let me go back and say good-bye to my family." Jesus replied, "No one who puts his hand to the plow and looks back is fit for service in the kingdom of God."

PRAYER

Lord, I come to you this day repenting of all the many excuses I have given for not being able to do Your work when You needed me to. I ask that You please forgive me, Lord. I receive the grace to take prompt action when to do whatever You ask me to do, in Jesus' name, amen.

NOTES ....

Starting a project is something everyone can do, but maintaining that project till finish is reserved for only a few. Excitement is often what pushes people to take a new challenge but before long, that excitement dies down and they abandon the challenge. At the start of the year, people make a lot of New Year resolutions. Some decide to sign up to go the gym thrice a week; others decide they will read through the entire Bible that year. But before long they start pulling back from those commitments. The reason is simply that their excitement has died down.

People who stay consistent are driven by passion and have a strong determination to see their dreams come true. Unless you are driven by passion and strong will power, you will never achieve anything meaningful in this life. The Bible records that Jesus made it a HABIT to always go out and pray DAILY on Mt. Olives. He also made it a lifestyle to go out and pray early in the morning before dawn. On Paul's part, it was HIS CUSTOM to go to the synagogue and teach the Word.

CONSISTENCY is not something you acquire overnight; it takes a conscious and deliberate effort on your part. You have to cultivate it and it becomes your habit. You will need to make sacrifices, go through discomfort and inconveniences if you want to attain CONSISTENCY. If you start a business and it seems not to be working keep pushing. CONSISTENCY is the SECRET of Achievers. If you start a fellowship and things seem tough, keep pushing, CONSISTENCY is the SECRET of Achievers. If you embark on reading through the Bible or studying a particular career or spending hours with the Lord, don't give up on the way, keep pushing: CONSISTENCY is the SECRET of Achievers. And before long, you will become accustomed to doing things that way.

Luke 22:39

Jesus went out as usual to the Mount of Olives, and his disciples followed him.

Acts 17:2

As was his custom, Paul went into the synagogue, and on three Sabbath days he reasoned with them from the Scriptures,

PRAYER

Father, I pray for the grace to be consistent in what I do. Lord, I ask that You will take away every discouragement that comes my way and causes me to give up every time I start a project, in Jesus' name, amen. I declare that from today, I will start achieving success in every area of my life, in Jesus' name, amen.

NOTES ....

....

....

The secret to a successful and stress-free ministry is to STAY IN YOUR LANE. Sometimes we wear ourselves out in ministry because we are trying to do everything. It is true that he who tries to do everything ends up doing nothing because he will be ineffective in all that he does. Even our Lord Jesus understood this principle very well. On His way to carry out an assignment, He was interrupted by a gentile woman who kept calling for His help. Jesus could have left where He was going and turned towards her direction but no: He STAYED IN HIS LANE. It took an extra effort for the woman to successfully get Jesus' attention.

A lot of us end up with stress in ministry because WE DO NOT KEEP TO OUR LANE. You must identify what is that unique assignment or group of people or location the Lord has sent you. As for Jesus, He knew He was sent ONLY TO THE LOST SHEEP OF ISRAEL. This took away much of the headache and heartache of trying to do everything and trying to go everywhere. It is a good thing to have a megachurch, but it may not be your assignment. Yours may be to disciple a few persons who will, in turn, build mega Churches: so stay on your lane. Healing ministry is great, but it may not be your lane. Yours may be teaching men to stick to the Healer even when healing doesn't show up. So stay in your lane. At the end of the day, we will be rewarded according to how well we stayed focused and not by how much we accomplished because some accomplishments are for self and not for the Lord.

Matthew 15:24

He answered, "I was sent only to the lost sheep of Israel."

PRAYER

Father, I commit Your servants into Your hands this day that You will help them to remain in the unique assignment You have given them. Lord, may You take away every spirit of competition and peer pressure around Your servants and help them to always remember that their reward will be based on how well they did and not on how much they did. Heavenly Father, may You also help me not to compare myself with others in all that I do, but that I will stay focused on what You have for me, in Jesus' name, amen.

NOTES ....

....

....

....

....

Jesus tells the story of a man who had two sons and he sent both of them to carry out a task for him. The first son boldly said he will not do it but later changed his mind and did it. Then the second son said He will do it but did not go. In the end, who do you think carried out the task? The one who said I will, but did not go or the one who said I won't, but later went? Of course, the latter.

We can clearly see this story playing out in our daily lives today. When the first son told the father that HE WILL NOT do the job, the father must have walked away concluding that this is a BAD CHILD. Then when he approached the second son and he responded that he will do it, the father must have showered praises on him; only to come back in the end and find out that, THE ONE HE CALLED BAD WAS ACTUALLY THE ANGEL and vice versa.

We must never rush into conclusions JUST BY HEARING what people tell us. As a Pastor or leader in any capacity, always go beyond what your members or workers told you. Do a little digging and verify to be sure that it is actually the way it was said. Because, TALK IS CHEAP and MANY CAN AFFORD it, but only real people accompany talk with ACTION.

Matthew 21:28-31

"What do you think? There was a man who had two sons. He went to the first and said, 'Son, go and work today in the vineyard.' "'I will not,' he answered, but later he changed his mind and went. "Then the father went to the other son and said the same thing. He answered, 'I will, sir,' but he did not go. "Which of the two did what his father wanted?" "The first," they answered. Jesus said to them, "I tell you the truth, the tax collectors and the prostitutes are entering the kingdom of God ahead of you.

PRAYER

Father, may you open our eyes to see people beyond their words. Lord, help me not to be a "man-pleaser" by saying things and making promises I cannot keep, but be someone that fears and honors You, in Jesus' name, amen.

NOTES ....

....

....

....

....

....

WEEK 01 | WISDOM NUGGET

STUDY THE WORD

Did you know that when you sit down with the Word, the world will stand up for you? In 2 Timothy 2:15, Paul advises Timothy to study: "Study to show thyself approved unto God, a workman that needs not to be ashamed, rightly dividing the word of truth.

PRAYER

✓ Father even as we begin this New Year, grant us the grace to sit down and study your word.

✓ Create in us a hunger for Your Word on a daily basis in Jesus name. Amen.

NOTES

....

....

....

....

....

....

....

....

....

....

....

All the people came together and decided to build a city with a tower whose top reaches heaven. Their aim was to make a name for themselves. They never bothered to inquire if God approved of that project. All building materials were acquired and men went to work. The project progressed at the speed of light and before long, the building had gone more than thirty stories high. In the eyes of everyone, this was a clear sign that God was with them. Well, that assumption was quickly corrected when the LORD Himself descended from heaven and put an end to the work.

Servant of God, just because people are flooding into your Church and the ministry is growing doesn't mean God is in it. If the foundation was not built on Christ, then it is only a matter of time and all that work will come crashing down. And just because everyone is screaming "wow, this can only be God," means it is actually God. You must MAKE SURE you have SEALED A DEAL with the Lord concerning that project before you ever lay the foundation stone. Because what men may call PROGRESS may just be WASTED EFFORTS in God's sight.

Genesis 11:6-8

The LORD said, "If as one people speaking the same language they have begun to do this, then nothing they plan to do will be impossible for them. So the LORD scattered them from there over all the earth, and they stopped building the city.

PRAYER

Dear Father, help me to always inquire from You before I embark on any project. Heavenly Father, may I never stop listening to Your voice with regards to the assignment You have given me. Despite the praises of men, I will always inquire to know what You think, in Jesus' name, amen.

NOTES

An adult does not have a problem with falling as long as NO ONE SEES HIM. But the moment he knows that someone SAW HIM falling, he is covered with shame. Jesus did not disarm the devil in secret, he did so publicly. Paul tells us in Colossians that Jesus DISARMED principalities and powers. What that means is, He took away all their arms and left Satan's entire arsenal empty. BUT this is what makes it even more humiliating: HE MADE A PUBLIC SHOW of that victory. Jesus made sure the defeat of the enemy was public so that you can always remind the devil of that day when he was Publicly Disgraced. If no one knew about it, the devil may come back and act as nothing happened. But since it was MADE PUBLIC, he is covered in shame and SHOULD NEVER THREATEN ANYBODY because we are all AWARE OF WHAT HAPPENED TO HIM THAY DAY. So NEVER let Satan intimidate you again. He is a fallen man and a fallen man has no power.

Colossians 2:15

And having disarmed the powers and authorities, he made a public spectacle of them, triumphing over them by the cross.

PRAYER

Lord, I thank You for the victory You have given us in the cross. Lord, I arise to the consciousness that Satan has been disarmed and publicly disgraced. By this act, I will never be intimidated or deceived by the devil. I have overcome the enemy because he is powerless. Thank You, Jesus, in Jesus' name, amen.

NOTES ....

....

....

....

....

....

....

....

....

....

As a believer, how you handle a fallen person will produce one of three effects in that person:-It can cause the person to REMAIN IN THE 'MUD'- It can cause him to RISE UP AND FIGHT YOU- or it can cause the person to RISE UP AND EMBRACE YOU. After God revealed David's sin to Nathan, he could have gone to the palace to DISGRACE the king. He could have summoned David's cabinet or even assemble the entire population and right there before them, expose to all that David committed adultery with Bathsheba (Uriah's wife). But Nathan decided to take another approach (mind you, GOD DID NOT TELL NATHAN HOW TO PASS THE MESSAGE), by using a story in which David ENSNARED HIMSELF.

When you reason with a fallen man and make him see the gravity of his own sins, it produces CONVICTION. But when you come into people's fallen state to pass judgment and Disgrace them, they will Hate and FIGHT YOU. When Joseph who was engaged to Mary learned of Mary's mysterious pregnancy, the Bible says he planned to CALL OFF THE RELATIONSHIP SECRETLY because HE DID NOT WANT TO DISGRACE HER. No wonder the Bible calls him a Righteous man. If it were to be one of us, we would tell the world of her wickedness and how she has been cheating on us. Some of us would even go back to Mary's parents to PAYBACK EVERY DIME WE'VE SPENT On THEIR DAUGHTER. But not Joseph, he chose NOT TO DISGRACE HER.

While I do not support the act of 'covering' people's sin, I also have never seen anyone that was disgraced and that disgrace led to repentance. Let our goal not be to bring DISGRACE to the fallen one, but to get them to a STATE OF REPENTANCE.

2 Samuel 12:5, 9, 19.

David burned with anger against the man and said to Nathan, "As surely as the LORD lives, the man who did this deserves to die! Why did you despise the word of the LORD by doing what is evil in his eyes? You struck down Uriah the Hittite with the sword and took his wife to be your own. You killed him with the sword of the Ammonites. Because Joseph her husband was a righteous man and did not want to expose her to public disgrace, he had in mind to divorce her quietly.

PRAYER

Heavenly Father, help me to see people with the eyes of love and not the eyes of condemnation.

NOTES ....

....

It's amazing to hear the way some of us pray to our Heavenly Father. You hear things like; "I COMMAND the hand of God to be released into this situation." "I COMMAND heaven to answer you now by force." "I COMMAND the finger of God to move in this situation." This is so wrong because God is not your mate. He is not your child or your servant. He is your Lord and that means MASTER. So the next time you pray, REMEMBER who you are talking to.

The words Jesus chose while praying teach us a lot. He had a humble attitude whenever He approached God in prayer. He also had Compassion as the base of every prayer He made. No wonder He had such great results. You can't get God to answer you when you come to Him in pride and arrogance. You must be humble and have reverence for God and also have compassion for those you're praying for. However, I must make it clear that when it comes to casting out demons and rebuking ugly situations, that's when we can command. Jesus teaches us to COMMAND demons and not God.

John 11:41

"So they took away the stone. Then Jesus looked up and said, "Father, I THANK YOU that you have heard me."

Matthew 9:36.

"When he saw the crowds, he had compassion on them, because they were harassed and helpless, like sheep without a shepherd."

PRAYER

Heavenly Father, I come to You today asking that You forgive me of every moment I have come into Your presence with arrogance. Lord, forgive me for my ignorance, in Jesus' name, amen. Lord, from today I will come into Your presence in humility and reverence for You are the owner of my life. And with this I know that my prayers shall produce great results, in Jesus' name, amen.

NOTES ....

....

....

....

....

....

....

....

....

Prior to the visit of some brethren, Peter used to eat with the Gentiles but when these men were around, he drew back for fear of criticism that he being a Jew eats with gentiles. Then we see a young Paul, a young apostle, rebuking Peter right to his face in the midst of their followers and Peter humbly apologizes for his mistake. If that were to happen today, Peter will never want to have anything to do with Paul. These days we see believers keeping malice with one another over very INSIGNIFICANT things. WORST of all are men of God who cannot talk good of one another or even sit on the same table because they had some kind of disagreement.

Going by our behaviors, I sometimes wonder if we plan on going to SEPARATE HEAVENS because if not, how then do we plan to live in THE SAME HEAVEN with the brother you don't talk to. May these actions of Peter and Paul trigger a chance within us today to know that we can DISAGREE but in the end, we still AGREE.

Galatians 2:11-14.

"When Peter came to Antioch, I opposed him to his face, because he was clearly in the wrong. Before certain men came from James, he used to eat with the Gentiles. But when they arrived, he began to draw back and separate himself from the Gentiles because he was afraid of those who belonged to the circumcision group." When I saw that they were not acting in line with the truth of the gospel, I said to Peter in front of them all, "You are a Jew, yet you live like a Gentile and not like a Jew. How is it, then, that you force Gentiles to follow Jewish customs?

PRAYER

Dear Lord, I pray for the grace to receive correction and rebuke whenever I am wrong irrespective of who is giving the rebuke. Lord, I pray that You will give me a heart of love. Lord, I pray that You will take away every spirit of enmity within the church today, be it among the ministers or among the congregation, in Jesus' name, amen.

NOTES ....

The body of Christ seems to be losing sight of a key ingredient of our faith which is Love. Our demonstration of love these days is determined by our perception of the one to whom we are showing love. If they are wealthy or can add to our lives, we show them love and respect. But if they have nothing to offer, we treat them with disdain. Unfortunately, we find this attitude right in the Church. It should not be so. The Church is supposed to be a place where everyone is treated not based on the kind of car they drive or the kind of home they live in or the kind of job they have, but based on the fact that we are all brothers and sisters from the same heavenly Father. We must love and respect everyone the same. Let us give no place for discrimination. Instead, let perfect love be seen in our midst.

James 2:1-4

"My brothers, as believers in our glorious Lord Jesus Christ, don't show favoritism. Suppose a man comes into your meeting wearing a gold ring and fine clothes, and a poor man in shabby clothes also comes in. If you show special attention to the man wearing fine clothes and say, "Here's a good seat for you," but say to the poor man, "You stand there" or "Sit on the floor by my feet," have you not discriminated among yourselves and become judges with evil thoughts?"

PRAYER

Our Most loving Father, teach us to love one another even as You have loved us before the foundation of the earth and sent Your only begotten Son to die for us. Lord, may You take away every form of discrimination taking place in the Church and let perfect love reign amongst Your people in Jesus' name, amen.

NOTES ....

....

....

....

....

....

....

....

....

....

WEEK 02 | WISDOM NUGGET

MOVE ON

You cannot achieve the successes of tomorrow if you are still mourning the failures of yesterday. Today choose to get up, shake off the dust and pick up the broken pieces of your life and move on. God is on your side and that's all that matters. "What shall we then say to these things? If God be for us, who can be against us?" Roman 8:31.

PRAYER

✓ Father in the name of Jesus Christ, I receive the grace to overcome my ugly yesterday. I declare that the failures of my past will never hold me down, in Jesus' name. Amen.

NOTES

....

....

....

....

....

....

....

....

....

How on earth can you perform a Healing Miracle and just SLIP AWAY UNNOTICED? Don't you know that's an opportunity for your fame to spread abroad? Don't you realize this is the kind of news that goes viral and makes you popular? If that were to happen today, we would order the cameraman to come closer and zoom in; we would ask the congregation to scream and make some noise because of the miracle; we would grant a press conference to let the world know God is using us. But this was not the case with our Lord Jesus. He chose to remain UNNOTICED.

In John 2, Jesus told His mom, "My time has not come." Jesus clearly understands the DANGER of becoming popular when it is not yet God's time for you to be popular. Many have made a shipwreck of their ministry by seeking popularity outside of God's will. Many started well but their desire for FAME has left them more frustrated than they could ever imagine. It is not every miracle God works through you that must be announced. Some cases require that you SLIP AWAY and fall before your heavenly Father and say, "Daddy you just shocked me again; take all the glory."

John 5:13

The man who was healed had no idea who it was, for Jesus had slipped away into the crowd that was there.

PRAYER

Heavenly Father, take away every desire for fame within me and let me not be seen, but let Jesus be seen, in Jesus' name, amen.
Father, I pray that you will keep your servants humble even when you do great miracles through them, in Jesus' name, amen.

NOTES ....

....

....

....

....

....

....

....

....

....

Jesus has just multiplied bread and fish and everyone has eaten to their satisfaction and even left some BROKEN PIECES of bread and fish on the grass on which they sat. As the crowd walked away, instead of Jesus and His disciples to abandon the leftover and walk away too, Jesus asked His disciples to go around gathering those pieces together. They ended up carrying twelve baskets full of bread and fish. Remember that just a moment before, Jesus prayed and multiplied bread. So He could have easily walked away leaving the leftover behind hoping that when another need arises, He will simply pray again and get another miracle. But not so with Jesus because He understood two things: First, Just because God multiplied bread yesterday doesn't mean He will always do so today. So I might have to survive tomorrow on the crumbs of yesterday's multiplication. Second, Even though I have no need for these crumbs, they could serve some families that are in hunger and starvation. So, take it along.

Let nothing be wasted. Many of us today are EXPERT WASTERS. And this runs from the PULPIT down to the PEW. Go down to Pastor's houses and see how foodstuffs are rotting in their food store whilst they have Church members who go for days without food. Check the garbage bins of Christians and see how much food is WASTED daily. The food they could have called in neighbors or even Church members and fed. Check your closets and wardrobe; see how many clothes and shoes (especially ladies) are lying in there that you've not used for more than three months. And worst of all, you're thinking of trashing them. Why not call in a sister or brother and give him/her that dress or shoe. And for some of us, we spend for today and forget about tomorrow. Money enters your hands and you rush to buy that 'fine suit, shoe, handbag, a gown which you saw that person wore on TV, not minding your income level and what you will eat tomorrow. OUR GOD HATES WASTE and any believer who delights in wasting resources must repent.

Matthew 14:20

They all ate and were satisfied, and the disciples picked up twelve basketfuls of broken pieces that were leftover.

PRAYER

Lord, I come to You today asking that You forgive me for all the things I have wasted. Lord, I repent and from today, I will be faithful with the resources You put in my hands in Jesus' name. Lord, help Your children to start sharing with other people and not only think of themselves in Jesus' name, amen.

NOTES

Write down anything you no longer use and name some people or places you can take them to for donation. Write ....

As soon as Abraham heard the voice of God to offer his son Isaac as a sacrifice, he got up EARLY the following morning and embarked on his journey. Had he waited much longer before carrying out the instructions, doubt and unbelief would have set in.

The longer you linger before executing God's instructions to you, the easier it is for you to end up NOT doing that thing? You will start by questioning what you heard, then you will doubt it, later you will PROCRASTINATE it and in the end, you will Abandon it. If you must achieve your dreams AND IN TIME, then you must be one who takes prompt action. If you want to study a career, start school now. If you want to do business, start now. It is only those with a SENSE OF URGENCY that arrive their destination on time. If God says go and you have wings, fly.

Genesis 22:3

Early the next morning Abraham got up and saddled his donkey. He took with him two of his servants and his son Isaac. When he had cut enough wood for the burnt offering, he set out for the place God had told him about.

PRAYER

Heavenly Father, help me to respond to Your instructions with a sense of urgency. I come against every attitude of procrastination in me, in Jesus' name, amen.

NOTES ....

....

....

....

....

....

....

....

....

....

Moses sent out twelve spies from the twelve tribes of Israel to go spy the land of Canaan. When they got there and saw the giants among the people, they became intimidated by their stature and because of that, they saw themselves as grasshoppers.

People around you cannot perceive you better than the way you perceive yourself. If you see yourself a failure, then everyone around you will start seeing you as a failure. If you think you are a "nobody," sooner or later you will start acting as a "nobody." And that's when people around you will start saying you are 'a good for nothing.' "It was only after the Israelite spies saw themselves as GRASSHOPPERS that they began to look in the eyes of the people as Grasshoppers" (Ps Robert J.).

It is time for you to start seeing yourself in the light of God's Word and not based on the circumstances in which you find yourself. You are more than what you are going through; you are seated with Christ in heavenly places (Eph. 2:6).

Numbers 13:33

"We saw the Nephilim there (the descendants of Anak come from the Nephilim). We seemed like grasshoppers in our own eyes, and we looked the same to them."

PRAYER

Gracious heavenly Father, I thank You for making me in Your image and for putting Your Spirit in me. Thank You for all the gifts and potentials you have put in me. Lord, from today, I will never see myself inferior to any situation, but I will rise up to face any challenge that comes before me, in Jesus' name, amen.

NOTES ....

....

....

....

....

....

....

....

....

....

Jesus was about to have a one of a kind experience on the mount of transfiguration. So He chose three of His disciples to take along for the awesome encounter. One of the reasons Jesus took just three of His disciples to the mount of transfiguration was because He wanted the events on that hill to remain a secret until an appointed time. And these three men did not disappoint Him. They kept the events of that day a secret till the death and resurrection of Jesus Christ.

As a servant of God, God will bring people your way who will open up their entire life to you. Wives will tell you things they've not told their husbands and vice versa; children will tell you things their parents know nothing about. Workers will reveal secrets they can't tell their bosses. They do these because they TRUST that as a man of God, you can keep their secrets. BUT UNFORTUNATELY, some of us Servants of God have carried people's secrets into the public. And there is nothing more tragic than having a man of God who can't keep your secrets, secret. If men cannot trust you with their secrets then there is no way you can know the deep things of God. The big question for everyone today is, can you be trusted with deep secrets?

Matthew 17:1-9

"After six days Jesus took with him Peter, James, and John the brother of James, and led them up a high mountain by themselves. Just then there appeared before them Moses and Elijah, talking with Jesus. As they were coming down the mountain, Jesus instructed them, "Don't tell anyone what you have seen, until the Son of Man has been raised from the dead."

PRAYER

Lord Jesus, I come to you this day asking you will forgive me for the moments I have not been able to keep the deep things that were shared with me. Lord give me the grace to keep peoples' private issues private in Jesus' name. Father may I be someone you can trust with deep secrets in Jesus' name.

NOTES

When you are gifted by God, you must watch out not to become A TOOL in the hands of men: You're a vessel FOR GOD. King Balak is terrified by the presence of ISRAEL around his nation. So he remembers and sends for the PROFESSIONAL 'Curser' by name Balaam to come to rescue his country. He even promised Balaam a huge reward for 'his SERVICES.' But God, however, stopped Balaam the prophet.

We should always remember that even though God gives diverse gifts to men, all His gifts are exclusively for His services. If you are gifted in RAISING FUNDS, do not become a tool in the hands of men to achieve their selfish desires for money. I perfectly understand the need for money in the Kingdom and that some have the grace to raise funds more than others. But that should NOT be YOUR PROFESSION. Anytime they see you on a flier, it has to do with raising money. Always remember that at the end of time, we shall be rewarded according to God's standards and not how many people you helped by RAISING FUNDS FOR THEM. Also, remember that men will use you like an orange. After squeezing the juice out of you and there is nothing left, they'd dump you in a trash can. So work at pleasing your Maker and not be a Tool in the hands of men, like Balaam.

Numbers 22:5, 6, 17.

..So Balak... "Sent messengers to summon Balaam son of Beor, who was at Pethor, near the River, in his native land. Balak said: "A people has come out of Egypt; they cover the face of the land and have settled next to me. Now come and put a curse on these people, because they are too powerful for me. Perhaps then I will be able to defeat them and drive them out of the country. For I know that those you bless are blessed, and those you curse are cursed." because I will reward you handsomely and do whatever you say. Come and put a curse on these people for me."

PRAYER

Father, I thank You for the spiritual gifts You have given me. I know that I did not get them because of my righteousness but simply by your grace. Lord, I thank You. Father, I pray that I will not use my gifts to glorify myself or to glorify men, but I will use them only for Your glory, in Jesus' name. May I not become a tool in the hands of men, but remain a vessel in Your hands Lord, in Jesus' name, amen.

NOTES ....

....

....

....

....

....

WEEK 03 | WISDOM NUGGET

STRONG SILENT TYPE

Choose to be the strong silent type. Let your actions speak louder than your words. People will remember your actions more than they will remember your words. There were moments Jesus refused to speak a word not because He was weak but because He chose to be the strong silent type. "But Jesus made no reply, not even to a single charge–to the great amazement of the governor." (Matthew 27:14).

PRAYER

- ✓ Father, in the name of Jesus, I receive the grace to tame my tongue. May I only talk when necessary.
- ✓ Lord, please help me to be a man or woman of action, in Jesus' name. Amen.

NOTES

....

....

....

....

....

....

....

....

Apostle Paul writes to the Romans in a time of severe persecution. Christians were being assassinated for their faith and this gave them every reason to look at the oppressor as REAL ENEMIES. It will be normal for them to wish these enemies dead and if possible, even pray for God to kill them. On the contrary, Paul says you are to love those very people who are persecuting you. The mystery in all these is that, while it may look foolish on your part; you are gaining a lot of credit in God's eyes. Here is God's recommendation on how to DEAL with your Enemies: He says do not take revenge for what anyone did to you. When you don't fight back, YOU GIVE ROOM for God TO FIGHT for you. When you go fighting your offenders, you Tie God's hands and He sits back and watches you struggle. If your enemy is hungry feed them, the Lord says. By this, you heap burning coals on their head. And finally, if you want to overcome your enemies, overcome their evil with LOVE.

Romans 12:19-21

Do not take revenge, my friends, but leave room for God's wrath, for it is written: "It is mine to avenge; I will repay," says the Lord. On the contrary: "If your enemy is hungry, feed him; if he is thirsty, give him something to drink. In doing this, you will heap burning coals on his head." Do not be overcome by evil, but overcome evil with good.

PRAYER

Merciful Father, I receive the grace to forgive my offenders and to let go of every wrong they've done to me. I commit them into Your hands Lord, and I ask that You deal with them as it pleases You, in Jesus' name, amen. Lord, give me the grace to love my enemies, in Jesus' name, amen.

NOTES ....
....
....
....
....
....
....
....
....
....

The whole nation sought a savior to bring down Goliath. Finally, David showed and cut off the Philistine's head. Everyone celebrated David including King Saul, who even went on to promote him. There was no problem until they got back home from battle and the whole nation gathered to welcome them. The women chanted saying: "Saul has slain his thousands, and David his tens of thousands." And this was the beginning of the problem between Saul and David Immediately the King felt INTIMIDATED and thought he was losing his throne to David who was just a teenager. The Bible records, "And from that time on Saul kept a jealous eye on David." To sum it up, Saul spent a greater portion of his life chasing David to kill him instead of fulfilling his purpose.

It will save you a lot of stress if you keep it at the back of your mind that no one can take from you the assignment God has put in your hands. When you allow insecurity to rule you, you turn to abandon your job and start FIGHTING people you think are a threat to you thereby not fulfilling purpose. Accept it or not, SOMEONE will always do better than you in a certain area, but that does not mean you have been dethroned. When men turn to celebrate your subordinates or praise that young minister more than you, that does not mean God has fired you. Stay focused and celebrate with them because many may have the gifts but lack the CHARACTER or ability to lead. So your throne is NOT AT STAKE.

1 Samuel 18:5-9

Whatever Saul sent him to do, David did it so successfully that Saul gave him a high rank in the army. This pleased all the people, and Saul's officers as well. As they danced, they sang: "Saul has slain his thousands, and David his tens of thousands." This made Saul very angry. "What's this?" he said. "They credit David with ten thousand and me with only thousands. Next they'll be making him their king!" And from that time on Saul kept a jealous eye on David.

PRAYER

Lord, I pray that you will purify my heart and keep it clean from any hate or jealousy. Father let the successes of others not be a threat to me. Help me to celebrate others when they succeed in Jesus' name, Amen.

NOTES ....

....

....

....

....

The herdsmen of Lot and Abram disputed over grazing territory. So Abram calls on Lot to choose from the whole countryside which way he will go and Abram will take the opposite direction. The Bible says "... Lot LOOKED up and saw that the whole plain of the Jordan was well watered, like the garden of the LORD, like the land of Egypt, toward Zoar..." According to Lot, he had chosen the best land because it looked green. Well, it turned out that Lot found himself in Sodom and Gomorrah which God destroyed.

As believers, it is dangerous for us to walk by sight instead of faith. Just because that brother or sister looks attractive doesn't mean that's the right mate for you. The job may have a good salary but if you only LOOK at that, you may end up with the wrong job. You must see through God's eyes if you want to succeed. If you go just by what you see, you will be misled, but if you follow the leading of the Spirit, you will celebrate in the end.

Genesis 13:8-10

So Abram said to Lot, "Let's not have any quarreling between you and me, or between your herdsmen and mine, for we are brothers. Is not the whole land before you? Let's part company. If you go to the left, I'll go to the right; if you go to the right, I'll go to the left." Lot looked up and saw that the whole plain of the Jordan was well watered, like the garden of the LORD, like the land of Egypt, toward Zoar. (This was before the LORD destroyed Sodom and Gomorrah.)

PRAYER

Lord God Almighty, I receive the grace to start walking by faith and not by sight. Lord, may I not follow what my eyes see but I will listen to the voice of Your Spirit in every decision I make, in Jesus' name, amen.

NOTES

The Lord has sent out 72 disciples into all the cities He was to enter. He gave them the authority to preach and heal the sick. Moments later, they all returned with great joy. The object of their joy was because "... DEMONS OBEY US in Your name..." In other words, of all the things that happened, this one stood out: demons obey us. Some of the other things that happened include, people believed their message of salvation, people got healed, some were comforted, hope was given and so much more. But NONE OF THESE was as important to them as the fact that demons obeyed them. Upon hearing this, Jesus was amazed and had to immediately correct them. He said to them: "However, do not rejoice that the spirits submit to you, but rejoice that your names are written in heaven." In simple words, the work of SALVATION IS MORE IMPORTANT than demons obeying you.

We must Re-examine some of the things we celebrate in church nowadays. How could we all be applauding and celebrating because a demon-possessed person said "Your man of God or your Church is the strongest in town." It is a waste of Precious Time to spend hours interviewing demons (sometimes wanting them to acknowledge that you're a real man of God). Simply cast them out. How is it that the one who stands to testify of how they've been transformed by the Word and are now born again receive less applauds than the one who says Papa prayed for him and demons ran out. Jesus says "...do not rejoice that the spirits submit to you, but rejoice that your names are written in heaven."

Luke 10:1, 17, 20.

After this, the Lord appointed seventy-two others and sent them two by two ahead of him to every town and place where he was about to go. The seventy-two returned with joy and said, "Lord, even the demons submit to us in your name." However, do not rejoice that the spirits submit to you, but rejoice that your names are written in heaven."

PRAYER

Heavenly Father, help us to fully understand the things that are dear to Your heart and to know that demons are under our feet. Lord, may we begin to value the salvation of men more than miracles of healing and deliverance, in Jesus' name, amen.

NOTES ....

....

....

....

....

....

They were his brothers and he had no reason to be suspicious. So he went on to share his dream with them hoping they would all celebrate or at least reason it out with him. But it turned out that he was so wrong. Joseph's brothers hated him "all the more" when he told them his second dream.

And from that day, the seed of hatred was sown in them. This will later result in them selling off Joseph as a slave. Had Joseph not told his brothers his dreams, he might not have suffered the things he suffered. The difference between Joseph's brothers and their father is that the brothers hated the dreamer but the father meditated on the dream. Some of those with whom we share our dreams may turn out to be our killers. The task of identifying who to share your dream is very important if you ever hope to achieve that dream. Until God tells you to share your dream with them, learn to stay mute.

Genesis 37:5, 6, 9, 11.

Joseph had a dream, and when he told it to his brothers, they hated him all the more. He said to them, "Listen to this dream I had: Then he had another dream, and he told it to his brothers. 'Listen,' he said, "I had another dream, and this time the sun and moon and eleven stars were bowing down to me." His brothers were jealous of him, but his father kept the matter in mind.

PRAYER

Heavenly Father, help me to know the right people I can share my dreams with. Help me to keep it a secret when I must do so, in Jesus' name, amen.

NOTES ....

....

....

....

....

....

....

....

....

....

Young David shows up to give his brothers some food on the battlefield. He hears Goliath's challenge and starts finding out what would be done to the person who kills Goliath. At this, Eliab his brother GOT SO ANGRY with him. The Bible says he "BURNED WITH ANGER" and referred to David as one with a wicked heart. David was so surprised that he asked Eliab "'Now what have I done?' 'Can't I even speak?'" The young man had done nothing wrong for his brother to address him as one with "WICKED HEART."

There are moments in life when men will suddenly rise to fight against you even when you've done nothing wrong. When this happens, try to ignore those fighting you and keep your eyes on where God is taking you. In the end, God will vindicate you and proof to the world that you were not guilty of all the accusations they labeled on you. He did it for David by lifting him up to become King; He can do same for you. Stay focused and don't fight back. God will fight for you and you shall hold your peace.

1 Samuel 17:28-29

When Eliab, David's oldest brother, heard him speaking with the men, he burned with anger at him and asked, "Why have you come down here? And with whom did you leave those few sheep in the desert? I know how conceited you are and how wicked your heart is; you came down only to watch the battle." "Now what have I done?" said David. "Can't I even speak?"

PRAYER

Righteous Father, you are the one who sees in secret and reward in public, Lord I pray that you will help to ignore the insults and lies spoken about me. Give me the grace to stay focused and know you are fighting for me in Jesus' name, amen.

NOTES

WEEK 04 | WISDOM NUGGET

COMPLEMENTARY NOT COMPETITIVE

The body of Christ must return to the consciousness that churches are not competitive but complementary. One plants and another waters but only God makes the harvest. "Therefore the man who plants and the man who waters both have the same purpose and each will be rewarded according to his work" (1 Cor. 3:8).

PRAYER

✓ Father, I pray that the body of Christ will return to the oneness that you instituted the church to demonstrate. I come against every spirit of competition in the hearts of your servants, in Jesus' name.

✓ I pray that the churches will start helping one another in any way needed so that together they can cause your Kingdom to manifest here on earth, in Jesus' name. Amen.

NOTES

....

....

....

....

....

....

At no other moment did we ever see Jesus so furious as He was in Matthew 21:12 when He entered the temple and drove out all who were buying and selling. Remember He was insulted, despised, called a demon-possessed and even spat on; but all these never got the Lord angry. The only thing that ever made Him beat people and chased them out of the temple was when He saw men PLAYING GAMES AND DOING BUSINESS IN GOD'S HOUSE.

It hurts God so bad to see His house (the Church) turned into a place of manipulation. God cannot stand it when poor souls who should be prepared for heaven are being manipulated to achieve SELFISH DESIRES. Jesus is unhappy when the house of God has become a place where we come and commercialize the gospel. We get so busy buying and selling our selfish desires that we care less about praying for the souls that are perishing. But I know it WON'T BE LONG before Jesus will again pick up a cane and flog these charlatans OUT OF HIS HOUSE. Therefore BE WARNED!

Matthew 21:12-13

Jesus entered the temple area and drove out all who were buying and selling there. He overturned the tables of the money changers and the benches of those selling doves. "It is written," he said to them, "'My house will be called a house of prayer,' but you are making it a 'den of robbers."

PRAYER

Our Father in heaven, I pray that You will look down on Your church with mercy. Lord, arise and do a cleansing in Your church in Jesus' name. Let all those buying and selling personal interest instead of doing Your work be chased out, in Jesus' name, amen.

NOTES ....

....
....
....
....
....
....
....
....
....

Jesus and Barabbas are presented to the people to choose who should be freed since it was their custom to grant amnesty to one prisoner every year. Barabbas should be no match for Jesus who has healed their children, raised their dead, multiplied bread, and fed them and done so many other good things for them. But when the moment of decision came for them to choose between the murderer and Jesus, they said give us the murderer and do away with this man Jesus.

That is the Unpredictable nature of MAN. If you ever want to consider man's nature before offering help, you'd end up NEVER helping ANYBODY. Some people may act nice towards you just for what they can get from you. You will only know your true friends in the day of trouble, not when everything is going fine. In order for you to live a peaceful life, you must accept the fact that MAN IS UNPREDICTABLE.

John 18:39-40

But it is your custom for me to release to you one prisoner at the time of the Passover. Do you want me to release 'the king of the Jews'?" They shouted back, "No, not him! Give us Barabbas!" Now Barabbas had taken part in a rebellion.

Acts 3:14-15

You disowned the Holy and Righteous One and asked that a murderer be released to you. You killed the author of life, but God raised him from the dead. We are witnesses of this.

PRAYER

Lord, in any way I have turned my back against those who have assisted me in the past, I ask for Your forgiveness and I decide this day to make things right with them, in Jesus' name, amen.

Lord grant me the grace to keep loving people even if they don't love me in return in Jesus name, amen.

NOTES ....

....

....

....

....

....

....

....

....

Spiritual prostitution seems to be the greatest weakness of the present-day church. God saw this in time past with His people and He passed across a message through Hosea who married Gomarrh, who kept leaving him for other men, to illustrate how Israel had abandoned their lover: GOD, for other men. When we got born again, we got married to Jesus. He became our lover: A JEALOUS LOVER. That means we are to live our lives in a way that satisfies Him. You no longer do the things you like to do because there is someone you must make sure you don't offend.

You can't be married to Jesus and on Sunday you are in church, Monday you are in a night club. That is spiritual adultery. Tuesday you went for prayers and Wednesday you are in a shrine or using fetish objects. That too is called spiritual adultery. Thursday prayer meeting you are drunk in the Holy Ghost, and Friday night you're under the power of alcohol. That is called spiritual adultery. On Saturday evening you go partying DRESSED LIKE the devil's bride, and on Sunday morning, you're dressed for other lovers: God.

How come you are a believer but your best companions do not speak your language or even want to hear about Christ. That also makes you an unfaithful bride to Christ your lover. Just as a husband wants his wife all to himself, the same way our God wants all of our attention. We must do things His ways and not our way. You cannot love God and love the world at the same time.

James 4:4

You adulterous people, don't you know that friendship with the world is hatred toward God? Anyone who chooses to be a friend of the world becomes an enemy of God.

Hosea 1:2

When the LORD began to speak through Hosea, the LORD said to him, "Go, take to yourself an adulterous wife and children of unfaithfulness, because the land is guilty of the vilest adultery in departing from the LORD."

Matthew 15:8

These people honor me with their lips, but their hearts are far from me.

PRAYER

Lord, I pray that You will help me to love faithfully. That I will do only the things You want me to do and yield completely to You in Jesus' name, amen.

Lord I pray that you will have mercy on me and forgive me for all the moments I have been unfaithful to you in Jesus name, amen.

NOTES ....

....

There are so many preachers on our pulpits today whom the devil has sifted like wheat and only their chaff is left. They look very much like they are serving God, but in reality, they do not know Him. We all know that Wheat is useful but the chaff is UNHEALTHY to consume. That's what Satan wanted to do with the disciples: sift out the grain (substance) and leave them like chaff. By doing this, Satan would have left them as empty vessels making noise but having no impact thereby producing camouflage Christians or what Rev. Chidi Okoroafor calls "unbelieving believers." Jesus saw this coming and decided to pray for His disciples.

When Satan sifts you like wheat, you start producing fake Christians, void of the knowledge of God's Word. When you have been sifted like wheat, you become a Preacher who preaches what he himself DOES NOT PRACTICE. You will preach holiness but live in a pool of sin. You will rebuke and discipline others meanwhile you're guilty of the very things you rebuke others for. When you become chaff, you will lack God's backing. And due to that, you will turn to fetish sources to get powers. When a man has been sifted, he loses consciousness of heaven and becomes very materialistic. You will want to acquire all that you can here on earth because the pleasures of this world have swallowed you.

Luke 22:31-32

"Simon, Simon, Satan has asked to sift you as wheat. But I have prayed for you, Simon, that your faith may not fail. And when you have turned back, strengthen your brothers."

PRAYER

Dear Lord, I pray, just as You prayed and delivered Peter from being sifted by satan, please deliver your servants in these last days in Jesus' name, amen. Lord, I come against any spirit of materialism that has taken over your people in the name of Jesus, amen.

NOTES ....

....

....

....

....

....

....

....

....

....

It is amazing how God places value on our giving. From a natural point of view, we often place value on gifts based on HOW MUCH they're worth. But this was not the case with our Lord Jesus. He recognized a poor widow's gift and placed the greatest value on it. I have also come to realize that it is not what you give a man that matters; it is the Attitude with which you give. You can't call a man a pig and then weeks later you present a gold necklace to him as a gift. The truth is even though it is an expensive gift, the recipient will not appreciate it because to him, "Pigs don't wear gold." And this is what most people don't understand. We think we can run people down, disrespect them, look and talk down on them, and then, in the end, WE BUY THEM back with our gifts. Let us remember that just as God values our attitude more than our gifts, man also values relationships more than gifts.

Luke 21:1-4

As he looked up, Jesus saw the rich putting their gifts into the temple treasury. He also saw a poor widow put in two very small copper coins. "I tell you the truth," he said, "this poor widow has put in more than all the others. All these people gave their gifts out of their wealth; but she out of her poverty put in all she had to live on."

PRAYER

Heavenly Father, help us to have an attitude of humility even when we are giving what we consider to be a lot to you. May we not be arrogant when we come to give to you or when we are giving to anybody in Jesus' name, amen.

NOTES

DON'T Get too Familiar with the One God has Anointed. You COULD Miss your Blessing. The Lord Jesus is moving all around doing miracles and setting the oppressed free and almost everyone who comes His way gets his/her breakthrough. Then He finally gets to His own home town. He preaches the same sermons, prays the same prayers BUT instead of the people receiving their miracles, they reacted differently. They capitalized on the personality of Christ and failed to see His Divinity. Because they watched Him grow up and walked around with Him, this made them not to put their faith in Him. They knew Him as the son of the carpenter, the firstborn child of Mary and so He could not be different from His age mates. And because of this, they missed their miracles. It is Dangerous to keep looking at an Anointed Person with the lens of yesterday, meanwhile God is dealing with him on the bases of Today. That you knew him ten years ago does not mean he is still the person you knew back then. Accept them for who they are now and see what God can use a common vessel to do. Never become too familiar with the one God is using.

Matthew 13:54-58

Coming to his hometown, he began teaching the people in their synagogue, and they were amazed. "Where did this man get this wisdom and these miraculous powers?" they asked. "Isn't this the carpenter's son? Isn't his mother's name Mary, and aren't his brothers James, Joseph, Simon, and Judas? Aren't all his sisters with us? Where then did this man get all these things?" And they took offense at him. But Jesus said to them, "Only in his hometown and in his own house is a prophet without honor." And he did not do many miracles there because of their lack of faith.

PRAYER

Father, in the name of Jesus Christ, may I not become too familiar with your servants irrespective of how close I know them. May I see them the same way you see Lord, in Jesus' name, amen.

NOTES ....

....

....

....

....

....

....

....

....

WEEK 05 | WISDOM NUGGET

PASTOR: AN OFFICE NOT A TITLE

Being a Pastor is an office not a title. An office is not a room in a building, it is a responsibility. A responsibility may not be what you like to do, it's what you're assigned to do. And keep it at the back of your mind that we all have a report to write at the end of our assignment. Those with good reports will be rewarded while those with bad reports will be fired.

PRAYER

- ✓ Lord, may you grant your servants whom you have called to be pastors to fully live up to the responsibilities of that high calling.
- ✓ Lord, help them to carry out their job with fear and trembling, remembering that they shall give an account to You in the end. I pray this in Jesus' name.

NOTES

(Write down the names of at least five pastors you want to be praying for).

....

....

....

....

In Acts 8:13-24; "Simon (the sorcerer) believed and was baptized. As he followed Philip, he was ASTONISHED by the great signs and miracles he saw. Then Peter and John laid their hands on the people and they received the Holy Spirit. When Simon saw that the Spirit was given through the laying of their hands, he OFFERED THEM MONEY and said, "Give me also of this ability so that anyone I lay my hands on may receive the Holy Spirit." Peter answered and said, "May your money perish with you because you thought you could BUY the gift of God with money. You have no part or share in this ministry BECAUSE Your HEART IS NOT RIGHT before God. Repent of this wickedness and pray to the Lord… for forgiveness."

Unfortunately, this is exactly what is happening in the body of Christ today. The language and the motive are exactly the same. "When we see the move of God's power, we offer the preacher money and say the same thing, "Give me this GRACE so I can operate in this dimension you operate." The only DIFFERENCE between us and Simon is the response we get from the one to whom we offer the money. Simon received a SHARP REBUKE that led to his repentance and his money was rejected. But for us today, we will receive "prayers and the laying of hands" to receive that grace and our MONEY is TAKEN without hesitation. And please don't get me wrong: desiring the gifts of the Spirit or giving money to a man of God IS NOT BAD as long as our motives are pure.

PRAYER

Heavenly Father, may you purify our motives and cause us to know that we cannot buy your gifts. Lord, may you put an end to every deception of commercializing your gifts in the Church today, in Jesus' name, amen.

NOTES

“Jesus sat down opposite the place where the offerings were put and watched the crowd putting their money into the temple treasury. Many rich people threw in large amounts. But a poor widow came and put in two very small copper coins, worth only a few cents. Calling his disciples to him, Jesus said, “Truly I tell you, this poor widow has put more into the treasury than all the others. They all gave out of their wealth; but she, out of her poverty, put in everything—all she had to live on.” (Mark 12:41-44).

Could it be that the person whom the Pastor looks up to as a major partner when it comes to giving is unknown by God because he could be giving money gotten from FRAUDULENT means? Could it be that the Politician who has a special seat in our church because of his giving is unknown by God because his wealth is gotten from embezzlement? Could it be that the family that is being praised by all for donating a church land or building is unknown by God because in His sight He sees them as unclean? Could it also be that the wretched looking brother or sister, mother or father; in our churches who never gain any recognition because they have little to offer when it comes to giving are seen as the most Righteous in God's sight? We must remember that man looks at outward appearance but God looks at the heart. Therefore in all that we do, we should aim at pleasing God and not man. 1 Sam. 16:7 says, “… People look at the outward appearance, but the LORD looks at the heart.”

PRAYER

Heavenly Father, may You help us in Your loving kindness to see people the way you see them. Let us not place value on people based on their possessions but let us see them with the eyes of love, in Jesus; name, amen.

NOTES

DO NOT PLACE YOUR FAITH IN OBJECTS...

Have you heard people testifying and saying they could not be attacked by demons because they wore the man of God's anointed Wristband or had Papa's Picture on their door? The problem with those kinds of Testimonies is that it leaves every other believer with the desire to also acquire those objects that can chase demons away. It even becomes worse when the man of God himself stands on pulpit to give Testimonies of what his anointed Wristband or sticker can do. How it saved people from ghastly accidents, sent thieves away and so on and so forth.

Don't get me wrong. I believe God can use ANYTHING at any time to do His will. But what God will NOT do is to now make the practice of using that object as a routine. That is why the Rod that He (God) used in parting the red Sea was not needed when they stood before river Jordan. After God spoke through a donkey, He did not do it again so that we don't start looking up to donkeys as God's mouthpiece (Num. 22:28). After Jesus put mud on a man's eyes to open them, He never used it again, so that we don't start a "MUD Doctrine" (John 9:6). The ONLY thing Jesus and the Apostles used Over and Over is the Word of God. This happened so that we can build our DOCTRINE Solely on THE WORD and not on Objects.

PRAYER

Lord, may you cleanse the Church of today from putting their faith in objects. Lord, may we put our faith in your Word and nothing else, in Jesus name, amen. Lord, may you set free every child of God who has been deceived to belief so much in wristbands, stickers, and any other objects more than they believe in your Word.

NOTES

....

....

....

....

....

....

....

....

....

““Jesus said to His disciples, “The masters of the Gentiles lord it over them (their followers); and those who exercise authority over them call themselves Benefactors. But you are not to be like that. Instead, the greatest among you should be like the youngest, and the one who rules like the one who serves”. Luke 22:25-26.

As children of the Kingdom of God, we must be different from the world. In the world, Leaders COMMAND their followers whereas in the Kingdom, Leaders SERVE their followers. Your greatness as a child of God is determined by how much you serve those the Lord brings your way and not by how bossy you are to those around you.

Jesus also told His disciples to emulate His example in serving others. He said: “Now that I, your Master and Teacher, have washed your feet (served you), you also should wash one another's feet” (serve one another). (John 13:14). I belief it is high time we reexamine our functions and see if we have been ‘Worldly' Leaders in the Kingdom of God or ‘Kingdom Leaders leading like the world.

PRAYER

Lord, may you grant me the grace to serve others just like You did. Father, help me to know that if You washed the feet of Your followers, then I must also be a servant. Father, may You help Your servants to not lead like the worldly leaders who lord it over their followers but to be like You who was a servant leader. I pray all these in Jesus' name, amen.

NOTES ....

....

....

....

....

....

....

....

....

....

We are called to be living testimonies unto the glory of God. But I'm afraid to say what we see and hear these days in the church is the very opposite. Christians testifying not to glorify God but to boost the reputation of their 'man of God.' Men of God standing on the altar and giving exaggerated Testimonies mixed with lies of how God is using them. To make things worse, we now ARRANGE Testimonies to suit our interests.

Some may call it "Faith-ing it out" when you say the pain is gone whilst it's still there. But in the following example, had this brother "Testilied" that he could see clearly after Jesus prayed the first time; he would have remained partially blind: seeing men like trees. But when " ...Jesus asked "Do you see anything?" he looked up and said, "I see people; they look like trees walking around." Once more Jesus put His hands on the man's eyes. Then his eyes were opened, his sight was restored, and he saw everything clearly. (Mark 8:23-25).

You cannot help God in doing His job. Just be honest with God and He will do a complete work in your life. It is not unbelief or doubt when you tell the preacher you still feel the pain after they've prayed for you. God wants you to be honest to yourself and be frank with Him. That's when He can do real business with you.

PRAYER

Heavenly Father, may You forgive me for all the moments I have not been sincere with You with regards to testifying about Your work in my life. Lord, have mercy on me for exaggeration during testimonies. Lord, help Your servants from telling lies and exaggeration when they talk of how much You are using them, in Jesus' name, amen.

NOTES ....

....

....

....

....

....

....

....

....

....

THE CHURCH IS A BURDEN TAKER NOT A BURDEN GIVER...

The Church of Christ is supposed to be a place where people who are heavy laden, can come and find rest. But I'm afraid to say the reverse is true nowadays. When a low or no income earner or the middle class is being bombarded with financial demands every month as they sit in our churches, then the church has become a Burden Giver and not a burden taker. We should not get to a point where our members start feeling uncomfortable to come to church because of the so many financial demands. Before they recover from contributing to buy a new car for the Pastor, you're already asking them to contribute for the Church land. And soon after that, they are contributing for a Revival program and thereafter is contributions for new chairs and so on and so forth. This becomes too burdensome on the members and it was never the approach of Jesus.

I'm not in any way against church members making contributions. Because that's the only way the Church can get projects done. But these contributions should not become a yoke on the people's neck. Jesus says in *Matthew 11:28-30: "Come to me, all you who are weary and burdened, and I will give you rest. For my yoke is easy and my burden is light."*

While we try to get our Church projects done, we must also pay attention to the spiritual and physical needs of the people in our congregations.

PRAYER

Lord, may You help us to do Your work in Your way in Jesus name. Father, help Your servants to not only pay attention on the projects they have for the church and forget the pressing demands of the people You have given them, in Jesus' name, amen.

NOTES ....

....

....

....

....

....

....

....

....

....

WEEK 06 | WISDOM NUGGET

DON'T DEMAND, IT EARN IT

Respect is not demanded; it is earned. You earn respect by taking responsibility. When you finally step up to the full responsibility of your person, respect will inevitably follow you. Stop demanding respect and start working to earn it.

PRAYER

✓ Lord, help me to live up to the full responsibility of who You have created me to be. Anything that is stopping me from fully becoming what You want me to be, please take it away, in Jesus' name. Amen.

NOTES

....
....
....
....
....
....
....
....
....
....
....
....
....

At one point the disciples of Jesus were confronted with a sick boy and they could not heal him. When the boy was finally brought to Jesus, He wept over the fact that His followers could not heal the sick boy. He had wished they could heal him and set him free. He had been with them for some time and thought them His Word and His ways. And most importantly, His time with them was soon going to run out. So He needed them to step up to doing the things He does because they will have to take over when He leaves. But they could not and this made Jesus weep. His reason for weeping was: "How long shall I be with you?"

Unfortunately for some of leaders today, they rejoice at the failure of their followers. When their subordinates fail in executing a task, they rejoice because that gives them the feeling they're the only ones who can do it and the Church or organization cannot do without them. What you fail to realize is that, you won't always be there. I'm sorry to say that many churches and ministries we see today will DIE THE DAY THE LEADER DIES unless the leaders start Training others to take after you. A good leader is one who trains someone to take over after he is gone away from that function and not see any vacuum.

Matthew 17:15-17.

"Lord, have mercy on my son," he said. "He has seizures and is suffering greatly. He often falls into the fire or into the water. I brought him to your disciples, but they could not heal him." "O unbelieving and perverse generation," Jesus replied, "how long shall I stay with you? How long shall I put up with you? Bring the boy here to me."

PRAYER

Heavenly Father, help me to be a leader who delights in the success of my subordinates and give me a heart that will train people to do the things I am good at. Lord, help Your church to be a training center where ordinary men and women can come in and get trained to start operating in the supernatural and that Church will not just be one man show but it will be You Lord, working though many to do Your work, in Jesus' name amen.

NOTES ....

....

....

....

....

....

....

....

It is rather unfortunate to say that some of us Preachers have decided to portray ourselves as 'Supermen' or some Deity who do not suffer the same things our church members or every other human being goes through. We make people believe we never get sick, we never get disappointments, we are never tempted (talk less of falling into sin or being wrong). But when in reality, there are moments we, men of God, do get afflicted in one way or the other. And because we have either given a false impression about who we are, we turn to PRETEND, HIDE, and LIE to people during our moments of affliction.

There is nothing wrong in admitting before your congregation that you are sick, weak, or going through a tough time and ask for their prayers. It is not a taboo for a Pastor to admit he is sick or to ask for prayer. If Jesus and Paul could ask for prayers from their followers during their days of trial, then you and I are not better off. As long as we are in this world, we will have tribulations and we all, including Pastors, will always need prayers.

Matthew 26: 40-41.

"Then he returned to his disciples and found them sleeping. "Could you men not keep watch with me (PRAY FOR ME) for one hour?" he asked Peter. "Watch and pray so that you will not fall into temptation. The spirit is willing, but the body is weak."

PRAYER

Lord God Almighty, may You grant us a humble heart to be able to come before one another and share our challenges and request for prayers. Lord help us to know that no one is too big to request prayers from others for and that Lord as we pray for one another, You will answer us in Jesus name, amen.

NOTES ....

....

....

....

....

....

....

....

....

....

If you love only those love you, you are not practicing Christianity. If you greet only those who greet you, then you are not shining your light as a Christian. Christianity is not a religion of self-centeredness but a place where everyone looks after the good of others. The Church should not be a gathering of people with many different factions where each group only looks after the interest of those within that group. You have a particular group of people you love and they're the only ones you visit, call, attend their events, bring them gifts, and shake hands with them. That is not Christianity and God is not glorified in such a place.

Jesus says in *Matt. 5:46-48: "If you love those who love you, what reward will you get? Are not even the tax collectors doing that? And if you greet only your brothers, what are you doing more than others? Do not even pagans do that? Be perfect, therefore, as your heavenly Father is perfect."* If we want to attain perfection in God's sight, then we must go on to love even those we consider our enemies.

PRAYER

Loving Father, please help me to love everyone including those who do not love me. May I walk in Your perfection by showing love to all who come my way, in Jesus' name, amen.

NOTES

No matter what you do, there will always be those who will never believe in you. As Jesus weeps over the death of Lazarus, some men stood by watching and gave a different meaning to what had happened. These same men had seen Jesus do miracles and probably some had even received a direct miracle from Jesus. At that time, Jesus to them was truly the Son of God. But when that "difficult or tough" moment came, they started singing a different song about the same Jesus they once respected. "Could not he who opened the eyes of the blind man have kept this man from dying?" they said.

Some people will only stick to you in the good times. They will say everything nice about you. BUT WAIT until the RAINY DAYS come then you'd know that men are so unpredictable. So it is needless trying to leave a good impression on people's minds about you. Human perception is subject to change at ANY TIME. THEREFORE in all you do, do it as UNTO THE LORD because you can never get everyone to love you.

John:11:37

But some of them said, "Could not he who opened the eyes of the blind man have kept this man from dying?"

PRAYER

Heavenly Father, grant me the grace not to relate with people based on what they will say about me but help me to live a life that is pleasing to You. Let my desires be to please You and not to give people good impressions about me, in Jesus' name, amen.

NOTES ....

The sole objective of the visit of the Pharisees was to TEST Jesus. They did not come to listen to Him teach, talk less of believing in Him. Testers come to Church like everyone else, but their motives are different. If we lack the spirit of discernment, I'm afraid we might spend our whole life trying to win over the WRONG people. The truth is, you can never win over a fault finder. Like the Pharisees came asking Jesus for a sign, it is needless trying to show skeptics the sign they're asking for. Because as soon as you're done showing them that sign, they'll ask for another sign, then another one until you eventually get tired. 'Testers' Never stay in one place no matter how hard you try to make them do. Jesus, understanding this, sighed deeply, and told them no sign will be given to them, then He moved on to another place.

Mark:8.11-13

"The Pharisees came and began to question Jesus. To test him, they asked him for a sign from heaven. He sighed deeply and said, "Why does this generation ask for a miraculous sign? I tell you the truth, no sign will be given to it." Then he left them, got back into the boat and crossed to the other side."

PRAYER

Heavenly Father, grant me the grace to identify people who come my way and are skeptics or just want to test me with regards to the things of God, who have no intention of believing in You; help me not to waste all my energy trying to proof God to them when they will never accept the truth. Help me to move away from such, in Jesus' name, amen.

NOTES ....

....

....

....

....

....

....

....

....

....

Stretching your hand and people are slain under God's power is all that your anointing can do? Calling names and identifying the situations of people through word of knowledge is all your anointing can do? Screaming "OUT IN THE NAME OF JESUS" and demons manifest and leave people is all your anointing can do? Well, if that be the case, then I must tell you that your anointing is INCOMPLETE. It is incomplete because it lacks the first ingredient of one who is truly anointed. And that ingredient is called "GOOD WORKS."

You cannot be ignoring your neighbors who go for days without food and claim you're anointed. You can't desire to wear the best suits and shoes while ignoring those wretched looking members in your church and claim you're anointed. The first thing, the Anointing does when it comes upon a person is, it gives him POWER TO DO GOOD. According to Revelations 22:12, Jesus will reward us according to our good works not according to how many miracles we performed.

Acts:10.38

" how God anointed Jesus of Nazareth with the Holy Spirit and power, and how he went around doing good and healing all who were under the power of the devil, because God was with him".

Revelation:22.12

"Behold, I am coming soon! My reward is with me, and I will give to everyone according his WORKS" (not his miracles).

PRAYER

Our Most loving Father, I receive the grace to do good to all who come my way, in Jesus name. Lord, help Your servants to understand that besides their anointing to do great miracles, good works is invaluable in Your sight.

NOTES

WEEK 07 | WISDOM NUGGET

HUMILITY IS NOT ATTRACTIVE

The simple reason most people don't want to be humble is because humility is not something very attractive. But it is the way of the Kingdom. God esteems humility so high that He says the humble will inherit the earth. "Blessed are the meek, (humble) for they will inherit the earth." (Matt. 5:5). I urge you and your household to choose humility.

PRAYER

✓ Father, we pray for the grace to remain humble in Your sight. Let our possessions or education not make us proud and abandon Your ways, in Jesus' name. Amen.

NOTES

....
....
....
....
....
....
....
....
....
....
....
....

A man who builds his entire ministry on prophecy WITHOUT the WORD is like a man who opens a restaurant just to serve appetizers. After taking the appetizer, your customers will finally SETTLE where they can get the REAL MEAL (The WORD). This could be the reason people don't stay in your church.

In John 4, we see Jesus using Prophecy as an appetizer to attract the woman at the well. When the woman who received the Prophecy went and brought the crowd telling them to come see the man who gave her an accurate Prophetic word, Jesus DID NOT continue with Prophecy to speak to the Crowd. HE SWITCHED TO THE WORD of God. At the end of the day, "MANY BELIEVED not because of the Word of Prophecy given to the woman, but because of the WORDS of Life spoken to them.

PROPHECY has NEVER and will never SAVE ANYONE; only the Word of God will. You can choose to either open a Church that serves appetizers (Prophecy) or a Church that serves a FULL MEAL(THE WORD). Both are good but the latter is what will establish a believer.

John:4.18-42.

The fact is, you have had five husbands, and the man you now have is not your husband. What you have just said is quite true." "Sir," the woman said, "I can see that you are a prophet... "Come, see a man who told me everything I ever did. Could this be the Christ?" They came out of the town and made their way toward him. And because of his WORDS many more became believers. They said to the woman, "We no longer believe just because of what you said; now we have heard for ourselves, and we know that this man really is the savior of the world".

PRAYER

Heavenly Father, help us to desire Your Word more than we desire prophecy. Make us to understand that all that we need is found in Your Word. Lord, help Your servants not to give their members what their itchy ears want to hear but to feed them with pure milk of Your Word, in Jesus name, amen.

NOTES ....

....

....

....

....

....

....

....

Cain out of his own will, brings a bad offering to God while his brother Abel of his own will, brings the best offering. God accepts that of Abel and rejects that of Cain. Cain becomes angry with Abel up to the point where he killed him. It was never Abel's fault for you to bring a bad offering. And it was not Abel who asked God to bless him and reject your offering.

The same behavior of Cain still happens amongst us today. You were best of friends with a brother or sister in Church until he bought his car; then you stopped talking with him. You were best of friends until your friend had a better job, house, scholarship, travelled abroad or got married; then you became enemies. The irony is he or she did not use your money to buy his car so why get angry? She did not marry your husband so why get angry?

The same question God asked Cain is what I also ask you today: "Why are you angry with your brother? Do you think you do well by being angry with your brother?" A genuine answer to this question could save your soul today. God bless you.

Genesis:4.5-8

But on Cain and his offering he did not look with favor. So Cain was very angry, and his face was downcast. Then the LORD said to Cain, "Why are you angry? Why is your face downcast? If you do what is right, will you not be accepted? But if you do not do what is right, sin is crouching at your door; it desires to have you, .. Cain attacked his brother Abel and killed him."

PRAYER

Lord purify my heart from any form of jealousy against my brothers and sisters in Jesus name. Make Your church a place where we can celebrate the achievements of one another in Jesus name. May we not be like Cain who brought a worthless offering to You.

NOTES ....

....

....

....

....

....

....

....

....

....

God's Mercy takes AWAY what we deserve (Punishment) and His Grace GIVES us what we don't deserve (Righteousness). His MERCY FORGAVE the thief on the cross, His GRACE GAVE him instant Access into heaven. His MERCY FORGAVE the prodigal son, His GRACE threw a PARTY for him. His MERCY CALLED blind Bartimaeus, His GRACE OPENED his blind eyes. His MERCY asked the man at the pool "do you want to get well?" His GRACE told him "Rise, pick up your bed and walk."

God's grace and mercy is also available for you today. No matter who you or what you have done. God can forgive you and receive you as His child. All you need to do say, "Lord I am sorry for all the wrong things I have done."

Scriptural references:

Lk 23:39-43, Lk 15:11-32, Mk 10:46-52, Jhn 5;1-15.

PRAYER

Dear merciful and gracious Father, I come to You today asking that You will look down on me with mercy. Grant me the grace to live the life You want me to live and to be the person You created me to be in Jesus' name, amen.

NOTES ....

"...These days we don't invite Preachers just because they can preach good or because they have special gifts of healing, deliverance or prophecy. There are Two main things you look for in any preacher you want to invite: 1) Can he raise funds? 2) Does he have a Church/ministry that I can also be invited? Everything else comes after but these two, MUST come first," said the big man of God as he advised young ministers who admire him. It was then I realized *Phil. 2:21* was still true today: *"For everyone looks out for their own interests, not those of Jesus Christ."*

How could you comfortably use the FLOCK of Christ to achieve your Selfish Interests? And we wonder why the present day believer lacks the spiritual stamina to resist the slightest temptation that comes their way. We wonder why we move from one revival to another, yet the hearts of the people are NOT REVIVED. We wonder why the sick come to revival meetings, sow seeds but go back even more sick than they came. The glory of God will not abide in a place where selfish desires have overthrown the desires of God. We must return to looking after the things that give God pleasure.

PRAYER

MAY YOUR GLORY RETURN TO YOUR HOUSE OH LORD starting from OUR HEARTS in Jesus' name. Purify our motives and cause us to look after your interest.

NOTES ....

Two of Jesus' Disciples came to Him expressing a desire to lead. This is what they said: *"Then James and John, the sons of Zebedee, came to him, "Teacher," they said, "we want you to do for us whatever we ask." "What do you want me to do for you?" he asked. They replied, "Let one of us sit at your right and the other at your left in your glory." "You don't know what you are asking," Jesus said. "Can you drink the cup I drink or be baptized with the baptism I am baptized with?"* (Mark 10:35-38). When the ten heard about this, they became indignant with James and John. Jesus called them together and said, "You know that those who are regarded as rulers of the Gentiles lord it over them, and their high officials exercise authority over them. Not so with you. Instead, whoever wants to become great among you must be your servant and whoever wants to be first must be slave of all. (Mark 10:35-43).

Jesus teaches us in these verses that the way up is down. Service and loyalty is what will get you up the leadership ladder. Keep serving faithfully where you are and you will soon get an upliftment.

PRAYER

Lord, help me to stay faithful in serving where You have placed me because I know You will always reward faithfulness, in Jesus' name, amen.

NOTES ....

....

....

....

....

....

....

....

....

....

As the congregation of Israel cried unto their Pastor Moses in front of the red sea, Pastor Moses acts like a man who is neither scared nor troubled. He goes on to encourage the people not to be afraid but be still and see God's power at work. In front of the people, Moses acts like all is well. Meanwhile DEEP DOWN within his heart, he is troubled and confused. He goes in the secret place of prayer and starts crying to God and that's when God comforted Him and showed the way forward.

If you knew half of what your PASTORS ARE GOING THROUGH, you will STEP UP YOUR PRAYERS FOR THEM. Even if they tell you all is well, sometimes it is not. So ALWAYS PRAY FOR THEM.

Exodus:14.13-15

Moses answered the people, "Do not be afraid. Stand firm and you will see the deliverance the LORD will bring you today. The Egyptians you see today you will never see again. Then the LORD said to Moses, "Why are you CRYING out to me? Tell the Israelites to move on.

PRAYER

Heavenly Father, may You uphold Your servants in their challenging moments and be their strength. Lord, You know them better and You are the only one that can truly comfort them. I pray You be there for them, in Jesus' name, amen.

NOTES

WEEK 08 | WISDOM NUGGET

FEED MY SHEEP

Copying and preaching someone's sermon while acknowledging your source is better than 60minutes of 'noise' making on a Sunday service. The Lord instructed His servants to feed His sheep and not starve them. The preacher must take time to prepare a sermon for God's people or at least get a good lesson from someone and present it to the congregation.

PRAYER

✓ Lord, grant Your servants insight into Your Word so they can properly feed Your sheep, in Jesus' name.

NOTES

....
....
....
....
....
....
....
....
....
....
....
....
....
....

It is unfortunate that in times of crisis, some people (Christians inclusive) choose to isolate themselves from the suffering masses and act like nothing is happening. Just because they assume there is no way they can be affected by the crisis. Some have this assurance because they live in fortified houses or they live far away from the crisis area. But what we fail to understand is that TRAGEDY makes no choices as to whom it should visit. Just as Mordecai reminded Esther that her position as Queen does not spare her from the coming CALAMITY, I am also Reminding everyone that if you don't rise up in Prayer and speak up for those in PAIN in times of crisis, then it's only a matter of time and you will also be needing someone to speak for you. God gave you that high office or that great wealth so you can be a voice to the voiceless and hope to the hopeless. So step up to that expectation and put a smile on the faces of many like Esther did.

Esther:4.12-14.

When Esther's words were reported to Mordecai, he sent back this answer: "Do not think that because you are in the king's house you alone of all the Jews will escape. For if you remain silent at this time, relief and deliverance for the Jews will arise from another place, but you and your father's family will perish. And who knows but that you have come to royal position for such a time as this?"

PRAYER

Father, help me to be a blessing to the people around me. Give me a heart for the people and make me a source of happiness to many, in Jesus name, amen.

NOTES ....

....

....

....

....

....

....

....

....

After preaching a long sermon all day, healing the sick, standing in the sun and most likely thirsty and hungry; Jesus ends His day by directing ALL HIS ATTENTION to see that people eat something. He could have walked away through the back door before the people would open their eyes, so that no one can touch Him. He could have been ushered to a special room to be served food and drinks (often special and different from what the common people would eat) while the CHIEF protocol would have his car or private jet ready for takeoff. These are the things we see preachers doing today. But our Lord did not disappear from the scene nor dare to send the people home hungry. All they had was a little bread and fish not even sufficient for Jesus and His disciples, but He was ready to give it up to feed the people.

You may say I don't have enough. Well the truth is, if you have the heart to do it, God will make the provision the same way He multiplied bread for Jesus. Have a heart for the people and God will make the provisions.

Mark6:36-38

Send the people away so they can go to the surrounding countryside and villages and buy themselves something to eat. "But he answered, "You give them something to eat." They said to him, "That would take eight months of a man's wages! Are we to go and spend that much on bread and give it to them to eat?" "How many loaves do you have?" he asked. "Go and see. "When they found out, they said, "Five-- and two fish."

PRAYER

Lord, give me a heart of compassion for people. Help me put food on the table of many around the world who have nothing to eat and as I desire to do this, I know You will make the provisions, in Jesus name, amen.

NOTES ....

....

....

....

....

....

....

....

....

....

Nicodemus comes to Jesus by night and begins his conversation by pouring out praises on Jesus. "...you come from God... no one can do these things you do unless God is with him..." For a Rabi (Teacher) of the Law to make those pronouncements about a person, it means that person was really a wonder.

I don't know what was on the mind of Nicodemus as he came to see Jesus. But right in the midst of his praises, Jesus responds to him. Notice Jesus did not respond to the PRAISES of Nicodemus; He responded to the NEED of Nicodemus. And that NEED was Salvation for his SOUL: "... You must be Born Again."

When men come to you for counseling or advice and begin by praising you, be careful that your conversation is not affected by those praises. Be honest with people and tell them the need of their soul which is a relationship with God through Jesus Christ. This is the only way we can SAVE the Souls of men.

John:3.2-3

He came to Jesus at night and said, "Rabbi, we know you are a teacher who has come from God. For no one could perform the miraculous signs you are doing if God were not with him." In reply Jesus declared, "I tell you the truth, no one can see the kingdom of God unless he is born again."

PRAYER

Father, help me to always see beyond the words of men and respond to the needs of their soul and not to their praises.

NOTES ....

....

....

....

....

....

....

....

....

....

A lot of times we wonder why we pray for the sick, they get healed but few months down the road, they fall sick again. The ministry of Jesus gives the answer to this question. Jesus healed so many people and some after their healing, decided to follow Him. Others decided to go after their own businesses. In *Luke 17:19,* after Jesus heals ten people, only one came back to thank Him. It turned out that this one guy got what his nine friends never got. And that is WHOLENESS. Jesus said to him, "… your faith has made you WHOLE." This means you can be healed but NOT made WHOLE.

To be healed means sickness has been taken away but to be made WHOLE means to take away sickness and also provide protection from any future attack from diseases. You can only get this protection if you stick to Jesus after you get your healing. But because many do not, they walk away and before long they get attacked by another disease and they are back where they were before their healing. If you want to be healed and made WHOLE, the secret is to STICK TO JESUS after your healing.

Matthew:8.15

He touched her hand and the fever left her, and she got up and began to SERVE HIM.

Luke:18.43

Immediately he received his sight and FOLLOWED JESUS, praising God. When all the people saw it, they also praised God.

PRAYER

Father, help me to stick to You both in health and in sickness. That I will not only run to You when I need Your healing and then walk away after that, but I will live all my days in Your presence, in Jesus name, amen.

NOTES ....

....

....

....

....

....

....

....

....

....

1 Corinthians 11:31 says; "But if we judged ourselves, we would not come under judgment."

Let's take a look at how Paul judged himself in Acts 20 by making the following statements: "You all know how I lived a clean life before every one of you... I escaped all the TRAPS the Religious folks set for me... I am INNOCENT of the blood of ALL MEN... I have Never tricked anyone to get their money... I have Never deceived anyone to get clothes for myself."

As I look at those statements, I ask myself how many of us can boast of all those things Paul said especially in this age when preachers and Christians alike do everything to covert people's wealth and possessions. The truth is, IF YOU JUDGE YOURSELF, YOU WILL NOT BE JUDGED. Examine yourself and make things right.

Acts:20.17-37

"From Miletus, Paul sent to Ephesus for the elders of the church. When they arrived, he said to them: "You know how I lived the whole time I was with you, from the first day I came into the province of Asia. I served the Lord with great humility and with tears, although I was severely tested by the plots of the Jews. Therefore, I declare to you today that I am innocent of the blood of all men. I have not coveted anyone's silver or gold or clothing. They all wept as they embraced him and kissed him."

PRAYER

Heavenly Father, forgive me of all the wrong things I have done. Lord, help me to live a righteous life that is pleasing to You, in Jesus' name, amen.

NOTES

Many times we hear people testifying of how they saw or encountered the Lord. And sometimes they sound very arrogant, boastful, and make it seem as if they walked into the presence of God with their hands in their pockets and had a conversation with God. But when you look at the men who encountered the Lord in the bible, the difference is clear. When Elijah saw God, he cried his eyes begging on the Lord to depart from him for he (Elijah), is a man of unclean lips. When John saw the Lord he fell face down and was dead (to fear) until the Lord tapped him and raised him up. After his ranting and preparing a long list of questions to ask the Lord, when Job finally saw the Lord he was unable to speak. Throughout the bible, anyone who Encountered the Lord had these MARKS:

1- BROKENNESS instead of Arrogance.
2- HUMILITY instead of PRIDE
3- MEEKNESS instead of "I know it all" attitude.

Therefore men don't need to hear your testimony to know you encountered the Lord, they just need to LOOK AT YOUR LIFE. Because when you truly meet God, you die to self.

PRAYER

Lord help me to encounter You in a way that will transform my life.
Father may You help us in our boastfulness and arrogance to truly know You and become humble in Jesus name, amen.

NOTES ....

....

....

....

....

....

....

....

....

....

WEEK 09 | WISDOM NUGGET

EVERY GLORY HAS A STORY

When you look at an army general and admire his stars be sure to also ask him to open up his shirt and show you his scars. There is no glory without a story. Keep on fighting the good fight and your reward will surely come. "And being found in appearance as a man, he humbled himself by becoming obedient to death—even death on a cross! Therefore God exalted him to the highest place and gave him the name that is above every name," (Philippians 2:8-9).

PRAYER

✓ Lord, help me not to quit on You during the tough moments of life. I will keep on trusting You no matter what because I know at the end of my story, I will see Your glory, in Jesus' name.

NOTES

....

....

....

....

....

....

....

....

Sometimes we just need to get back to the ABCs of the Gospel because the gospel is truly as simple as ABC. Jesus in the following scripture encourages us to show hospitality. The most striking statement is in the response Jesus gave when He was asked, 'when did they see Him and helped Him?' He says whatever you did to THE LEAST OF THESE MY BROTHERS, you did to me.

Beloved it is very easy to go visit the wealthy brother or sister who is in the hospital than the poor one who can never repay you in any way. It is very easy to provide help to that wealthy man or woman when they ask because you know he will surely pay you back tremendously. But what of the poor person who can never pay you back? The kind of hospitality Jesus values the most is hospitality shown to those who can never repay you. Jesus says visiting, clothing, feeding, and caring for such is likened to caring for JESUS HIMSELF.

Matthew:25.35-40

For I was hungry and you gave me something to eat, I was thirsty and you gave me something to drink, I was a stranger and you invited me in, I needed clothes and you clothed me, I was sick and you looked after me, I was in prison and you came to visit me.' "Then the righteous will answer him, 'Lord, when did we see you hungry and feed you, or thirsty and give you something to drink? When did we see you a stranger and invite you in, or needing clothes and clothe you? When did we see you sick or in prison and go to visit you?' "The King will reply, 'I tell you the truth, whatever you did for one of the least of these brothers of mine, you did for me.'

PRAYER

Lord, help me to be hospitable to everyone who comes my way. Give me a heart that looks after the poor, in Jesus' name, amen.

NOTES ....

....

....

....

....

....

....

....

....

....

As we look at the life of Jesus, we see a man with tremendous power and authority, yet He lived a very simple life. He made everyone feel comfortable around Him irrespective of their socioeconomic status. He called little children to come to Him; He ate with sinners; He ministered to the rich; He constantly visited the poor, and amongst His disciples He acted like a friend and not a MASTER.

Beloved are you "easy to be with?" Are you the kind of Dad who walks into the house and all the kids run into their rooms? Are you the kind of man or woman in Church who never talks to certain brethren or invites them to your house because they look wretched? Are you the kind of Pastor who talks rudely to your followers and even slap them sometimes (believe me this happens) because you are their spiritual leader? Are you the kind of Pastor who lords it over his Church? Are you 'EASY TO BE WITH' or people feel 'UNEASE AROUND YOU?' Let us all learn from Jesus.

1Peter5:3 "

One of his disciples, whom Jesus loved, was at the table, leaning against Jesus' breast".

John 13:23.

"..not lording it over those entrusted to you, but being examples to the flock."

PRAYER

Most Loving Father, help me to become a person that others will feel very comfortable to be around. Whatever is not right in my character, help me make the right adjustments, in Jesus' name, amen.

NOTES ....

....
....
....
....
....
....
....
....
....

Your giving may be accepted and applauded by men meanwhile in the sight of God, it is unacceptable. In the verses below, Paul points out two Types of Givers: Those who sow to please the flesh and those who sow to please the Spirit. A flesh-pleasing giver gives to the Pastor to seal his mouth from condemning his or her misconduct. A Spirit-pleasing Giver gives to the Pastor out of Love and to meet a need. A flesh pleasing sower gives so men can see him and revere him as a wealthy man. Also that he may gain the favor of men. A Spirit-pleasing Giver gives to an individual who can never repay him or add anything to him/her. In his conclusion, Paul says Flesh-Pleasing giving will harvest DESTRUCTION while the Spirit-pleasing Giver will reap Eternal life. As we look at ourselves through the lens of these scriptures, the question is, WHAT KIND OF GIVER ARE YOU?

Galatians 6:6-8

Anyone who receives instruction in the word must share all good things with his instructor. Do not be deceived: God cannot be mocked. A man reaps what he sows. The one who sows to please his sinful nature, from that nature will reap destruction; the one who sows to please the Spirit, from the Spirit will reap eternal life.

PRAYER

Father, may You purify my motives when it comes to giving. Let my giving not be to please men but may it be to glorify Your name, in Jesus' name, amen.

NOTES ....

....

....

....

....

....

....

....

....

....

Naaman has come with leprosy all the way from another country. The prophet gives him a VERY SIMPLE instruction: "go and deep yourself seven times in the Jordan and be healed." But No! Naaman gets offended with the instructions. WHY? He said, "I thought he will come outside and call on the name of the LORD his God, wave his hand over the spot and cure me of my leprosy." So he turned to return home with his disease but for his servant.

Do you know there are believers who will only believe they're healed if the prophet gives them objects like WATER, OIL, FRUIT, HANDKERCHIEF, etc.? Do you know there are people who think God has touched them only WHEN THE PREACHER PUSHES THEM DOWN? Do you know there are people who will only like a Prophet who COMMANDS THEM LIKE SLAVES, and gives them FASTING ASSIGNMENTS?

The Pastor who PRAYS A PRAYER OF FAITH AND DECLARES GOD'S WORD is NOT believed to be God-sent. As unfortunate as it may sound, man likes it when it is complicated but not so with our God.

2 Kings 5:10-11

Elisha sent a messenger to say to him, "Go, wash yourself seven times in the Jordan, and your flesh will be restored and you will be cleansed." But Naaman went away angry and said, "I thought that he would surely come out to me and stand and call on the name of the LORD his God, wave his hand over the spot and cure me of my leprosy.

PRAYER

Lord help me to believe in the simplicity of Your ways in Jesus name.

NOTES

Jesus' parable teaches of a tree that produced no fruit for several years. The planter got tired of coming and not finding fruit on the tree. He was going to cut it down but the gardener pleaded with the owner to give it one more year and if the owner comes back and finds no fruit, then he can cut down the tree. In this parable you are the tree and God is the planter. Jesus is the gardener giving you GRACE to live another day in that sin: hoping you can repent. The reason you didn't die in that sickness or accident is because Jesus wants you to repent. The reason you have been having near misses but still alive is because God wants you to draw closer and become productive with your life. But the grace of God has an end. His Spirit will not wrestle with us forever. If your creator comes back ONE MORE TIME and still finds you living in sin (unproductive), He will have no choice but to cut you down. REPENT NOW because time is not on your side.

Luke:13.6-9

Then he told this parable: "A man had a fig tree, planted in his vineyard, and he went to look for fruit on it, but did not find any. " 'Sir,' the man replied, 'leave it alone for one more year, and I'll dig around it and fertilize it. If it bears fruit next year, fine! If not, then cut it down.' "

PRAYER

Father I thank You for Your mercy and for always giving me a second chance. Lord I repent of my sins and I pray that you give me the grace to be productive for You in Jesus name, amen.

NOTES ....

....

....

....

....

....

....

....

....

....

TRYING TO HELP GOD IS A DANGEROUS THING...

God had promised Abraham and Sarah a great family and a bright future. But after waiting on God and not seeing result, they decided to take another route by having a child with Hagar, hoping it will still lead to the promise. Unfortunately for them, that was the beginning of their end, had God not stepped in.

Beloved, ARE YOU TRYING TO HELP GOD because it looks like He is delaying to act concerning what He promised? Did God promise you a great Church and you are trying to deceive people from other churches to pull them into your church? It is Dangerous trying to help GOD. Has God promised to use you in the miraculous and you are now trying to use charms to achieve that because it seems God is slow? Did God promise you marriage and you're now wearing clothes that expose your body parts and trying to seduce men because you think time is not on your side? I tell you it is Dangerous to try to help GOD. Wait on the Lord and He will show up for you at the right time.

Genesis 16:2

So she said to Abram, "The LORD has kept me from having children. Go, sleep with my maidservant; perhaps I can build a family through her." Abram agreed to what Sarai said.

PRAYER

Father help me to fully depend on You and not lean on my understanding in Jesus name, amen.

NOTES ....

....

....

....

....

....

....

....

....

....

WEEK 10 | WISDOM NUGGET

GO FOR A NAME NOT A TITLE

God told Abraham, "I will make you into a great nation, and I will bless you; I will make your name great, and you will be a blessing." When man exalts man, he gives him a title, but when God exalts a man, He gives him a name. A name is for posterity while a title will only last for as long as you occupy the office that bears that title. I choose to go for a name and not a title. The power we have today as believers is in the Name of Jesus not in all the titles Jesus has. And believe me, Jesus has so many titles but demons will only run out when you mention the name: JESUS. See Philippians 2:9-11. I choose to go for a name and not for titles.

PRAYER

✓ Father, in the name of Jesus I pray that You will give me a name in the land of the living. Lord, may the obsession for titles and positions not overwhelm me, in Jesus name. Lord, I come against every strange spirit that has taken over Your children today, causing them to be running after titles. I declare that they will return to being who You want them to be, in Jesus' name, Amen.

NOTES

....

....

....

....

Read Revelation 3;19-20. Let us break this verse down a little to gain some more understanding of what Christ is telling us. "Those whom I love" can only mean those who are in Christ. "To reprove" in this context means "convict." "To be zealous" means "desire after very strongly, to covet." So, Christ is saying: "Those who are in Me, I convict and discipline. So in turn, desire Me, covet Me and repent of your sins. Christ is standing at the door of your heart, knocking. He is the beautiful voice of the shepherd calling us, His sheep. We recognize that voice. That voice to us is more beautiful than a thousand birds singing in unison; more lovely than all the compositions played by man. Even more heart warming than that of my mother when she would sing to me as a child. A voice that changes hearts and minds, and brings forth hearts of flesh that once were stone. He promises that, not only will He talk to us, He will come IN to us, in our hearts, in our minds and live there. He will sustain us, nourish us with His Word, with His voice and with His power. An eternal communion awaits us, one just to lay at His feet and revel in the awe of a Creator so powerful that the very stars hang from the sky by His Word alone. Brothers and sisters, that is our eternity. How glorious it will be.

Revelation 3:19-20.

"Those whom I love, I reprove and discipline, so be zealous and repent. Behold, I stand at the door and knock. If anyone hears my voice and opens the door, I will come in to him and eat with him, and he with me."

PRAYER

Lord, I open up my heart to You and I ask You to come and dine with me. Direct my life and all that I do because I know that You will lead me only to the good paths, in Jesus' name, amen.

NOTES ....

FOLLOWING CHRIST IS NO BED OF ROSES...

As Jesus feeds the hungry, heals the sick, and delivers the oppressed, it was evident that He was no ordinary man. He had become the kind of person everybody will want to identify with. In this particular situation, some young men looked at Jesus doing ministry and desired to be with Him. They saw the fame, the prestige, the POWER, INFLUENCE, and the FOOD that could come their way if they followed Jesus. So they decided to come submit to Him. As they tendered in their applications, Jesus saw their motives and told them: Let it known to you even birds have a place to sleep but I have nowhere to lay my head. In order words, Ministry is NOT a bed of Roses as you may think.

Beloved, just because you see the glitter on a ministry or the success of a Church, it doesn't mean it's all easy. There are struggles you can never see until you get in. Therefore count the cost before you login.

Matthew8:19-22

Then a teacher of the law came to him and said, "Teacher, I will follow you wherever you go." Jesus replied, "Foxes have holes and birds of the air have nests, but the Son of Man has no place to lay his head." Another disciple said to him, "Lord, first let me go and bury my father." But Jesus told him, "Follow me, and let the dead bury their own dead."

PRAYER

Father I thank You for the grace to be called Your child. Lord help me to follow You in both good and bad times in Jesus name, amen.

NOTES ....

Jesus is informed of the sickness of his dear friend Lazarus. But He stayed back until his friend died and was buried and Jesus only showed up four days later. As Jesus shows up, Martha tells Him if He had been around, her brother would not have died. To Martha, Jesus has come late; at a time when ALL HOPE IS GONE. Even though Jesus tried to get her to believe He could raise Lazarus back to life, Martha refused to believe until Jesus went on to raise the dead man back to life. The truth is there was really NO HOPE with Lazarus' situation. But that did not stop God. God's Word is able to make alive every dead situation. We must learn to BELIEVE GOD even if EVERYTHING LOOKS IMPOSSIBLE.

John11:21

"Lord," Martha said to Jesus, "if you had been here, my brother would not have died. John11:23 Jesus said to her, "Your brother will rise again."

PRAYER

Heavenly Father, help me to believe Your word even when the words do not make sense in Jesus name, amen.

NOTES ....

....

....

....

....

....

....

....

....

....

"Be careful not to do your 'acts of righteousness' before men, to be seen by them. If you do, you will have no reward from your Father in heaven. "So when you give to the needy, do not announce it with trumpets, as the hypocrites do in the synagogues and on the streets, to be honored by men. I tell you the truth, they have received their reward in full. (Matthew 6:1-2). Jesus is not saying in the above verses that we should not show our good deeds in public. A closer look at the text will reveal to us that Jesus had a different message. He said, "...do not do your good deeds before men TO BE SEEN BY MEN." In the next verse He says do not blow a Trumpet when you help SO AS TO BE HONORED BY MEN. With this, you can clearly see that the problem IS NOT displaying your CHARITY but THE MOTIVE for which you display is core. If you do good to people and show it publicly to be praised, then it is WRONG. BUT if you show it PUBLICLY to CREATE AWARENESS and Even Get more support, then it is ok. God wants us to feed the hungry, clothe the naked and give shelter to the homeless but our motive for doing that should not be to gain the praises of men.

PRAYER

Merciful Father, give me a heart of love to care for the people and purify my motives so that I don't do this to get the praises of men but to please You, in Jesus' name, amen.

NOTES ....

....

....

....

....

....

....

....

....

....

THIS WILL BE YOUR CROWN IN HEAVEN…

If one were to ask the question: who do you think will receive a great crown in heaven? Many will say: It is the one who has raised the dead, opened blind eyes and deaf ears and the one who has thousands of members in His church. BUT from God's perspective, all these is wrong.

Paul says the ONLY THING that will glorify a person and give him a crown in heaven is THE SOULS YOU ESTABLISH IN CHRIST. Paul says he will labor for his disciples to see Christ formed in them; because on the last day, it is those he nurtured in the Lord that will be his glory in God's presence.

Don't be carried away by all the distractions you see around you. A person who successfully nurtures ONE SOUL to maturity in the Lord is better than the one with ten thousand members who live in sin.

1 Thessalonians 2:11-20

For you know that we dealt with each of you as a father deals with his own children, encouraging, comforting and urging you to live lives worthy of God, who calls you into his kingdom and glory. For what is our hope, our joy, or the crown in which we will glory in the presence of our Lord Jesus when he comes? Is it not you? Indeed, you are our glory and joy.

PRAYER

Father help me to win souls for Your kingdom and to disciple them to maturity in You for this will be my crown when You return in Jesus name, amen.

NOTES ....

....

....

....

....

....

....

....

....

....

Desiring to receive an Impartation from God or a man of God is never a bad thing. But the way you go about it can either be good or bad. Elisha was given one requirement if he going to receive an Impartation from Elijah: he must see Elijah when he is taken up. For Elisha that means one thing: CONSISTENCY IN SERVICE.

He has to stay close to Elijah at ALL TIMES. He has to follow Elijah EVERYWHERE he goes. Even if Elijah went to rest room, Elisha has to stick around because he did not know what time Elijah would be taken up. If you must receive that Impartation from the one you so admire, you must BE CONSISTENT in your commitment to the things God has put in your charge. Work faithfully and tirelessly knowing that your reward is on the way.

You cannot be INCONSISTENT in service and expect to receive an Impartation.

2 Kings 2:9-10

When they had crossed, Elijah said to Elisha, "Tell me, what can I do for you before I am taken from you?" "Let me inherit a double portion of your spirit," Elisha replied. "You have asked a difficult thing," Elijah said, "yet if you see me when I am taken from you, it will be yours--otherwise not."

PRAYER

Most gracious Father, help me to be a faithful servant who is consistent at in his service to You. Lord take away any form of distraction that will want to sway me away from serving You faithfully in Jesus name, amen.

NOTES

....

WEEK11 | WISDOM NUGGET

SINGERS MUST SING THE WORD

Christian music today seems to be losing its taste. Gospel singers are now singing more like worldly musicians. But we are called to be different in both our message and our style. When you start singing the Word, you start sinking the world. Dear gospel minister, sing the Word.

PRAYER

- ✓ Lord, help those whom You have into this noble office as Levites (singers) to fully understand their calling and walk in it. Let every distraction be taken away from them so they can stay focused on their calling.
- ✓ I come against every spirit of the enemy that is trying to infiltrate our churches through music. We shut you out, in Jesus' name, Amen.

NOTES

....
....
....
....
....
....
....
....

The subject of wrestling with enemies (both physical and spiritual) cannot be missed when you talk to believers nowadays. It is preached on almost every pulpit and prayed about in almost every prayer meeting. But why on earth are we serving the ALL POWERFUL GOD and yet we're tormented by enemies? God in His Word does not deny the existence of demonic forces. And so anyone who tries to deny the fact is only operating in error. But even though God acknowledges the presence of demons, He also guarantees His children victory over the enemy. In order for you to experience that victory, God requires that you obey the following instructions. He says: "SIT AT MY RIGHT HAND TILL I have make your enemies YOUR FOOTSTOOL."

Most of us want our enemies to be subject to us but WE DON'T WANT TO SIT BESIDE THE FATHER. God cannot make your enemies your footstool when you're still on your feet: you must SIT. You cannot be moving ahead of God and tell Him to subdue your enemies. You must SIT and let God act. You cannot make God do it within your own timeline. You must sit until the Lord FINISHES, even if it takes ten months or ten years. If God couldn't change the Order for His own Son Jesus when He told Him to sit at His right hand; then you should not think the instructions will be any different for you.

Psalm:110.1

The LORD says to my Lord: "Sit at my right hand until I make your enemies a footstool for your feet."

Matthew:22.44

"'The Lord said to my Lord: "Sit at my right hand until I put your enemies under your feet.

PRAYER

Father help me to be patient and trust You to put an end any demonic activities in my life. Help me to be able sit at Your side and just trust You with my life in Jesus name, amen.

NOTES

A body has many parts but they all work in unity. So is the body of Christ. Let no one think he or she is more important than others. I will let the following scripture speak for itself. 1 Corinthians 12:14-27. Now the body is not made up of one part but of many. As it is, there are many parts, but one body. The eye cannot say to the hand, "I don't need you!" And the head cannot say to the feet, "I don't need you!" On the contrary, those parts of the body that seem to be weaker are indispensable, and the parts that we think are less honorable we treat with special honor. And the parts that are unpresentable are treated with special modesty, Now you are the body of Christ, and each one of you is a part of it.

In the body of Christ, you need me and I need you.

PRAYER

Loving Father, help us to be united in love and in purpose so we all together will accomplish great things for Your kingdom in Jesus name. Lord we come against any spirit of disunity in the body of Christ in Jesus mane, amen.

NOTES

"After the circumcision, there is need to sit down and be healed. No need to rush and hurt ourselves as we fulfill His will." (Pastor Crystabelle Ferim). To be circumcised means to be set apart. And to be apart is synonymous to being called. When God calls a man or gives you a prophetic word saying you've been called into ministry, there is need for you to understand when He actually wants you to start. This is because between the 'CALLING Time' and 'Manifestation Time,' lies the PREPARATION TIME. You can't skip this time and expect to succeed. There is No need to rush into ministry because it's not about who started first; it's about who FINISHES WELL.

Moses waited forty YEARS in the wilderness before starting ministry yet his impact lives till today. Jesus (who was God Himself), prepared for thirty YEARS before starting ministry, yet His impact lives till today. Apostle Paul spent over fourteen YEARS preparing before starting ministry yet his impact lives on till this day. There is no need to rush. Ministry is not a marathon.

Habakkuk2:3

For the revelation awaits an appointed time; it speaks of the end and will not prove false. Though it linger, wait for it; it will certainly come and will not delay.

Galatians 2:1

Fourteen years later I went up again to Jerusalem, this time with Barnabas. I took Titus along also.

PRAYER

Heavenly Father, help me to walk patiently with You. Guide my steps so that I don't rush ahead of You into something You have not prepared for me in Jesus name. Lord help Your church today to learn how to wait on You before they take any action.

NOTES ....

....

....

....

....

....

....

....

....

....

Did God lie when He told Adam and Eve they would die if they ate the Fruit? Because we all know they ate the fruit but stayed alive. Sometimes the only way to get insight into God's Word is by asking SERIUOS questions. The TRUTH is GOD DID NOT LIE because Adam and Eve both DIED. They did not die a physical death but they died in many different ways. First of all, they died a spiritual death which was separation from the presence of God. When they heard God coming towards them, they RAN AND HID themselves. "Whenever you start running away from your Creator, you're dead spiritually." (Dr. Tony Evans). Secondly, they DIED emotionally. Fear came over them. A person who is FEARFUL is a dead person. They also died psychologically. They saw that they were naked. They had no clothes before their fall but didn't see their nakedness. But after their disobedience they saw that they were naked. When you die psychologically, you start seeing things different from the way you have always seen them. THEREFORE, NEVER DISOBEY God's Instructions because even when it looks like you got away with it, the consequences will catch up with you.

Genesis 3:3-8

but God did say, 'You must not eat fruit from the tree that is in the middle of the garden, and you must not touch it, or you will die.'" Then the eyes of both of them were opened, and they realized they were naked; so they sewed fig leaves together and made coverings for themselves. Then the man and his wife heard the sound of the LORD God as he was walking in the garden in the cool of the day, and they hid from the LORD God among the trees of the garden.

PRAYER

Merciful Father, I receive the grace to fully obey Your instructions and to live in Your presence all the days of the life. Lord take away every spirit of disobedience from my life and from Your church in Jesus name, amen.

NOTES

It's NOT the Number that turned out for Altar Call; it's how many LASTED! As Jesus came close to the end of His earthly ministry, He started speaking the most important things so that His disciples will remember when He leaves. He told them the very essence why He called them is TO GO AND BEAR FRUIT (make Disciples). And not just people who will brand themselves as Christians for a week or two, but people who will STAND FIRMLY for Christ till He returns.

The question we must ask ourselves today is: are we really raising FRUIT THAT ABIDE or we are simply excited about the Multitudes that come out and raise their hands and repeat a prayer after preacher? God wants us to bear fruits that last.

John 15:16

You did not choose me, but I chose you and appointed you so that you might go and bear fruit--FRUIT THAT WILL LAST--and so that whatever you ask in my name the Father will give you.

PRAYER

Heavenly Father, help me to be a soul winner and the souls I will win will be souls that last in Jesus name, amen.

NOTES ....
....
....
....
....
....
....
....
....
....

It is very important for us to remind ourselves that even though our God is a God of love and mercy, He is also a God of wrath. In His love and mercy He sent His Son Jesus to die for our sins so that we can believe in Him and be saved from our sins. But those who refuse to find refuge in Jesus will have no place to hide when God eventually punishes the world. It is because of these things the anger of God is coming: self-glorification, Selfish desires, immorality, jealousy and everything that does not glorify God. When this is taken care of, you won't have to worry about the Day of the Lord's judgment.

Colossians 3:5-6

Put to death, therefore, whatever belongs to your earthly nature: sexual immorality, impurity, lust, evil desires and greed, which is idolatry. Because of these, the wrath of God is coming.

PRAYER

Merciful Father, help me to live a life of righteousness so as to be ready for Your coming. Lord help us and give us the grace to put to death the things that belong to our sinful nature in Jesus name, amen.

NOTES ....

....

....

....

....

....

....

....

....

....

WEEK 12 | WISDOM NUGGET

DOWN PAYMENT FOR THE FUTURE

The sacrifice you make today is the down payment for the glories you will enjoy tomorrow. Choose the discomforts of today in exchange for the comfort of tomorrow, knowing that unless you sow, you can never harvest. Don't make the mistake of Esau who forsook his glorious future (birth right) for temporal pleasure (a plate of stew). "Look, I am about to die," Esau said. "What good is the birthright to me?" But Jacob said, "Swear to me first." So he swore an oath to him, selling his birthright to Jacob. (Gen 25:32-33).

PRAYER

- ✓ I choose this day not to settle for temporary pleasure and forsake my future. I will rather go through hardship for this moment and wait for the glorious future God has for me.

- ✓ Lord, I pray You help anyone going through tough moments right now. Lord, help them to know that they're only making a sacrifice which they will live to enjoy in the future.

NOTES

....
....
....
....

The easiest way we sin these days is in our thoughts and our words. It is easy to smile at a brother or sister in Church while cursing them in your heart. The Pharisees looked very holy in front of everyone, but inwardly, Jesus says they are sinners. He tells His disciples "BE ON YOUR GUARD" against this. Meaning it's something that can creep in without you noticing. We must keep this in our minds: There is nothing concealed that will not be disclosed. What you have said in the dark will be heard in the daylight. What you have whispered in the ear in the inner rooms will be proclaimed from the roofs. Righteousness begins when we maintain consciousness of DIVINE PRESENCE. Even though the person you're talking about is not present and may never know what you said about him/her, there is always a HIDDEN CAMERA called the Holy Spirit who sees and hears all that you say and do. Therefore let your righteousness not be like that of the Pharisees but do all AS THOUGH THE LORD IS PRESENT because HE IS INDEED PRESENT right there.

Luke 12:1-3

Meanwhile, when a crowd of many thousands had gathered, so that they were trampling on one another, Jesus began to speak first to his disciples, saying: "Be on your guard against the yeast of the Pharisees, which is hypocrisy. There is nothing concealed that will not be disclosed, or hidden that will not be made known. What you have said in the dark will be heard in the daylight, and what you have whispered in the ear in the inner rooms will be proclaimed from the roofs.

PRAYER

Heavenly Father, help me to live every single day of my life with a consciousness of Your divine presence so that I may not sin against you in Jesus name. Lord help Your church to have unconditional love for one another.

NOTES ....

....

....

....

....

....

....

....

....

....

It is possible to lead many into Heaven and you end up in hell. When we get into some kind of leadership positions, it's easy for us to quickly identify weaknesses in people's lives and discipline them. We can easily offer them materials to read and counseling to restore them. And in the end, a lot of them actually get restored. But that's not the greatest success story of any leader. Paul says it is possible for you to get others into heaven but you yourself end up in hell. So he says, in as much as he preaches to others, he also watches over himself lest he falls. This is because the greatest tragedy of the Kingdom will be preachers who sent many to heaven buy they themselves ended up in hell.

1 Corinthians 9:24-27

Do you not know that in a race all the runners run, but only one gets the prize? Run in such a way as to get the prize. Therefore I do not run like a man running aimlessly; I do not fight like a man beating the air. No, I beat my body and make it my slave so that after I have preached to others, I myself will not be disqualified for the prize.

PRAYER

Gracious Father, grant me the grace to watch myself as I live my days on earth. Let me not be fast to see the sins in the lives of others and not see how messed up my own life is. Help me Lord to make heaven at the end of the day in Jesus name, amen.

NOTES ....

....

....

....

....

....

....

....

....

....

"The major cause of the recent devastating California wild fire is greatly linked to UNDERGROWTH. It is those small trees and shrubs growing under tall trees that quickly caught the fire and spread it up to the forest trees. HAD THERE BEEN NO UNDERGROWTH, the impact would have been less." (Reporter on N.P.R radio). Undergrowth refers to, "A mass of bushes, small trees, and plants, especially growing under the trees in a forest:"

David a seventeen year old kid has just cut off the head of Goliath. As the soldiers returned home, the women sang saying, "Saul has slain his thousands, and David his tens of thousands." As a result of this, Saul is filled with jealousy. "And FROM THAT TIME on Saul kept a jealous eye on David" the Bible records. We would later find out how Saul made many attempts to kill David. But all those attempts stemmed out of THE JEALOUSY that lay deep down in him. When you NURTURE jealousy for someone, it starts growing shrubs in you that will produce hatred and will someday destroy the green vegetation of God. I call it Undergrowth because no one can see it until they go deep down into the forest of your heart. Meaning you can smile with them but your heart is against them. Clear out every undergrowth (jealousy) in your heart because that is what will bring down your beautiful green forest when it catches the fire of hatred.

1 Samuel 18:7-9

As they danced, they sang: "Saul has slain his thousands, and David his tens of thousands." Saul was very angry; this refrain galled him. "They have credited David with tens of thousands," he thought, "but me with only thousands. What more can he get but the kingdom?" And from that time on Saul kept a jealous eye on David.

PRAYER

Father may You help me not to nurse jealousy in my heart for anyone. Purify and sanctify my heart towards everyone Lord in Jesus name, amen.

NOTES ....

....

....

....

....

....

....

....

Rehoboam takes over as king after Solomon. His people came to him pleading for their labor to be reduced since Solomon had done that to build the great kingdom he had. The young king goes to his elders for advice and they told him to do as the people say else the people might rebel against him. But Rehoboam went on to find out from HIS FRIENDS who gave him BAD ADVICE. Tell them "My father laid on you a heavy yoke; I will make it even heavier. My father scourged you with whips; I will scourge you with scorpions.'" His friends advised. Well, in the end, Rehoboam lost that kingdom all because of his TOXIC FRIENDS. The saying is true: "Show me your friends and I will tell who you are." If all the friends around you bring nothing but negativity to the dialogue table, then you got wrong friends. They're toxic because they destroy everyone they come in contact with and that includes you.

1 Kings 12:4-11

"Your father put a heavy yoke on us, but now lighten the harsh labor and the heavy yoke he put on us, and we will serve you." They replied, "If today you will be a servant to these people and serve them and give them a favorable answer, they will always be your servants." But Rehoboam rejected the advice the elders gave him and consulted the young men who had grown up with him and were serving him. My father laid on you a heavy yoke; I will make it even heavier. My father scourged you with whips; I will scourge you with scorpions."

PRAYER

- *Lord help me to carefully select my friends and only walk with people who can bring positivity to my life. Keep away toxic friends from my life in Jesus name, amen.*

NOTES ....

....
....
....
....
....
....
....
....
....

Jesus is out doing ministry when a GENTILE woman came to Him requesting help for her child. At first, Jesus IGNORES her by staying quiet. But as she persisted, Jesus responds by telling her: "I was sent only to the lost sheep of Israel." In other words, I don't want to be derailed from MY ASSIGNMENT. Where you are asking me to come is NOT part of my assignment. But after much persistence, Jesus however granted her request (He is omnipotent and can do as He wills). But here is the lesson for you and me: Never let anyone DERAIL you from what God has called you to do. If you were called to pastor in rural areas, stick to your assignment and DON'T TRY TO BECOME A CITY PASTOR because you will fail. If you were called to lead just a few, DON'T START DREAMING of a mega church because God's grace won't be made available for an assignment He did not give you. Therefore let everyone operate according to the MEASURE of grace that is given to him.

Matthew 15:22-25

A Canaanite woman from that vicinity came to him, crying out, "Lord, Son of David, have mercy on me! My daughter is suffering terribly from demon-possession." Jesus did not answer a word. So his disciples came to him and urged him, "Send her away, for she keeps crying out after us." He answered, "I was sent only to the lost sheep of Israel." The woman came and knelt before him. "Lord, help me!" she said.

PRAYER

- *Heavenly Father, help me to stick to the unique assignment You have called me to do. Lord takeaway every kind of pressure from the lives of Your children these days that makes them want to drift into doing what You have not called them to do in Jesus name, amen.*

NOTES

David has sinned with Bathsheba and has plotted with Joab to kill her husband Uriah so he could marry her and cover for his sins. But after all these, God sent Prophet Nathan to go address David for his sins. Remember David is king. Had Nathan come to David and POUR OUT THE REBUKE DIRECTLY, David would have ordered the death of Nathan. But the Prophet came with a story and made the King to pass his own judgment upon himself and then Nathan opened up. In the end, David is humbled and repents. God can give you a message but will not tell you how to deliver it. Experience and wisdom is required from you to put that message across rightly. It is possible to speak the mind of God and still get beaten or killed simply because of a wrong way of delivery. A message that was meant to bring a transformation in a person can instead be received with hostility simply because of HOW IT WAS PRESENTED. Therefore, in all that you get, get understanding.

2 Samuel 11:27, Chapter 12:1-9

After the time of mourning was over, David had her brought to his house, and she became his wife and bore him a son. But the thing David had done displeased the LORD.

The LORD sent Nathan to David. When he came to him, he said, "There were two men in a certain town, one rich and the other poor. The rich man had a very large number of sheep and cattle, David burned with anger against the man and said to Nathan, "As surely as the LORD lives, the man who did this deserves to die! Why did you despise the word of the LORD by doing what is evil in his eyes? You struck down Uriah the Hittite with the sword and took his wife to be your own. You killed him with the sword of the Ammonites

PRAYER

- *Lord I receive wisdom from You on how to communicate with the people You bring my way. Let my words be filled with wisdom and bring meaning to the hearers in Jesus name, amen.*

NOTES ....

....

....

....

....

....

....

....

WEEK 13 | WISDOM NUGGET

CALLED TO FEED THEM NOT FEED ON THEM

As Preachers and Pastors, we must avoid walking into our churches and seeing our congregation as a cash cow from where we will enrich ourselves. Failure to do this will negatively affect our presentation of God's Word to the sheep He has given us. You are called to feed them and not to feed on them.

PRAYER

✓ Lord, we pray that Your servants will not get caught in the temptation of seeing their congregations as a source for them to make fast cash but that they will genuinely love to see their growth spiritually.

✓ Lord, any challenges in their lives that maybe causing them to try to use their calling for the wrong reasons, may You take it away, in Jesus' name, Amen.

NOTES

....
....
....
....
....
....
....
....

Jesus stops under a tree and tells Zacchaeus He will be guest at his house that day. The man gladly receives Jesus even though the people murmured that Jesus was eating with tax collectors. As they sat down eating at the table, Jesus did not preach any sermon. He did not even speak a word, but JUST HIS PRESENCE brought CONVICTION upon the sinner which led to his repentance. "Look, Lord! Here and now I give half of my possessions to the poor, and if I have cheated anybody out of anything, I will pay back four times the amount." Zacchaeus said.

If there is one thing we need in these last days to change our generation, it is DIVINE PRESENCE. A preacher can talk from morning till night and everyone is clapping, but without DIVINE PRESENCE there'd be NO impact. A carrier of Divine Presence just needs to show up somewhere; even without saying a word, demons will run out of people and conviction will overwhelm everyone. GO FOR DIVINE PRESENCE.

Luke 19:5-9

When Jesus reached the spot, he looked up and said to him, "Zacchaeus, come down immediately. I must stay at your house today." All the people saw this and began to mutter, "He has gone to be the guest of a 'sinner.'" But Zacchaeus stood up and said to the Lord, "Look, Lord! Here and now I give half of my possessions to the poor, and if I have cheated anybody out of anything, I will pay back four times the amount." Jesus said to him, "Today salvation has come to this house, because this man, too, is a son of Abraham.

PRAYER

Lord, release Your overwhelming presence upon me. Let me carry Your power of Your presence everywhere I go and that men will encounter You when they come in contact with me, in Jesus' name, amen.

NOTES

Permit me begin with this statement from Paul: "For we are God's workmanship, created in Christ Jesus to do good works, which God prepared in advance for us to do." (Eph 2.10). It is very easy to get caught in the web of religious boastings even without knowing. After all, we got inspired by other great men of God who shared their testimonies of how they fasted, went on retreats, sow seeds and THEN GOD GAVE THEM POWER. So you also took that route; went on long fasts and sowed seeds and now 'you see results.' So why won't you boast. Why won't you feel special and demand reverence? Look at your; miracles, accurate prophecies, healings, breakthroughs, even look at the size of your church. All these did not come cheap. YOU PAID THE PRICE you will say.

But the simple truth is that you did not receive all what you have because of what you did? You are who you are and all what you have is as a result of ONE THING: God's GRACE Not your Works. But you may ask what of those who don't have these proofs. Well, Paul says: you were prepared in advance to do what you do. Each one of us has a unique task God had prepared us IN ADVANCE to do. So in all you Do and Achieve, DO NOT BOAST for it is Christ who works in you by His Grace.

Ephesians 2:8-10

For it is by grace you have been saved, through faith-- and this not from yourselves, it is the gift of God--not by works, so that no one can boast. For we are God's workmanship, created in Christ Jesus to do good works, which God prepared in advance for us to do.

PRAYER

Lord Almighty, help us to always remember that we are who we are and have what we have because of Your grace. Help us to stay humble to You in Jesus name, amen.

NOTES ....

....

....

....

....

....

....

....

....

....

Mighty, anointed, strong, and brave Samson assumed he had become a superstar in displaying God's power. He now believes no matter how he lives his life, 'power will still flow.' So he ends up with Delilah who wanted to trade his anointing for silver and gold. Samson tricks her a couple of times just to preserve his oil. But after a while, Samson became careless with his unction. After telling Delilah his secret, the Philistines came upon him and "...He awoke from his sleep and thought, "I'LL GO AS USUAL and shake myself free." But he did not know that the LORD HAD LEFT HIM.

ARE YOU STARTING TO TAKE GOD'S ANOINTING FOR GRANTED? You used to spend hours praying before a ministration, but now you leave from watching soccer or a movie straight to the pulpit. You will soon discover like Samson that THE OIL IS GONE. You used to see sin and run away, but now you see sin and find scriptures to justify it. Well, very soon it will not be business as USUAL. You used to depend solely on God's power but now you are mixing powers because you claim your friends are all doing same. Well, one of these days you may not survive the Philistines AS USUAL. Because You LOSE RELEVANCE THE the Day you start taking God's ANOINTING for GRANTED.

Judges:16.20

Then she called, "Samson, the Philistines are upon you!" He awoke from his sleep and thought, "I'll go out as before and shake myself free." But he did not know that the LORD had left him.

PRAYER

Father, help me not to take Your anointing on my life for granted, in Jesus' name, amen.

NOTES ....

....

....

....

....

....

....

....

....

....

The Spirit can RESTRICT You from Preaching. In as much as God's Word must be preached to all people right to the ends of the earth, there are moments God will restrict a person from Preaching for one reason or the other. This was the case with Apostle Paul and his team as they were stopped twice from preaching in certain cities. God knows the hearts of all men and when He sees that your audience will not yield to His Word, He can restrict you from preaching to them.

God could be restricting you from one place and sending you to a more open group of persons somewhere else. Therefore, you must be led by the Spirit of God even when it comes to who you can share the gospel with.

Acts 16:6-8

Paul and his companions traveled throughout the region of Phrygia and Galatia, having been kept by the Holy Spirit from preaching the word in the province of Asia. When they came to the border of Mysia, they tried to enter Bithynia, but the Spirit of Jesus would not allow them to. So they passed by Mysia and went down to Troas.

PRAYER

Precious Holy Spirit, I pray for Your guidance when it comes to sharing Your Word. Lead me to the people and places You have prepared for me to share Your Word and as I do so, let there be a great harvest, in Jesus' name.

NOTES

Sometimes people make statements like: If he claims to have the healing gift, why then is he himself sick? If God is using him to change lives why has he not changed the lives in his own family? If he prays for people and they receive breakthroughs then why is he himself struggling? These questions did not begin today because even the Pharisees told Jesus, "Physician, first heal yourself." Apostle Paul also struggled with this because as a mighty healer, he never expected that he could be sick. But it happened that he fell sick and after praying three times for healing and getting no answer, he finally came to terms with the fact that, God's power can flow through you without flowing within you. This is because His anointing upon a man is for service and not just for himself. God does this to remind us that He is the one working miracles through us and it is not our own power. This will keep us humble and not cause men to look up to the man of God but to look up to the God of the man.

2 Corinthians 12:7-9

To keep me from becoming conceited because of these surpassingly great revelations, there was given me a thorn in my flesh, a messenger of Satan, to torment me. Three times I pleaded with the Lord to take it away from me. But he said to me, "My grace is sufficient for you, for my power is made perfect in weakness." Therefore I will boast all the more gladly about my weaknesses, so that Christ's power may rest on me.

PRAYER

Heavenly Father, I thank You for Your anointing upon my life. Lord I arise to the consciousness that Your anointing on me is to serve people and not for myself. Therefore Lord keep me humble to always look up to you for Grace, in Jesus' name, amen.

NOTES ....

....

....

....

....

....

....

....

....

....

Sometimes we get overwhelmed by the assignment God has given us that we literally pour out our frustration in the wrong places. But when the task becomes difficult, complain to the task giver not to the task itself. This was the SECRET OF MOSES in dealing with the Israelites. They were such a difficult people to handle, but every time Moses faced difficulties with them, HE WENT TO THE LORD FOR HELP.

If God has made you a leader over people; that is a task He has given you to carry. Anytime those people become too difficult for you to handle, always go back to the Lord who gave them to you. Never pour out your frustration and complains to the task (those you are leading) pour it out to the task giver.

Exodus 17:4.

Then Moses cried out to the LORD, "What am I to do with these people? They are almost ready to stone me."

Exodus 14:15.

Then the LORD said to Moses, "Why are you crying out to me? Tell the Israelites to move on.

Numbers 11:2.

When the people cried out to Moses, he prayed to the LORD and the fire died down.

PRAYER

- *Lord help me to always look up to you for help in accomplishing the task You have given me in Jesus name, amen.*

NOTES ....

....

....

....

....

....

....

....

....

....

WEEK 14 | WISDOM NUGGET 05/04/2020

NO PLACE FOR JEALOUSY

The sky is too wide for two birds to collide. For that to happen, the birds are either blind or they have been shot. The disciples of John came and reported a situation to John that would have brought about a clash between John and Jesus. But John gave no place for jealousy. You too must do same. “They came to John and said to him, “Rabbi, that man who was with you on the other side of the Jordan - the one you testified about - well, he is baptizing, and everyone is going to him.” To this John replied, “A man can receive only what is given him from heaven.” (John 3:26-27).

PRAYER

- ✓ Father, kill every seed of jealousy that maybe growing in me.
- ✓ Lord, may I look out for the good of others even when it makes me uncomfortable.

NOTES

....
....
....
....
....

Everywhere Apostle Paul went with his team to share the Word of God, their audience listened to them as Servants of God and took everything they said as God's instructions. That's ok to do until you meet those who claim to be God's mouth piece yet they teach another gospel. The Bereans DISTINGUISHED themselves in that; they did not just swallow everything Paul told them. They received Paul's message but then went on to EXAMINE IT to see if IT IS IN LINE WITH GOD'S WORD. Paul commended them for this.

In these last days when many wolves have gone out there in sheep clothing, it is very important that you examine every teaching you get out there to see if it lines up with all scripture. Don't just assume a Dr. in theology, a Bishop, an Apostle or a Right Rev. is enough to compel you to follow their teachings blindly. Go back and examine it to make sure it fits in with the rest of scripture. So much has happened nowadays that we all are now compelled to take every teaching out there with a pinch of salt.

Acts:17.11

Now the Bereans were of more noble character than the Thessalonians, for they received the message with great eagerness and examined the Scriptures every day to see if what Paul said was true.

PRAYER

Lord, help me to have the attitude of the Berean Christians so that I will not walk in error. Lord, deliver the body of Christ from all forms of deception as we examine every teaching in light of Your Word.

NOTES ....

....

....

....

....

....

....

....

....

....

A situation arose in Corinth among the brethren. Some said they belong to Paul and others said Appollos. Paul could have used this incident to his advantage. It could have been a moment for him to draw huge followers to himself. Rather he rebuked them and told them Christ is not divided and said neither him nor Appollos died to save them: only Christ died so they must follow Christ and not men.

There will be no place for all the division in the body of Christ today if we could have the same mindset as Paul. We would not restrict our members from attending other church programs and even talk down on other genuine ministers. We will not delights in comparing ministers and saying which one is better than the other. Our focus should be Christ and wherever Christ is preached by whosoever, we should gladly celebrate.

1 Corinthians 1:11-15

My brothers, some from Chloe's household have informed me that there are quarrels among you. What I mean is this: One of you says, "I follow Paul"; another, "I follow Apollos"; another, "I follow Cephas"; still another, "I follow Christ." Is Christ divided? Was Paul crucified for you? Were you baptized into the name of Paul? I am thankful that I did not baptize any of you except Crispus and Gaius, so no one can say that you were baptized into my name.

PRAYER

Heavenly Father, help Your church to be united in purpose. Lord takeaway every division in the body of Christ today and give us the spirit of unity and focus on Christ, in Jesus' name, amen.

NOTES ....

....

....

....

....

....

....

....

....

....

At some point in the ministry of Jesus, He made statements that baffled His followers. What He said was so weird that it made Him lose more than half of His followers. How could they stay with a person who says they must eat His flesh and drink His blood? But even though so many left him that day, He did not reverse or withdraw the statement He had made. This is because, what the people understood was not what He intended.

The same thing happened when he told the Pharisees "before Abraham was (born), I am!" They picked up stones to stone Him because they said Jesus was not even up to fifty years old and He said He was before Abraham. Again their understanding was not the intended meaning of Jesus. So He ignored them and left the scene. It is needless trying to explain yourself over and over to some people who completely misunderstand what you said and instead of asking for explanations, decide to come up with a different meaning to your message. As long as your intentions were good and you had a different meaning to what you said, ignore and walkaway. The truth will eventually be known at the end of the day.

John 6:54-59

Whoever eats my flesh and drinks my blood has eternal life, and I will raise him up at the last day. Your father Abraham rejoiced at the thought of seeing my day; he saw it and was glad." "You are not yet fifty years old," the Jews said to him, "and you have seen Abraham!" "I tell you the truth," Jesus answered, "before Abraham was born, I am!" At this, they picked up stones to stone him, but Jesus hid himself, slipping away from the temple grounds.

PRAYER

Lord, help me to ignore and walk away when people misunderstand me and say things that I did not say, in Jesus' name, amen.

NOTES ....

A small shepherd boy leaves the jungle and heads to the battlefield to give his brothers food. Just at that instant, Goliath comes out to mock the army of God. God sends David to take him down and that is exactly what happened. The moment that happened, DAVID'S entire destiny changed. FROM THAT DAY, the shepherd boy became a PALACE BOY. His friends changed, his meals changed, his clothes changed, and everything about him changed ON THAT ONE DAY.

All of humanity was heading to a DEAD END; on a highway to destruction BUT on ONE DAY, JESUS the Christ was born and that changed the destiny of all men who believe in Him. Whatsoever you might have been going through in life, IT TAKES JUST ONE DAY for God to turn that story around. I pray TODAY will be your ONE DAY for a Turn around.

Luke 2:11

TODAY in the town of David a Savior has been born to you; he is Christ the Lord.

1 Samuel 17:57

As soon as David returned from killing the Philistine, Abner took him and brought him before Saul, with David still holding the Philistine's head.

1 Samuel 18:2

From THAT DAY Saul kept David with him and did not let him return to his father's house.

PRAYER

Lord, I know You can do the impossible in one day; let this day be the day of a turnaround in my life and in the lives of those who desire a breakthrough from You Lord, in Jesus' name, amen.

NOTES

God gives Moses very simple instructions on how to get water from the rock. Moses starts by doing exactly what God said but he DERAILED along the way. The instructions were:

- Take the Staff. Gather the Assembly. SPEAK to the Rock; it will pour out water.

Moses did the above But ADDED the following:

- He Rebuked the congregation. "Listen you rebels.." he said.
- Moses raised his arm and struck the rock twice with his staff.

Then God said to Moses and Aaron: "Because you did not trust in me enough to honor me as holy in the sight of the Israelites, you will not bring this community into the land I give them."

This simple mistake from Moses made him not to enter the promised land. When God gives us instructions, we must carry them out EXACTLY as He said them. Your followers MAY NOT KNOW you have disobeyed God and thus are still celebrating the miracle of water, but that will not avert God's discipline.

Read Numbers 20:7-12

PRAYER

Lord, may You help me to obey Your Word and carry out Your instructions exactly as You gave them, in Jesus' name, amen.

NOTES ....

....

....

....

....

....

....

....

....

....

King Nebuchadnezzar had a dream no one could narrate or interpret. This placed Daniel's life along with all the wise men at risk of being executed. But Daniel went to the Lord for help and got what the King needed. After Daniel interpreted the dream, the King decided to promote him and give him many gifts. Daniel could have gladly received all that and walked away. But HE THOUGHT OF HIS FRIENDS and requested that they too be promoted and the King did. This is proof of a man who has the good of others on his mind.

It was easy for him to say, I labored for this breakthrough alone, I prayed and fasted alone, where were my friends when I spent sleepless nights because my life was in danger? But that was not Daniel. He had a heart for people. When you see that job opportunity do you ever care to inform your brother? When you come across that piece of information that can be beneficial to someone you know, do you ever care to inform them? Let's learn from Daniel and try to pull others along with us when we climb life's socio-economic ladder.

Daniel:2.48-49

"Then the king placed Daniel in a high position and lavished many gifts on him. He made him ruler over the entire province of Babylon and placed him in charge of all its wise men. Moreover, at Daniel's REQUESTED the king appointed Shadrach, Meshach and Abednego administrators over the province of Babylon, while Daniel himself remained at the royal court."

PRAYER

Lord, give me a heart that looks after the good of others. Take away every selfishness from my heart, in Jesus' name, amen.

NOTES ....

WEEK 15 | WISDOM NUGGET 12/04/2020

CAN YOU STAND WEALTH AND POWER

There is a kind of humility that poverty imposes on a people: but give a man WEALTH and POWER and you'd see a revelation of his True Character. The true test of your commitment to God is not in your broke days; it is in the days when your barns are full. Can God still count on you when you are wealthy as much He did when you were broke? "When the young man heard this, he went away sad, because he had great wealth. Then Jesus said to his disciples, "Truly I tell you, it is hard for someone who is rich to enter the kingdom of heaven. (Matt. 19:22-23).

PRAYER

✓ Father, please guide my heart not to forget You even in my prosperity.

✓ Lord, always help me to remember that I am who I am because of You, in Jesus' name, Amen.

NOTES

....
....
....
....

The Church of Christ is supposed to be reaching the souls that are lost out there in the world and not snatching the ones that have been found and are sitting in a church somewhere. Don't you know that a kingdom divided against itself cannot stand? (Mk 3:24). When Paul and Silas came into the city, it was the kingdom of darkness that lost a member (Acts 16:19). Let us not make the mistake of trying to snatch members from other churches into our church and think we are having church growth. Our call is to reach the unsaved and not to snatch the saved.

Acts 16:19.

When her owners realized that their hope of making money was gone, they seized Paul and Silas and dragged them into the marketplace to face the authorities.

PRAYER

Father, help the Church to come to the consciousness of what You have called us to do. Help us to truly reach out to the lost out there who have not known You, in Jesus name, amen.

NOTES

A Church without POWER (God's power) is like a building without a roof. You can paint it, decorate it, put a new carpet and dress it with the most expensive furniture; it will still LOSE ALL its OCCUPANTS on a RAINY Day. Such a building is only good for good weather. Oh that God will anoint His servants with power the same way He anointed Jesus of Nazareth with the Holy Ghost and Power (Acts 10:38). It is only when we have received power that we can boldly speak His Word. Acts 1:8 says ..and you shall SPEAK MY WORD in Jerusalem, Judea, Samaria and the rest of the world. We must continue to cry to God for a church filled with His power because His power is the only thing that will make a difference in this generation.

PRAYER

Heavenly Father, we commit Your Church into Your hands and ask that You fill it with Your Holy Spirit and with Power in such a way that everyone who comes in will go back with a touch, in Jesus' name, amen.

NOTES

Just the other day I watched a video of a preacher illustrating freedom and deliverance with the use of a key and padlock. He had asked all his members to bring padlocks to Church which they all did. The message was: the moment he prays and they unlock the padlocks; everywhere they were tied, they will immediately be unlocked. I wept as I watched the performance unfold in what is supposed to be the house of God. Some will defend this act calling a "prophetic act". The only problem with such practices is that it can go to very wild extremes. If everything can be used as a prophetic sign, then I won't be surprised if one of these days church members are asked to bring caskets to Church to use it as "prophetic act" to bury their enemies. A heart that truly seeks God believes God by faith and not by physical so-called "prophetic acts" which ties to people's faith to objects instead of God. Jesus says: *"..A wicked and adulterous generation seeks for a sign.." Matt 16:4*. He also asked "*..when the Son of man comes, will He find faith on earth?.." Luke 18:8*. Faith in God is all you need.

PRAYER

Merciful Father, please have mercy on Your church and save Your children from the deception of the Devil. Lord take away every scale that has blinded Your children and driven them away from Your true word into falsehood and bring them back to the light in Jesus name, amen.

NOTES

Like the people of Israel, sometimes it seems as if your life has taken the wilderness route on the journey to freedom. Israel could have taken a direct route and made it to their Promised Land in about two weeks but God decided to take them through the wilderness. But why would God choose such a long route when there was a shorter, more obvious direct route? Why did the Iraelites linger in the wilderness and ended up with a journey that lasted forty years? God wanted to teach them some very important lessons.

While in the wilderness, the Israelites learned how to trust and depend on God alone. They learned patience and endurance as well as how to govern themselves. By the time they finally got to Canaan, no opposition was able to stand their way. The reason your struggles still linger is because God is working out some things for your good and preparing you for an unprecedented victory. Hang in there and trust God and it won't be long before you sing your victory song.

Exodus 33:14.

The LORD replied, "My Presence will go with you, and I will give you rest."

PRAYER

Lord, I thank You for the grace to trust You even in my struggles. I know that You are working things out for my good and I will rejoice in the end. I trust You with my life and I know You will never fail in Jesus' name, amen.

NOTES ....

What is on your mind? The outcome of your life is a result of your thoughts. What you think is what you become. "Getting out of drugs and quitting smoking is a mind thing. Laying aside the garment of fornication and adultery is a mind thing. If you think you're broke, you're gonna be broke" (Bishop TD Jakes). The heart is the central processing unit of every human being. Change your thoughts and you'd change your life.

Proverbs 23:7

for as he thinks within himself, so he is. "Eat and drink!" he'll say to you, but his heart won't be with you.

PRAYER

Father help me to have the right thoughts in my heart. Thoughts that will make me a better person and not thoughts that will destroy me. Clean up my heart and give me a brand new heart that will think godly in Jesus name.

NOTES ....

....

....

....

....

....

....

....

....

....

To deliberately and continuously live in sin and say "we are in the era of grace" or even quoting Eph. 2:8-9, "*we are saved by Grace through faith... not by the things we do*" is like setting your house on fire or deliberately crashing your car because you have Insurance to cover for it. Well the truth is, it will only be too late for you when the Insurance company pulls out the OTHER DETAILS of your policy. The same book which has Eph. 2:8-9 also has Rom. 6:1-2 *("What shall we say then? Shall we continue in sin, that grace may abound?. God forbid. How shall we, that are dead to sin, live any longer therein?")*.The Bible is a whole book. Read all of it to get the complete picture. Don't just read the first page of your insurance policy and make conclusions. There are more IMPORTANT details inside.

Ezekiel 18:20.

"The soul that sins shall die.."

PRAYER

Gracious Lord, help me not to take Your grace for granted. I receive the grace to live a righteous life for You, in Jesus' name, amen.

NOTES ....

....

....

....

....

....

....

....

....

....

WEEK 16 | WISDOM NUGGET 19/04/2020

BE SURE THE WORD SAYS IT

There are many things we hear being preached in churches today which are not in line with God's Word. But no matter how sweet it sounds, if the Word does not say it; don't believe it. Colossians: 2:8 says: "See to it that no one takes you captive through hollow and deceptive philosophy, which depends on human tradition and the basic principles of this world rather than on Christ."

PRAYER

- ✓ Lord, deliver me from any form of deception today, in Jesus name.
- ✓ Lord, deliver the church from false teachings that are not founded in the Word, in Jesus' name.

NOTES

....
....
....
....
....
....
....
....
....

AVOID TESTIMONIES THAT GLORIFY MEN AND NOT GOD...

It appears these days if you must qualify to be among those to give a testimony in Church, you must include the Pastor's name or use the words; "this commission." The following statements should not be missing if you want to PASS the screening process: "...but ever since I joined this commission or stepped my feet into this place..." "...as soon as Papa laid his hand on me or prophesied to me, everything started working well..." The screeners are well drilled to select only those whose testimonies promote the Pastor or the commission. This leaves me wondering if God is still the giver of such testimonies. Well maybe He's not in some cases and that's why the testimonies are either full of lies and exaggeration or they are short lived. If we are truly testifying of "what the Lord has done," then let us give Him ALL the glory and none of it to man because God will not share His glory with any man.

Isaiah 42:8.

I am the LORD: that is my name: and my glory will I not give to another, neither my praise to graven images.

PRAYER

Dear Lord, may You save us in this generation and take us out of perversion in Jesus name, amen.

NOTES

King Saul was still in the Palace when God told Samuel to go to the house of Jesse and anoint Him a king for He has rejected Saul as king. May I remind us that, the Crowd may still be celebrating and clapping for you meanwhile Heaven has closed your file. God does not send out a communiqué when He fires His employee; you will only discover on Pay Day that you have NO SALARY and your termination letter will read: *"Depart from Me for I know you not, thou worker of iniquity"* (Matt. 7:23). Therefore as you labor for God in any capacity whatsoever, be sure to carry out your functions with fear and trembling.

1 Samuel 16:1.

The LORD said to Samuel, "How long will you mourn for Saul, since I have rejected him as king over Israel? Fill your horn with oil and be on your way; I am sending you to Jesse of Bethlehem. I have chosen one of his sons to be king."

PRAYER

Lord, Help me to Keep my eyes on You alone as I serve You. Help Your servants not to get their approval from men but from You, in Jesus' name, amen.

NOTES ....

....

....

....

....

....

....

....

....

....

God has called us and sent us into the world to make disciples for Him and not fans for ourselves. It is dangerous for any minister to have a church full of fans instead of disciples. Fans will clap for anything they hear coming from the one they admire. But just because the Crowd is clapping for you doesn't mean you're making headline news in heaven. One other thing you must know about fans is that they are very unpredictable. The same crowd or fans that shouted "Hossana to the Son of David" as Jesus entered Jerusalem was the same crowd that shouted "Crucify Him and give us Barrabas" a few days later. Therefore raise disciples and not fans.

Matthew 21:8-9.

A very large crowd spread their cloaks on the road, while others cut branches from the trees and spread them on the road. The crowds that went ahead of him and those that followed shouted, "Hosanna to the Son of David!" "Blessed is he who comes in the name of the Lord!" "Hosanna in the highest heaven!"

Luke 23:21.

But they kept shouting, "Crucify him! Crucify him!"

PRAYER

Lord help us to be disciple makers which is what You have called us to do in Jesus name, amen.

NOTES

The Lord GIVES Seed to the Sower and Bread to the Eater. The GIFT is the same but the receiver gives it a meaning. Tom receives it and calls it SEED while Jerry calls it BREAD. Down the road Tom becomes rich because he planted (invested) the seed and Jerry becomes poor because to him it was bread which he ate and there is nothing left. Then Jerry starts crying to God saying: "Oh Lord change my situation, oh Lord why me? Look at Tom whom I grew up together with and went to the same college; he is far better off than me. Why have You abandoned me Lord?" What you don't know is that you both received the same gifts from God but you decided to waste your portion in eating and drinking, buying new clothes and shoes, traveling, buying that latest car, while Tom was busy investing the seed he received. And now he is better off. The saying goes: you can't eat your cake and have it. Choose to be an investor and not a consumer.

Ecclesiastes 11:1.

Cast your bread upon the waters: for you shall find it after many days.

PRAYER

Lord I receive the grace to invest in my future. I will not only think about temporary pleasures but I will set my eyes on future and invest in in Jesus name, amen.

NOTES ....

....

....

....

....

....

....

....

....

....

People often say "I was pushed to the wall and that's why I reacted the way I did." Permit me use this illustration from Pastor Raymond Gobum. He says if you take an orange fruit; throw it high in the air and let it drop to the ground, pick it up and hit it against the wall, put it in an oven and broil it, thereafter take it out and squeeze the juice out of it, taste it and you'd notice it will still taste sweet. On the other hand when take a lime or lemon and wash it carefully, lay it on a king size bed, place it under a fan to keep it cool and thereafter, squeeze out its juice and taste of it, it will taste SOUR!! So what you give out (your reaction) is not as a result of how you were treated; it is simply a manifestation of the kind of liquid (nature) that resides in you. It is either SWEET or SOUR.

This illustration changed my life entirely. Jesus displayed this by His death as was prophesied in Isaiah *53:7 "He was oppressed, and he was afflicted, yet HE OPENED NOT HIS MOUTH: he is brought as a lamb to the slaughter, and as a sheep before her shearers is dumb, so HE OPENED NOT HIS MOUTH."* Let us crave for the nature of Christ to fully dwell in us.

Philippians 2:5.

You must have the same attitude that Christ Jesus had.

PRAYER

Loving Father, help me to become more and more like You in the way I love and relate with. Lord takeaway any nature in me that does not reflect Your nature, in Jesus' name, amen.

NOTES

Ephesians 4:11-12 says, "And he gave some, apostles; and some, prophets; and some, evangelists; and some, pastors and teachers; For the perfecting of the saints, for the work of the ministry, for the edifying of the body of Christ:" When God gave those different gifts to men, it was NEVER for the Purpose of COMPETITION or to show who is Superior to the other; the gifts were given to complement one another. So we may be DIFFERENT in Functions (Titles) but we are all of equal importance. We are all members of the same body carrying out different functions for the good of THE SAME body.

"The eye cannot say to the hand, "I don't need you!" And the head cannot say to the feet, "I don't need you!" (1 Cor 12:21). Therefore let the APOSTLE NOT think he is more Important than the PASTOR (Teacher), neither should the PROPHET think he is more important than the EVANGELIST. The Worldly system has polluted our belief system by its way of competition but we of the Kingdom must learn to live by the standard of God's Word.

PRAYER

Father, help Your servants to not be caught up in unnecessary competition as to who is important than the other but united, knowing they are all members of one body, in Jesus' name, amen.

NOTES

....

....

....

....

....

....

....

....

....

....

WEEK 17 | WISDOM NUGGET 26/04/2020

WRITE NOBODY OFF

A keen look at the heroes of faith will tell you that God's Heroes are NOT those who were Flawless: they are those who were SELFLESS. Time will fail me to tell you about the great names in Hebrew chapter 11. They had a lot of mess in their lives but God cleaned them up and used them. So don't write anybody off when the owner of the pen has not given you permission.

PRAYER

✓ Lord, I come to You in humility knowing that I am not perfect in my ways but I believe that You will bypass my weaknesses and grant me your strength to becoming who You have made me to be.

✓ Lord, help me not to look at people based on their deeds but to see them with the eyes of love, in Jesus' name.

NOTES

....

....

....

....

....

....

....

"Someone told him, "Your mother and brothers are standing outside, wanting to see you." He replied, "My mother and brothers are those who hear God's word and put it into practice." (Luke 8:20-21). The House of God is different from your living room or your private corporation where you and your family can run things the way you like. In the Church, we ALL report to the Boss of the Church: Christ Jesus. So don't make the mistake of putting your wife first, your children second, your brothers/sisters third, your in-laws fourth, and then all else can come after. Jesus' mother and brothers did not understand that and thought Jesus will drop what He was doing to rush to them or maybe bring them to the front and give them a special seat. But not so with Jesus. In God's house, the things of God must be put first and done in the way God wants.

PRAYER

Lord, help us to do Church Your way and not our way knowing that it is Your work and not our work, in Jesus' name, amen.

NOTES

....

BEWARE OF BRIBERY AND CORRUPTION...

King Balak is scared of the Israelites and sends for Balaam the prophet to come curse them. But God refrained Balaam from going. He heeded to God's voice until money and gifts changed hands. We must be careful not to heed to the power of MONEY and GIFTS but heed to the VOICE OF GOD. *"The elders of Moab and Midian left, taking with them the fee for divination. When they came to Balaam, they told him what Balak had said. But God said to Balaam, "Do not go with them. You must not put a curse on those people, because they are blessed." The next morning Balaam got up and said to Balak's princes, "Go back to your own country, for the LORD has refused to let me go with you." Then Balak sent other princes, more numerous and more distinguished than the first. ..because I will reward you handsomely and do whatever you say. Come and put a curse on these people for me." But God was very angry when he went, and the angel of the LORD stood in the road to oppose him. Balaam was riding on his donkey, and his two servants were with him".* (Num. 22: 7-22). As a servant of God, you must beware of bribery and corruption.

PRAYER

Lord, keep my heart from being deceived by men and help me overcome the power of money in Jesus' name. Help Your servants not to run after money but to yield to Your voice in Jesus' name, amen.

NOTES ....

....

....

....

....

....

....

....

....

....

When people get questioned as to why their followers seem to be worshipping them, the common excuse we get is "I didn't force anybody to bow, kneel, prostrate or honor me the way they do." The Truth is you can always stop people from doing what they do. Statistics have proven that someone who is truly humble (including unbelievers) cannot stand and watch others adore or bow to him. He will resist them in every way he/she possibly can. If this is true with unbelievers, how much more of servants of God? Remember that no matter the excuses we give, we will not be judged based on what people did to us; we will be judged based on how we reacted to what was done to us. If you didn't REJECT it, then you ACCEPTED it.

Acts 14:14-15.

"But when the apostles Barnabas and Paul heard of this, (the people were trying to worship them/sacrifice to them), they tore their clothes and rushed out into the crowd, shouting: "Men, why are you doing this? We too are only men, human like you. We are bringing you good news, telling you to turn from these worthless things to the living God, who made heaven and earth and sea and everything in them."

PRAYER

Lord, may You keep molding us until we truly conform to the image of Your Son Jesus Christ. Take away every pride from our heart and give us the grace to stop men from making us their god in Jesus' name, amen.

NOTES ....

....

....

....

....

....

....

....

....

....

When we go through difficult times or we suffer for God, it is easy to think that God has abandoned us or we are the only ones going through that rejection. Elijah thought same until God's message came to him informing him of God's reserve army. Elijah had a feeling of abandonment not knowing that while he was resisting Baal in one part of the country, there were seven thousand prophets in another part facing the same battle and not giving up. God wants you to know this day that you are not the only one going through that problem. There are many people in other places you have no idea of, who are going through the same challenge as you, and are not giving up. So you too must not give up.

1 Kings 19:14,18

He (Elijah) replied.. I AM THE ONLY ONE LEFT, and now they are trying to kill me too." Yet I (THE LORD) RESERVE SEVEN THOUSAND in Israel-- all whose knees have not bowed down to Baal and all whose mouths have not kissed him."

PRAYER

Gracious Father, I thank You for the grace to live for You no matter the pressure that has come my way. Lord I declare this today that I will not give up, in Jesus' name, amen.

NOTES

....

Apostle Paul says in Galatians 1:16-17... when God called me, "..I did not immediately CONSENT with ANY MAN, nor did I go up to Jerusalem to see those who were apostles before I was, but I went immediately into Arabia and later returned to Damascus." It is amazing how much energy some ministers of the gospel spend these days trying to CONSENT with men. Some have travelled hundreds of miles just to seek Connections. Others have given out huge sums of money to men just to get connections. And this is especially true for young ministers. The truth is that you really don't need to go this route. If only you can stay focused and work on the calling you have, the same connections you're seeking will soon start SEEKING YOU.

When you spend time impacting communities and newspapers begin to report how you're transforming gang members into preachers, drug dealers into noble men; then you'd fall on the list of those the city wants to honor. And before you know it, you have gained media attention. At this time, all the people you admired will come desiring to connect with that young man who is all over the media. Paul stayed on his assignment and at the right time, he was able to meet anybody he wanted to meet.

PRAYER

Lord help us to be patient and wait on Your time in our lives in Jesus name.

NOTES ....

....

....

....

....

....

....

....

....

....

But Elisha said to him, "*Was not my spirit with you when the man got down from his chariot to meet you? Is this the time to take money, or to accept clothes, olive groves, vineyards, flocks, herds, or menservants and maidservants*? (2 Kings 5:26). From Elisha's question to Gehazi, it's clear he gets angry with Gehazi not because he collected the gifts but because of the time he had collected them. That implies if Gehazi had collected those gifts at an appropriate time, it would not have been a problem. By implication Elisha is saying, now that you have not even started ministry, is this the time to be running after Gifts? Is this the time to be requesting money from people before prayer? Is the time to be trying to wear suits and shoes that cost thousands of dollars: now that your church is still trying to get established? Is this the time to be placing a price tag on anyone who desires to have you preach in their program: now that you're barely able to deliver a good sermon? Then what will you do when you eventually become so popular? Is this the time to request to be lodged in the most expensive hotel: now that you're still growing in ministry? God delights in giving us all the above but when you lust after them it leads to sin.

PRAYER

Father, help us not to lust after the pleasures of this world but to be satisfied with that which we have, in Jesus' name, amen.

NOTES ....

....

....

....

....

....

....

....

....

....

WEEK 18 | WISDOM NUGGET

WHAT ARE YOUR CONTRIBUTIONS

May I state here that you will be remembered for your contributions not your qualifications. While it is good to go to school and have all the qualifications, humanity does not celebrate a piece of paper; it celebrates tangible contributions that bring change and improvement. What are you contributing to your world? How are you making your community a better place? That is what you will be remembered for.

PRAYER

- *Father, help me to be a contributor to the development and betterment of my community and the world at large, in Jesus' name, Amen.*

NOTES

....

....

....

....

....

....

....

....

....

....

In 1 Thes 3:2, 1 cor 4:17, Phil 2:19, Apostle is saying the same thing: I will send Timothy to take my place. Paul is sending Timothy to represent him in some major events that needed his presence. Paul understands he cannot do everything by himself and so decided to delegate some authority to Timothy. We too must do same if we want to have a successful ministry. It cannot be you alone leading prayer meeting, counseling, preaching. You are out of town on Friday and Saturday and you have to risk your life in Overnight Driving just to preach in your Church on Sunday morning; looking tired and worn out. You may think you're doing ministry that way but the truth is you're REDUCING your lifespan. Learn from Apostle Paul and delegate some Authority by sending others to replace you in some events.

PRAYER

Lord, help us to do ministry the right way. Give us the wisdom to share out the load on us so that others can also be blessed as they serve You, in Jesus' name, amen.

NOTES

AN HONEST FRIEND IS A TRUE FRIEND...

Many people today instead of being sincere with one another, they'd rather choose the path of flattery. We see things that are wrong about people and choose to ignore them or we carry it away and talk about it at their back just because we don't want to hurt their feelings. And if we're not careful, we might be deceived to think that the silent people in our lives are our best of friends not knowing they are killing us at our backs. Get this truth: He who is outspoken is better than the one who conceals his thoughts and acts in front of you like he or she agrees with all you do or say when internally, they don't.

Galatians:2.14

When I saw that they were not acting in line with the truth of the gospel, I said to Peter in front of them all, "You are a Jew, yet you live like a Gentile and not like a Jew. How is it, then, that you force Gentiles to follow Jewish customs?

PRAYER

Father, help us to choose our friends based on their motives and NOT just their words. Lord, give me a heart that will accept honesty instead of flattery, in Jesus' name, amen.

NOTES ....

....

....

....

....

....

....

....

....

....

AVOID EXAGGERATIONS IN YOUR TESTIMONIES...

In Acts chapter five, a man and his wife sold their property and decided to bring the money to God. Ananias was enlisted among those with a Testimony that Sunday. He had been listening to others stand in front of the Church and give shocking testimonies of how they sold their possessions and brought all the money to God. So that day he decided he was also going shock the Church with his testimony. He told the Church he sold his land and "here is ALL THE MONEY : Not even a dime is left behind," he must have said. The congregation must have jumped on their feet with thunderous hallelujahs to the Lord. While the congregation was excited, the Lord told Peter that Ananias' testimony was full of lies. And Ananias and his wife died on the spot as a result of trying to give an exaggerated testimony (*Acts 5:1-11*).

When you say you opened blind eyes: are you really sure it happened as you said it? Are you really sure that immediately you entered his office he granted you the job or visa WITHOUT INTERVIEW as you said it? The next time you stand to testify, REMEMBER Ananias and Saphira who tried to SHOCK GOD with their Testimony but ended up being SHOCKED BY GOD. If the SHOCK of human energy (electricity) can kill, then the SHOCK of God's energy is a real danger. It is better to testify or pledge and return to your seat with NO APPLAUSE than trying to give a SHOCKING TESTIMONY and end up like Ananias and Saphira.

PRAYER

Lord, help us to be truthful when we stand to testify for Your glory. Take away from Your church every spirit of lies telling, in Jesus' name, amen.

NOTES ....

....

....

....

....

....

....

....

....

....

But why the sudden change of attitude? What has your friend done that got you so angry that you never want to have anything to do with him/her? You guys have been good friends for years and as a matter of fact, just few days ago, you were smiling at each other and having fun together. So why the sudden change of attitude despite all the evidence to show there is no reason to be mad with your friend?

There are lost friendships in your life you can never repair because the reason for their attitude towards you is far beyond your imagination. People may be angry with you because you offended them or they've heard rumors about you which are often false. Others may just not like you anymore because you dared to get out of the box in which they had placed you. As long as you did not offend anyone, you must learn to move on with your life because no matter how hard you try, you can never get some people to like you. They have made up their minds and nothing can change it.

Luke 23:21.

But they kept shouting, "Crucify him! Crucify him!"

PRAYER

Lord, give me the grace to keep my eyes on You alone. Help me not to be moved by what men say but by what You say Lord, in Jesus' name, amen.

NOTES ....

....

....

....

....

....

....

....

....

....

He is called by many as the thief on the cross. But I call him the man who cheated hell. He had killed many innocent people and everyone looked forward to the day he would be arrested and executed. And above all, they longed for the day he will meet the Devil in hell. But as unbelievable as it happened, this guy made it into heaven just in the nick of time. I can imagine victims of his criminal acts: people he shot and killed while on earth looking at him in heaven and telling God, "this guy can't be here."

Some of the people we have written off here on earth may make it to heaven and some of those we think are saints may end up languishing in hell. Therefore anyone who thinks he stands, let him take heed lest he falls. And please let's learn not to write people off but pray for them.

Luke 23:43.

Jesus answered him, "Truly I tell you, today you will be with me in paradise."

1 Cor 10:12.

Therefore let him that thinks he stands take heed lest he fall.

PRAYER

Lord, help me to run the Christian race with endurance until I make it to heaven. May I not write anybody off but pray for them because with You even the worst of sinners can be saved.

NOTES ....

....

....

....

....

....

....

....

....

....

If we use the following approach to correct people, I guarantee you that we will get TREMENDOUS Results. Nobody likes it when all you see about them is NEGATIVE. At that point, they build a RESISTANCE against you and will never adhere to the rebuke you give them. Find something good about them. Start from there then progress to the rebuke.

PAMPER: "You have persevered and have endured hardships for my name, and have not grown weary." HAMMER: "Yet I hold this against you: You have forsaken your first love." (Rev. 2:3-4). PAMPER: " ... You did not renounce your faith in me, even in the days of Antipas, my faithful witness, who was put to death in your city-- where Satan lives." HAMMER: "Nevertheless, I have a few things against you: You have people there who hold to the teaching of Balaam, who taught Balak to entice the Israelites to sin by eating food sacrificed to idols and by committing sexual immorality." (Rev. 2:13-14).

PAMPER: "I know your deeds, your love and faith, your service and perseverance, and that you are now doing more than you did at first." HAMMER: " Nevertheless, I have this against you: You tolerate that woman Jezebel, who calls herself a prophetess. By her teaching she misleads my servants into sexual immorality and the eating of food sacrificed to idols." (Rev. 2.19-20).

We can see from this approach that the one who is being rebuked with accept correction because you have first pointed out something positive about them.

PRAYER

Loving Father, I receive wisdom from You to always find something good about people before I point out anything wrong in Jesus name.

NOTES ....

....

....

....

....

....

....

....

....

....

WEEK 19 | WISDOM NUGGET

IT WON'T ALWAYS BE YOU

Are you the richest in your community, church, or workplace? Stay humble: you won't always be the richest. Are you the smartest? Stay humble: you won't always be the smartest. Maybe your car is the latest model. Stay humble: that car won't always be the latest. Is your beauty the talk of the day? Please, be humble, because even Beauty fades away. Solomon had tested all these things and he concludes by saying all of it is vanity upon vanity. "Meaningless! Meaningless!" says the teacher. "Utterly meaningless! Everything is meaningless." (Eccl 1:2).

PRAYER

✓ Heavenly Father, help me to see myself as a vessel in your hands and that all that I am and I have if from you. Lord help me to remain humble and to know that I am nothing without grace in Jesus name. Amen.

NOTES

....

....

....

....

....

IF YOU ARE SPIRITUAL, PROVE IT...

For many of us today, the proof of our spirituality is by pointing out or exposing the weaknesses or sins of others. We think by doing this, everyone will see our exposed brethren as sinners and see us as the guy who never sins. Sometimes we go as far as making statements like "You should be ashamed for calling yourself a Christian and doing such a thing." Others will say, "I knew that someday you'll be caught up in something like this." Well to you who says so, if you knew that, then the right thing to have done would have been finding a way to make sure that day never came.

Paul says to the Galatians, the proof of your spirituality is your ability to RESTORE the sinner and not to DESTROY them. He even says you must do that GENTLY. This is because no man is a spiritual giant. It takes just a second without God's grace for you to crash into sin beyond repairs. So while correcting those who err, watch yourself lest you also be tempted.

Galatians:6.1

Brothers, if someone is caught in a sin, you who are spiritual should restore him gently. But watch yourself, or you also may be tempted.

PRAYER

Merciful Father, I receive the spirit of love and the grace to love my brethren unconditionally. Lord, help Your children who are struggling with sin and deliver us out of that snare in Jesus name, amen.

NOTES ....

....

....

....

....

....

....

....

....

....

THE GOSPEL SHOULD CARRY NO PRICE TAG…

The fact that you charge a fee before they can get you to minister, tells me that you didn't get your spiritual gift for free and God is not the source. The GIFTS of God are Free and He commands us to also give it out freely. We live in a time when men place a price tag for the gifts of God and God is not pleased with that. And just because it has been going on for long or it is being done by some great man of God, doesn't mean it is right. The word is clear on this subject and it must be respected. Jesus sent His disciples out with the following command: *"Heal the sick, raise the dead, cleanse those who have leprosy, drive out demons. Freely you have received, freely give"* (Matthew:10.8).

PRAYER

Merciful Father, we ask for Your forgiveness in any way we have sinned against You by selling Your free gifts to us. Lord, have mercy and clean Your Church from such practices, in Jesus' name, amen.

NOTES

Imagine we lived in the time when we all had read about the coming of the messiah and looked forward to that. We had many who came claiming to be that coming One. They performed a few signs here and there and had themselves some followers. But not too long, the self-acclaimed messiah died and that was his end. And then we wake up one morning and hear of a certain young lady named Mary who has become pregnant and is claiming that she will birth the Coming Messiah. Joseph will be a laughing stock to the all his peers saying he is about to marry a woman that was impregnated by some unknown person. Worst of all, Jesus is born and grows up. He behaves like every other child; crying around, creeping and being fed. It is with this picture in mind that I came to the conclusion that I would not have believed in Jesus if I lived in His days.

But today, you and I can look at that ONE GREAT EVIDENCE that swallowed up all the above events: HIS EMPTY GRAVE, and say He is indeed God. We can also look at the whole picture from start to end and know that it was God working in it all. We have no reason not to believe Jesus today.

Luke:23.37

..and said, "If you are the king of the Jews, save yourself."

PRAYER

Thank You Lord for the privilege to be living in this generation. Lord, open the eyes of those who have not known You to come to the truth, in Jesus' name, amen.

NOTES ....

....

....

....

....

....

....

....

....

....

As humans, we have that tendency of always surrounding ourselves with people that massage our egos by singing our praises. But the truth is if you ever want to go far in life, you will need to have somebody beside you who can look at you in the face and tell you the truth; not what you want to hear. God requires honesty from us and this means doing things that may not be liked by everybody. Pleasing men is not a bad thing, but before you please men, first make sure God is pleased. Because if you only focus on pleasing men, Paul says you are not a servant of God but a servant of men.

Galatians 1:10.

"For do I now persuade men or God? or do I seek to please men? for if I yet please men, I should not be the servant of Christ."

PRAYER

Heavenly Father, help me to live my life to please you even if this means displeasing the people around me.

NOTES

Eli the priest was fast to condemn Hannah of drunkenness when in reality the woman had a great need. Sometimes we are too fast in seeing what to condemn in people instead what to pray for. We are blind to the reality of the needs of the people God brings our way?

Beloved, when a pastor starts making a mistake of a Praying woman for a drunk, it tells you how far that Pastor has gone away from the Lord. There are many in our pews and on our streets today with great needs but we are blind to the reality of their needs. We look at them in a shallow way and only see the drugs and substance abuse meanwhile what they're really after is satisfaction for their soul.

1 Samuel 1:13-15

Hannah was praying in her heart, and her lips were moving but her voice was not heard. Eli thought she was drunk and said to her, "How long will you keep on getting drunk? Get rid of your wine." "Not so, my lord," Hannah replied, "I am a woman who is deeply troubled. I have not been drinking wine or beer; I was pouring out my soul to the LORD.

PRAYER

Lord, open my eyes to see people beyond their looks or what they do and see the real.

NOTES

As Jesus' ministry expanded and gained more grounds, he realized how complex His work had become. The large crowds that followed Him also came along with many challenges. Some were angry he healed on a Sabbath. Others said he had a demon and even his disciples questioned why he spoke with a Samaritan. When John came he did not eat or drink but lived in the wilderness. And everyone said surely he has a demon because a normal person will like to mingle with others. Well, Jesus came drinking and eating with men and they said he is a drunkard and mingles with sinners. Having observed all these, Jesus came to one conclusion: man is complicated.

Don't try to change your skin color because a brother said I can only marry a fair lady. Because by the time you become fair, he will now be searching for a lady who has a PhD. Don't try to move your Church service time from morning to evening because someone said he will prefer evenings; because by the time you do that, their new excuse will be 'I work nights.' Man is so complicated and can never be satisfied by another man. So just do what the Lord leads you to do and leave the rest for God.

Matthew:11.18-19.

For John came neither eating nor drinking, and they say, 'He has a demon.' The Son of Man came eating and drinking, and they say, 'Here is a glutton and a drunkard, a friend of tax collectors and "sinners." 'But wisdom is proved right by her actions."

PRAYER

Lord, I receive grace to do what You have called me to do. Help me to become more like You in my nature, in Jesus' name, amen.

NOTES ....

....

....

....

....

....

....

....

....

....

WEEK 20 | WISDOM NUGGET

QUOTE FROM PASTOR CHRIS

"How come you are wealthy and the person taking care of your kids dresses in rags. You come to Church looking nice and clean, your wife looking gorgeous yet the one carrying your baby is so untidy. You're making a fool of yourself." (Pst. Chris Oyakhilome). The simple message here is that, love even those who are not of your household.

PRAYER

- ✓ Lord, help me to show love even to those who can never pay back in any way.
- ✓ Let the love of God dwell so richly in me, in Jesus' name.

NOTES

....
....
....
....
....
....
....
....
....
....
....
....

Another word for sincere love is GENUINE love. If your love is Sincere it means, it is UNCONDITIONAL. It is not the type which when things go right you call him Daddy and when things go wrong, you call him Devil. Sincere love is not influenced by circumstances, it is unshakable. This kind of love is kind, it seeks the good of others more than self, it keeps no record of wrong, it does not boast, it is not rude, not easily angered, it perseveres (1 Cor 13). This is the kind of Love Apostle Paul calls SINCERE LOVE.

Romans:12.9

"Love must be sincere. Hate what is evil; cling to what is good."

PRAYER

Lord, help me to grow in unconditional Love, in Jesus' name, amen.

NOTES

The ministry of Jesus attracted large crowds because of the miracles He performed. Men, women, and children came from all over to partake in the events that were unfolding before their very eyes. In one passage the bible records: "…His FAME spread across the country…" In another place He had over 5.000 men minus women and children. Despite all these, Jesus never rejoiced because of the popularity He had gained. He was not out for popularity but after discipleship. Jesus knew too well that you can be very popular but have no true disciples.

We must never make the mistake to think that now that you're popular enough, it is enough reason for you start a church. Running a Church requires disciples and not just fans. Like Jesus who said: you must eat my flesh and drink my blood and the crowd walked away from Him; it takes only one statement or action from you and all your so-called followers will desert you. Therefore while you have the consciousness of your popularity, keep in mind that you have just a handful who can boldly say, "…where else can we go from you?..."

John:6.53

Jesus said to them, "I tell you the truth, unless you eat the flesh of the Son of Man and drink his blood, you have no life in you

.

John:6.66

From this time many of his disciples turned back and no longer followed him.

PRAYER

Lord, help me to make disciples and not go after fans, in Jesus' name, amen.

NOTES ....

....

....

....

....

....

....

....

....

....

Running a Church is not like running a private business. In your business, everyone reports to you and you have the final say. But with the Church of God, you (founder) report to God through the Holy Spirit and only God has the final say. You were only made a caretaker by Jesus Christ who is the true owner of the Church. He owns the Church because He bought everyone in there with His precious blood. Therefore as the general overseer, you must remember that you have a boss to report to on the last Day.

Acts:20.28

Keep watch over yourselves and all the flock of which the Holy Spirit has made you overseers. Be shepherds of the church of God, which he bought with his own blood.

PRAYER

Heavenly Father, I thank You for the privilege You have given us to be partakers in Your work. Lord help us to do Your work with the consciousness that we are just caretakers, in Jesus' name, amen.

NOTES ....

If I were asked what the greatest sin is, I would have said things like; murder, adultery, fornication or occultism. But Jesus shocks His disciples as He tells them the one thing heaven considers a taboo. He says if anybody causes a little one who believes in Him (new convert) to stumble, it will be so terrible for that person that it would have been better for him to be thrown into the sea with a heavy stone around his neck. This is because, when a new convert is discouraged from the faith and eventually backslides, he/she may never be come to the faith again. Therefore, we must watch ourselves ESPECIALLY how we deal with BABES in the Lord.

Don't go talking down a man of God or fellow brethren to a new convert because they will assume all men of God or brethren will be the same. And once they make that conclusion, they will have no reason to abide in the faith. And when this happens, that person's blood is upon your head.

Matthew:18.6

But if anyone causes one of these little ones who believe in me to sin, it would be better for him to have a large millstone hung around his neck and to be drowned in the depths of the sea.

PRAYER

Gracious Father, help me not to be a stumbling block to anyone's faith. Let me not be the reason why someone will leave the faith but help me to be an encouragement to everyone I come across, in Jesus' name, amen.

NOTES ....

““The easiest way to stop the flow of God’s blessing into your life is to use what God provides JUST for yourself” (Dr Tony Evans). When God starts blessing a man, He does so in view of the needs of the people that will come around that person. In order words, God makes you rich so that you can be a channel of blessing to those in need around you. But because most of us don’t see God’s big picture for our prosperity, we turn to be selfish with the blessing He has given us. Never think that God blesses you just for ‘you:’ you’re blessed to be a blessing to many.

Genesis:12.2

“I will make you into a great nation and I will bless you; I will make your name great, and you will be a blessing.

PRAYER

Heavenly Father, I arise to the consciousness of the fact that You have blessed me so I can be a blessing to many in need. I receive the grace to start blessing as many as I come across who are in need. Forgive me for the times I have been selfish with Your blessings, in Jesus' name, amen.

NOTES ....

....

....

....

....

....

....

....

....

....

Apostle Paul encourages Timothy to not let anyone look down on him because he was young. But what is most important is that he shows him clearly how to do that. Paul's message to Timothy was: The way to not let anyone look down on you as a young man is by being exemplary in Your Speech, in life, in love, in faith and in Purity. If you speak well, live an organized life, love unconditionally, walk in faith and have a pure life: you won't need to command anybody to respect you; you automatically gain their respect. So it is not about going around and telling people to respect you. It is about doing things in a very mature and responsible way and people will be compelled to respect you irrespective of your age.

1 Timothy:4.12

Don't let anyone look down on you because you are young, but set an example for the believers in speech, in life, in love, in faith and in purity.

PRAYER

Heavenly Father, help me to be the ideal leader You have made me to be. Let me do things in a mature and responsible way that men will look and see a godly man in me, in Jesus' name, amen.

NOTES ....

....

....

....

....

....

....

....

....

....

WEEK 21 | WISDOM NUGGET

THEY BELONG TO JESUS

As spiritual leaders, the people God gives us are for us to teach them the ways of God and prepare them for the coming of their master. We must never draw men so much to ourselves that it becomes difficult to hand them back to Jesus. They are God's people and not our people.

PRAYER

✓ Lord, give me the mindset of a shepherd and make me remember that I am not the owner of the people you bring my way.

✓ Lord, help your servants toady not to be guilty of taking men away from You, but that they bring to You, in Jesus' name. Amen.

NOTES

....
....
....
....
....
....
....
....
....

The mistake that most people make when they become wealthy is to think their wealth came to them as a result of their hard work or their smart business ideas. While it is partially true that there is no success without hard work, it is also true that without the blessing of God upon a man, he cannot get true riches. God's Word has the following advice for us: Don't make the mistake to "*say my strength and the power of my might has gotten me this wealth ...but you shall REMEMBER the Lord your God for it is Him who gives you the power to make wealth...*" (Deuteronomy 8:17-18). The Word Remember here is not just to have memories of someone. It talks of having reverence for a person. In other words God is saying you shall revere or serve Me for I AM the one who gives you power to make wealth.

PRAYER

Lord, help me to serve You and honor You for giving me the power to make wealth, in Jesus' name, amen.

NOTES ....

....

....

....

....

....

....

....

....

....

As humans it is very easy for us to place a high value on things that are of less importance in God's sight. We try to compare people based on the things they have done or the wealth they have. We often miss a very important ingredient called love. Apostle Paul says it is possible to give all your possessions to the poor and even offer your body to burnt but you don't have love. The one who has the Greatest Respect in God's sight is he who shows love. So if you want to be highly respected in God's sight, be a man or woman of love. And by that, I mean unconditional love.

1 Corinthians 13:3.

And if I give all my possessions to feed the poor, and if I surrender my body to be burned, but do not have love, it profits me nothing.

1 Corinthians 13:13

"And now these three remain: faith, hope and love. But the greatest of these is love."

PRAYER

Loving Father, I receive the grace to love all who come my way. Let everything I do be done in love, in Jesus' name, amen.

NOTES ....

In as much as it feels good to go drop your loads on someone and walk away, the Bible teaches otherwise. Many have been deceived today to think that the man of God is the one to carry their burdens to God. You're asked to bring your Prayer Request so he carries to the mountain in exchange for a fee. Politicians hire Prophets to live in their homes during elections in order to carry their Burdens to God, all in exchange for a fee. Other Pastors out of a pure heart wear themselves out trying to carry the burdens of members. The truth is that no man, whosever, has the ability to carry the burdens of another man. For such a person is even unable to carry his own burdens: what more of another's?

As far as burden carrying is concerned, only one man; JESUS has that ability. Our job as Shepherds therefore is to help put down the burdens of our members at the foot of the cross where Jesus takes them away. Moses tried to carry his people's burdens but it so weighed him down and he ended up missing Canaan. Don't burn yourself out trying to do what only Jesus can do. Drop it at the cross and move on.

Matthew 11:28-29

"Come to me, all you who are weary and burdened, and I will give you rest. Take my yoke upon you and learn from me, for I am gentle and humble in heart, and you will find rest for your souls. For my yoke is easy and my burden is light."

PRAYER

Lord, I thank You for dying on the cross in my place to take away my burdens. Therefore any load of distress that is still sitting on me, I lay it all down at the cross. I will not look to man but I will look up to You, in Jesus' name, amen.

NOTES ....

....

....

....

....

....

....

....

....

....

"All that demonstration of healing was fake. If not why did the person fall sick again and even died?" We often hear people make such statements when a sick person comes to Church for prayer, gets prayed for and the person stands up to testify of their healing and later falls sick again or dies. Unbelievers and even some believers turn to think that such a person was never healed in the first place.

I will like to draw our attention to **Luke 11:26:** *"Then it goes* (talking of a demonic spirit when it goes out of a person) *and takes seven other spirits more wicked than itself, and they go in and live there. And the final condition of that man is worse than the first."* When a person gets healed or delivered, that person must stay in the righteousness of God. This is because when the demon of sickness leaves a person, he will come back after some time to visit that body. If he comes and finds sin, he will go and get seven other demons worse than him and come live in you. So in the end, the problem is not with the healing or the one who prayed, the problem is with the one who was prayed for.

Luke:11.24-25

"When an evil spirit comes out of a man, it goes through arid places seeking rest and does not find it. Then it says, 'I will return to the house I left.' When it arrives, it finds the house swept clean and put in order.

PRAYER ——————————————————

Lord, help me to maintain my healing from You. Let me always keep my heart clean and orderly so the devil will always be kept away, in Jesus' name, amen.

NOTES ....

....

....

....

....

....

....

....

....

....

Jesus and His disciples show up at a country side and immediately large crowds gather to hear Him. The Preacher mounts the stage and preaches a great sermon. Prayer is made and it is time for the people to go home. But Jesus calls a back stage meeting with His inner circle. What He brings up in that meeting is quite UNUSUAL: "This people have come a long way and if we let them go hungry, they may collapse on the way." That is the LAST THING any crusade organizer will want to pay attention to.

Permit me share with you what would have been the subject of discussion in that back stage meeting if it were today's crusaders: "Look at the crowds that showed up. You all know how much we've spent for this crusade. If we let these huge crowds go away WITHOUT COLLECTING AN OFFERING, we may not have the same crowd tomorrow. So let's collect an offering or make an appeal now." As a man of God, what do you see in the crowds that gather to hear you? Do you see YOUR OFFERINGS (your money) or do you see THEIR NEEDS?

Mark:8.1-3

During those days another large crowd gathered. Since they had nothing to eat, Jesus called his disciples to him and said, "I have compassion for these people; they have already been with me three days and have nothing to eat. If I send them home hungry, they will collapse on the way, because some of them have come a long distance."

PRAYER

Compassionate Father, give me a heart of compassion for the needy people You bring my way. Lord, take away every spirit of exploitation from the hearts of Your servants in Jesus' name, amen.

NOTES ....

....

....

....

....

....

....

....

....

....

The presence of the Israelites makes Balak the King so uncomfortable that he decides to go hire Balaam the Prophet to come and spiritually assassinate the Israelites. Unfortunately for both of them, God disrupted their plan. Let no man think he or she has the power to take away the life of another person. If God is for you, no man can be against you. No one can curse the one God has blessed. Let the entire kingdom of darkness gather against you, they will still not succeed because God is on your side and He will fight for you. God has blessed you and no man can curse you. And for those who take pleasure in praying for the death of others, God has not called us to be Spiritual Assassins.

Numbers 22:22

But God was very angry when he went, and the angel of the LORD stood in the road to oppose him. Balaam was riding on his donkey, and his two servants were with him.

PRAYER

Heavenly Father I thank You for the secret battles You are fighting for me. I thank You for being my defender when the enemy rises against me. Lord may You continue to defend Your children in Jesus name, amen.

NOTES ....

....

....

....

....

....

....

....

....

....

WEEK 22 | WISDOM NUGGET

A CHILD OF GOD, NOT THE FATHER OF GOD

Our attitude in prayer matters a lot. When we come to God in prayer, we must come as CHILDREN of God and NOT as FATHERS OF GOD. Prayer is not commanding God. Prayer is communicating with God the same way a child speaks to the father. We must come in humility and reverence not in pride and arrogance.

PRAYER

- *Father, forgive me for the moments I have come before You in arrogance and even commanding You to give me my desires.*

- *Lord, have mercy on the church for the arrogance we have displayed in Your presence during prayers. May we start having reverence for You when we come to pray, in Jesus' name, Amen.*

NOTES

....
....
....
....
....
....
....
....
....

It is easy to point our fingers at others saying they are proud. But as we look at the words of Apostle Paul, we may have to reexamine ourselves. In very simple words, Paul reveals to us what pride is. He says a proud person is one who is not willing to associate with people of Low Position. He is one who has an exaggerated sense of self importance. If you only associate with people who have the same educational qualification as you, you are a proud person. If you see yourself to be the most important person and everyone should bow to you, then you are proud. Whether you're a Pastor or Church member, we must examine ourselves and find out who we associate with and how we place value on ourselves in the midst of others. God does not work with proud people.

Romans 12:16.

Live in harmony with one another. Do not be proud, but be willing to associate with people of low position. Do not be conceited.

James 4:6.

But he gives us more grace. That is why Scripture says: "God opposes the proud but shows favor to the humble."

PRAYER

Lord, help me to be humble and be able to associate with people of low position. Take away every spirit of bride in the hearts of Your children, in Jesus' name, amen.

NOTES

We often pray asking God to fill us with His power. But as we read Acts chapter one, we will realize that we don't get power by asking God for power. We get power when we receive the Holy Spirit. And we get the Holy Spirit by asking the Father. We ask through prayer and wait on Him to give us what we have asked. So if anyone needs God's power, let him go to God in prayer and ask for the Holy Spirit to fill him. Because when the Holy Spirit comes, He brings power.

Acts:1.4

" ...He gave them this command: "Do not leave Jerusalem, but wait for the gift my Father promised, which you have heard me speak about.

Acts:1.8

But you will receive power when the Holy Spirit comes on you; and you will be my witnesses in Jerusalem, and in all Judea and Samaria, and to the ends of the earth."

PRAYER

Heavenly Father, fill me with Your precious Holy Spirit. Let my entire being be overwhelmed with Your presence and I know when this happens, I will be filled with Your power. Thank You Lord for filling me with Your Spirit and Your power, in Jesus name, amen.

NOTES

Villagers in a small village brought a blind man to Jesus for healing. Jesus takes the man's hand and walks him out of the village away from all the people who brought him. He went to spit on the man's eyes and prayed for him and the man received his sight. The encounter ends with Jesus telling the healed man to go straight to his house and not enter the village.

In other portions of scripture, Jesus heals in public and even explains why He did it. But in this case, He heals in secret and keeps it secret. The reason I think is because Jesus never wanted anyone to build a doctrine on the METHOD He used in healing the man. Jesus was led by the Spirit to spit on the man for his healing. BUT in order to make sure no one copies the practice, He did it in secret; away from the people.

We must never build a practice out of something God instructed us to do just for a single instance. That you gave the man water to drink and he became healed does not mean you should build a doctrine of giving people water for their healing.

Mark 8:22-26

They came to Bethsaida, and some people brought a blind man and begged Jesus to touch him. He took the blind man by the hand and led him outside the village. When he had spit on the man's eyes and put his hands on him, Jesus asked, "Do you see anything?" Once more Jesus put his hands on the man's eyes. Then his eyes were opened, his sight was restored, and he saw everything clearly. Jesus sent him home, saying, "Don't go into the village."

PRAYER

Lord, help Your servants to pay attention to Your instructions. Let us obey Your voice and act according to Your instructions, in Jesus' name, amen.

NOTES ....

....

....

....

....

....

....

....

....

....

Jesus tells His disciples … "I saw Satan fall like lightning from heaven (Luke 10:18). This statement alone holds the key to your spiritual authority. By knowing that Satan has fallen, it puts you in a place of authority over the devil. Knowledge is power and what you don't know controls you. You could be the heir of an estate but working as a cleaner in that same estate until the day you get to know what belongs to you. Most believers are treated that way by the devil. He deceives them to think that Satan has so much power over them but in reality we are dealing with a fallen angel. Now that we have been reminded that Satan has fallen, we must rise and take our place of authority in Christ Jesus.

Luke 10:17

The seventy-two returned with joy and said, "Lord, even the demons submit to us in your name."

Luke 10:18

He replied, "I saw Satan fall like lightning from heaven'

PRAYER

Lord, I thank You for the victory You have given me over the devil. I declare that Satan has no power over me because he is a fallen angel. I walk in victory, in Jesus' name, amen.

NOTES ....

....

....

....

....

....

....

....

....

....

When men start reasoning God's Word with their minds and not their hearts (spirit), they easily fall prey to the Devil. This was the same strategy Satan used to deceive Eve in Genesis 3:1 when he asked her: "...did God really say…?" That statement did put Eve into a position of questioning God's instructions instead of obeying them. I fear when men start rationalizing God's Word and try to use their intellect to figure out if what God says actually makes sense. Some will say there are about four billion people in the world who are not Christians. Do you really think a loving God will just send all these people to Hell? Others may say do you think God will sacrifice His only begotten Son on the cross for you and a "small sin" will keep you out of heaven? The truth is that God's Word gives very clear answers to those questions and God will not lower His standards because He has honored His Word more than His name. Believe His Word without questioning it and you will not be deceived like Eve.

Genesis 3:1,19

Now the serpent was more crafty than any of the wild animals the LORD God had made. He said to the woman, "Did God really say, 'You must not eat from any tree in the garden'?" ...For the wisdom of this world is foolishness to God. As the Scriptures say, "He traps the wise in the snare of their own cleverness."

PRAYER

Heavenly Father, may I never take Your Word for granted or try to start using my brain to reason what You say before I obey. I choose to obey You even if the words don't make sense because You are never wrong. Lord, save Your people from being deceived by Satan, in Jesus' name, amen.

NOTES ....

....

....

....

....

....

....

....

....

John, in his account tells us about a man called Joseph of Arimathea saying he was a disciple of Jesus. But John adds that; he was a SECRET DISCIPLE because HE FEARED THE JEWS. He was the one who brought down Jesus' body from the cross and buried it. Notice that, just because he was a secret disciple did not make him a lesser disciple. He was accepted by Jesus as a disciple even though he did not publicly follow Jesus. Becoming a disciple of Christ is a matter of the heart and not just the outward display of carrying a bible, singing Christian songs or belonging to a local Church. There are people who cannot proclaim their faith in Jesus publicly because of their family background, their former religion, or their government: but in their hearts their trust is in Jesus Christ. Jesus ACCEPTS such and calls them His disciples. God knows that not everyone has been given the grace to suffer as a martyr for Christ. There are some who will secretly worship in spirit and in truth. If you are one of such, don't let the enemy deceive you that God does not accept you because He does. But if you are a secret disciple of Jesus, it should be for Fear and not for Shame.

John 19:38.

Later, Joseph of Arimathea asked Pilate for the body of Jesus. Now Joseph was a disciple of Jesus, but secretly because he feared the Jews. With Pilate's permission, he came and took the body away.

PRAYER

Father, I thank You for the privilege to worship You openly and freely. Lord ,I pray for the many who are secretly following You in the Arab world, China, India, Russia, North Korea and other nations where there is no religious freedom, Lord, comfort them and keep them, in Jesus' name, amen.

NOTES ....

....

....

....

....

....

....

....

....

....

WEEK 23 | WISDOM NUGGET

NOT EVERYTHING MATTERS

If you NOTICE *everything*, you will be a man of many sorrows. But if you also IGNORE *everything*, you will be an Excellent Mediocre. Therefore: see everything, ignore what is Trivial and focus on what is Important. There are some things you just need to let go. See or hear them and act like you did not see or hear them.

PRAYER

✓ Father, give me the grace not to be moved by everything that I see or hear happening around me. Let me only react to what is important, in Jesus' name. Amen.

NOTES

....
....
....
....
....
....
....
....
....
....
....
....
....

Nobody is called to reach the whole world: We're all called to reach our UNIQUE World 'S'. No matter how popular and influential you may think you are, there are people you will never reach and they will never know you. That's why Jesus said: "Go into ALL the world..." The world all signifies that are many communities or groups of people that need to be reached. By this He meant everyone should go into their UNIQUE communities or spheres of influence. There is a world of Bankers that only bankers will reach. There is a world of Mechanics that only Mechanics will reach. There is a world of Hair dressers that Pastors can never reach. Therefore we must not all become PASTORS because if we do, there are MANY WORLD'S' we will not reach. Play your part in your corner and be satisfied with it because God counts on you to carry His Word to that world in which you belong. Remember that even the greatest of preachers is not known all over the world.

Mark 16:15

"He said to them, "Go into all the world and preach the good news to all creation."

PRAYER

Father help me to reach the people You have placed around me with the gospel. Let me be effective in my world because You count on me for their salvation in Jesus name, amen.

NOTES ....

....

....

....

....

....

....

....

....

....

God's Word admonishes us not to love the world or anything in it. If anyone loves the world, the love of the Father is not in him. And this is proof that a man loves the world: He craves for what is sinful; he lusts after worldly things and above all; He boasts of what he has and what he has done.

Nowadays, most of us are exhibiting our boasting in a very subtle way. We act like we are testifying of God's blessings but in reality, WE ARE BOASTING OF WHAT WE HAVE AND WHAT WE HAVE DONE. No man can really boast of anything because all we have is given to us by the Lord. John says if any one does this, then the love of the Father is Not in him.

1 John 2:15-16

Do not love the world or anything in the world. If anyone loves the world, the love of the Father is not in him. For everything in the world-- the cravings of sinful man, the lust of his eyes and the boasting of what he has and does-- comes not from the Father but from the world.

PRAYER

Loving Father, help me to be humble and acknowledge that no matter how much I have, it all came from You. Let no trace of boasting be seen in me, in Jesus' name, amen.

NOTES ....

....

....

....

....

....

....

....

....

....

The reason why the Church of today cannot confront her Ahab is because of sin within the Church. Prophet Nathan could never have confronted David to rebuke him of adultery if he had his own sin partner at home. Elija could never have confronted Ahab to rebuke him for idolatry if he himself practiced idolatry.

We cannot expect the Church to confront the government on embezzlement when the clergy themselves are engaged in changing figures. How do you expect the so-called Prophets to rebuke the government for practicing occultism when they themselves stand on pulpits in the day and stand in cults at night? How can the Church leaders rebuke the government for practicing favoritism when favoritism and nepotism is at its peak within the church? Righteousness is the pump that fuels the engine of boldness in us. If that pump is broken you cannot see boldness. It is only the righteous that shall be bold a lion.

Proverbs 28:1

The wicked man flees though no one pursues, but THE RIGHTEOUS ARE AS BOLD AS A LION.

1 Kings 17:1

Now Elijah the Tishbite, from Tishbe in Gilead, said to Ahab, "As the LORD, the God of Israel, lives, whom I serve, there will be neither dew nor rain in the next few years except at my word."

PRAYER

Lord, take me back to the place of righteousness in Jesus' name. Help Your Church to be a place of righteousness so that we can have the boldness to face and correct what is wrong, in Jesus' name, amen.

NOTES

When the ten lepers cried out to Jesus for mercy, Jesus could have called them unto Himself and healed them as He did in other cases. But instead He told them: "Go, show yourselves to the priests." Does this mean that Jesus was commending the Priests who served in the temple? Certainly not because these are the very people who never believed He was the Son of God. As a matter of fact, it was the Chief priest who actually did everything to see that Jesus was killed. So why would Jesus send lepers to these people who do not agree with Him. Jesus sent them to the Priest because He acknowledged the office of the Priest. In the Old Testament, it was only the Priest who could attest that a person was healed of leprosy and eventually restore that person. Jesus understood that even though the Priest in His days had lost touch with God, He still had to respect the God ordained office.

There will be times when the leader occupying that office is someone who does not like you or is someone young enough to be your last child. Still do your best to respect him/her because it's not about the Officer, it's about the Office.

Luke 17:12-14

As he was going into a village, ten men who had leprosy met him. They stood at a distance and called out in a loud voice, "Jesus, Master, have pity on us!" When he saw them, he said, "Go, show yourselves to the priests." And as they went, they were cleansed.

PRAYER

Father, help me to have respect for people even if the people don't respect or recognize what I am doing.

NOTES

Pastor Eli (the Priest) like any other Pastor was glad that God had given him sons who will succeed him in ministry. These sons grew up and unlike some kids, Eli's sons ACCEPTED to join the ministry. They began serving as Pastors in the Temple. Every day they woke up on time, got dressed for service, set up the temple, and began serving as the people came in. Everyone including Eli knew they were serving God but in reality they were. Before long, they began to sleep with women at the temple and defiled God's offering.

It is very possible to be ACTIVE in God's house but have no relationship with the Holy Spirit. I know that sister calls you Daddy, makes your coffee Sunday mornings, sings in the choir and even leads a group; but you must never take those activities for spirituality. Just because that brother comes to church very early and is so involved in the things of God, does not mean he is spiritual. It is possible for the minister to be travelling all over for the gospel and yet he has no real intimacy with God. Never allow activity for God to mean connection with God. The end result of such is the kind of disaster that Eli's sons brought to the temple.

1 Samuel 2:22-23.

Now Eli, who was very old, heard about everything his sons were doing to all Israel and how they slept with the women who served at the entrance to the Tent of Meeting. So he said to them, "Why do you do such things? I hear from all the people about these wicked deeds of yours.

PRAYER

Father, help me to have a daily relationship with You. Lord, may I not become so busy with religious activity that I don't deepen my walk with You. Draw Your children closer on a daily basis in Jesus' name, amen.

NOTES

....

....

....

....

....

....

....

....

....

Jesus has performed great signs in Jerusalem and so many people now believe in Him. But He knows that these one believed simply because they have seen miracles and the day they don't see any miracle, they will all walk away. So Jesus decided not to entrust Himself to such. Even though He accepted them, He could not put them in His inner circle because they are not dependable.

Many maybe singing your praises and pledging their support to you now that things are going well: don't depend on that. You still must carefully select who you can bring into your inner circle. Everyone can stand with you when life is good but when things get tough, you need men who are resilient. That's why Jesus entrusted Himself only to a selected few. We must learn to do same.

John 2:23-25

Now while he was in Jerusalem at the Passover Feast, many people saw the miraculous signs he was doing and believed in his name. But Jesus would not entrust himself to them, for he knew all men. He did not need man's testimony about man, for he knew what was in a man.

PRAYER

Lord help me to carefully select the people I can commit myself to and walk with in Jesus name, amen.

NOTES ....

....

....

....

....

....

....

....

....

....

WEEK 24 | WISDOM NUGGET

THERE IS A PROCESS

You are asking God to give you in one month what He gave another man after fifteen years. You must know that the results you see involve patience and dedication. Take your time and go at God's speed and you too will someday be the admiration of many. Never be in a rush to make it. "There is a time for everything, and a season for every activity under the heavens." (Ecclesiastes 3:1).

PRAYER

- ✓ Loving Father in heaven, I thank You because You have the best in mind for me. Therefore, I will trust You to bring that which I desire at the right time.
- ✓ I refuse to be in rush and try to go ahead of God. I pray this, in Jesus' name. Amen.

NOTES

....
....
....
....
....
....
....
....
....

Simon Peter has come to believe in Jesus and followed Him for more than three years. He has seen Jesus display tremendous power calming the raging seas and calling the dead back to life. He knew more than anyone else that Jesus had all it takes to protect them. But "what in the world was Peter doing with a sword?" (Chuck Swindol). Why do you need a sword when you are walking with the strongest man on earth who is God Himself?

Peter's behavior teaches us just one lesson: many have come to Christ but they are still using the methods and tools of the world to solve Spiritual Problems. Now that you are a child of God, you should not be visiting shrines or carrying objects from witch doctors on your body. You cannot continue to keep a sin partner and call yourself a believer. Just as Jesus told Peter "Put your sword back 'where it belongs" I also say to you today, Put all those things back where they belong. Get rid of them in any way possible because "those who live by the sword shall die by the sword." If you choose to live by those things, you can be sure those very things will kill you someday.

Matthew 26:50-52

Jesus replied, "Friend, do what you came for." Then the men stepped forward, seized Jesus and arrested him. With that, one of Jesus' companions reached for his sword, drew it out and struck the servant of the high priest, cutting off his ear. "Put your sword back in its place," Jesus said to him, "for all who draw the sword will die by the sword.

PRAYER

Lord help me not to live a double life. Now that I am in You, let my whole life submitted to You. I denounce everything from the world and I fully yield to Your ways in Jesus name, amen.

NOTES

One unique feature about our God is that even though He is unchanging, His methods do change from time to time. He can show up as a pillar of fire in one place and as a cloud in another. The mistake we often make as humans is that of creating a pattern of how God operates based on one incident of His deliverance. While preaching in a city, men were sent to kill Paul and the information was relayed to him. He could have said: I am going nowhere, the same God who delivered me from ship wrecks and from the bite of serpents will defend me when these men get here. He did not do that: Paul had to run for his life. He understood that just because God saved you in one way yesterday doesn't mean it will always be the same. Many have died because when God expected them to run, they stayed back. Our task as believers is to ALWAYS FIND OUT HOW/WHAT God wants us to do in EACH SITUATION.

Acts 9:23-25

After many days had gone by, the Jews conspired to kill him, but Saul learned of their plan. Day and night they kept close watch on the city gates in order to kill him. But his followers took him by night and lowered him in a basket through an opening in the wall.

PRAYER

Precious Holy Spirit, lead me into the ways of the Father. Let me do only what God wants me to do, in Jesus' name, amen.

NOTES ....

After their failure, He chose to teach His disciples how to succeed instead of sounding mysterious about what He does. It is unfortunate that most leaders enjoy it when their followers fail. This way, they can maintain their grip of influence on those who look up to them. They think if everyone is able to do it, then no one will come to them for anything. So they bury the secrets of their success and always sound mysterious or tell you everything else but the truth. When Jesus' disciples asked why they could not deliver the boy, He gave them a CLEAR AND DIRECT answer: "You lack faith." In other words, faith is my secret: if you get it, you too can do the same things that I do.

The proof of a great man of God is not in how many signs or miracles he did but in how many people he raised to operate in the same divine gifts he has.

Matthew 17:16-20

I brought him to your disciples, but they could not heal him." "O unbelieving and perverse generation," Jesus replied, "how long shall I stay with you? How long shall I put up with you? Bring the boy here to me." He replied, "Because you have so little faith. I tell you the truth, if you have faith as small as a mustard seed, you can say to this mountain, 'Move from here to there' and it will move. Nothing will be impossible for you."

PRAYER

Lord help me to be able to transfer what You have blessed me with unto the next generation in Jesus name, amen.

NOTES ....

Let the Word speak for itself as you read the following verses of scripture: Matthew 24:38-42 says… For in the days before the flood, people were eating and drinking, marrying and giving in marriage, up to the day Noah entered the ark; and they knew nothing about what would happen until the flood came and took them all away. That is how it will be at the coming of the Son of Man. Two men will be in the field; one will be taken and the other left. Two women will be grinding with a hand mill; one will be taken and the other left. "Therefore keep watch, because you do not know on what day your Lord will come.

PRAYER

If you want to receive Jesus as your Lord and Savior, you can make the following prayer: Heavenly Father, I come to you this day as a sinner and I ask that You forgive me of my sins. I believe in Your son Jesus Christ that He came and died to take away the punishment for my sins and that He rose from the dead and ascended into heaven and is coming back to take me to heaven. Thank you for receiving me as Your child, in Jesus' name. Lord, I receive grace to live every day of my life with an expectation of Your return, in Jesus' name.

NOTES

The King of Israel requested his friend King Jehoshaphat to accompany him to war. Jehoshaphat agrees but requested that they first inquired of the Lord. The king of Israel then brought in four hundred prophets who all said it was ok. But Jehoshaphat insisted they inquired from another prophet. Israel's king said there is one more prophet called Micaiah from whom they can inquire. But he said "I hate him because he never prophesies anything good about me." In the end Micaiah was brought in and he said God was against their move. Well he ended up in Jail and the king went to war and never returned.

Just because somebody sings your praise doesn't mean they love you; they could just be doing that for the benefits they get. The people you may think are your haters may actually be the ones you need around you. Those who hail you seek your attention but those who love you seek your good. We must not make the mistake of trading those who hail us for those who love us.

1 Kings 22:5-8

But Jehoshaphat also said to the king of Israel, "First seek the counsel of the LORD." So the king of Israel brought together the prophets-- about four hundred men-- and asked them, "Shall I go to war against Ramoth Gilead, or shall I refrain?" "Go," they answered, "for the Lord will give it into the king's hand." But Jehoshaphat asked, "Is there not a prophet of the LORD here whom we can inquire of?" The king of Israel answered Jehoshaphat, "There is still one man through whom we can inquire of the LORD, but I hate him because he never prophesies anything good about me, but always bad. He is Micaiah son of Imlah." "The king should not say that," Jehoshaphat replied.

PRAYER

Father, help me to be open to the right people in my life. Take away every wrong companion around me and only allow the people who can help me make good decisions, in Jesus' name, amen.

NOTES ....

....

....

....

....

....

....

A group can never make any progress if everyone thinks he or she is more important than the others. God requires us to have an attitude of humility and treat one another with respect and dignity. There is nothing wrong with having a high self-esteem. In fact a person with a low self-esteem cannot achieve anything significant in life. What Paul is saying in the following scripture is that: do not think of yourself to be something more than what you truly are. Because when this happens pride sets in. But rather be humble and know that you are who you are because of the grace of God.

Romans 12:3

For by the grace given me I say to every one of you: Do not think of yourself more highly than you ought, but rather think of yourself with sober judgment, in accordance with the measure of faith God has given you.

PRAYER

Heavenly Father, I receive the grace to stay humble and not see myself to be more important than others. I thank You for making me who I am and giving me all that I have, in Jesus' name, amen.

NOTES ....

....

....

....

....

....

....

....

....

....

WEEK 25 | WISDOM NUGGET

AVAILABILITY IS MORE THAN ABILITY

God is giving MORE Attention to AVAILABILITY than to ABILITY. His Word says if you are willing and obedient, you shall eat the fruit of the land. Just avail yourself and God will give you the ability. "If you are willing and obedient, you will eat the good things of the land" (Isaiah 1:19).

PRAYER

✓ Dear Father, help me to avail myself in Your hands for You to use me, in Jesus' name.

NOTES

....

....

....

....

....

....

....

....

....

....

....

....

....

....

....

The rise of false preachers and fake prophets had already been predicted by Jesus. He spoke a parable of a man who planted a good vine but an enemy came and sowed weeds. Jesus uses the parable to send home a clear message on how to deal with the 'Fakes' in our midst. The servants asked the owner, "Should we go and uproot the weed" immediately we notice it? The answer was: leave both to grow together till the Harvest. On that day, He Himself (the Owner) will then separate the weed from the wheat. This is "'because while you are pulling the weeds, you may root up the wheat with them."

Do you know by preaching and calling who is fake, you may end up making baby believers to see every prophet and preacher as fake? Sooner or later, they may backslide and say there is no genuine preacher out there: they are all fake. When Jesus says let them grow together He means, focus on teaching your Christians the true Word and by that truth, they will tell right from wrong.

Matthew 13:27-30

"The owner's servants came to him and said, 'Sir, didn't you sow good seed in your field? Where then did the weeds come from?' "'An enemy did this,' he replied. "The servants asked him, 'Do you want us to go and pull them up?' "'No,' he answered, 'because while you are pulling the weeds, you may root up the wheat with them. Let both grow together until the harvest. At that time I will tell the harvesters: First collect the weeds and tie them in bundles to be burned; then gather the wheat and bring it into my barn.'"

PRAYER

Gracious Father, help me to love Your true Word and depend solely on it. Save Your people from every falsehood and bring them to the truth of Your Word, in Jesus' name, amen.

NOTES ....

....

....

....

....

....

....

....

....

....

LET GIVING BE DRIVEN BY LOVE...

Just because you give doesn't mean you Love. You can give so much without actually loving the people you are giving to. Some politicians give because they expect votes from the ones they are giving to. Others give to show off their wealth and to gain fame. Apostle Paul says it is possible for a person to give out everything he/she has and even offer his body to be burnt, but still DOES NOT HAVE LOVE. If your giving will be recognized by God, it must come out of a heart of love for the ones to whom you are giving. Anything short of that, Paul says it shall profit you nothing.

1 Corinthians:13.3

If I give all I possess to the poor and surrender my body to the flames, but have not love, I gain nothing.

PRAYER

Loving Father, help me to have genuine love for humanity. Let everything I do be done out of a heart of love, in Jesus' name, amen.

NOTES ....

....

....

....

....

....

....

....

....

....

You will be absolutely right in saying God is no respecter of persons. The mistake we often make is to use that scripture to cover up for our disrespect of human authority or the elderly. But that scripture is referring to God and not to man. When it comes to a man to man relationship, God requires us to give honor to whom honor is due. If your anointing has no respect for grey hair, then there is something wrong somewhere. As children of God, we must be exemplary in both our speech and our attitude towards one another. Writing the book of Luke, Luke addresses Theophilus as MOST EXCELLENT THEOPHILUS (Luke 1.3). We should give respect to those who deserve it.

Acts 10:34

Then Peter opened his mouth, and said, Of a truth I perceive that God is no respecter of persons:

PRAYER

Lord, give me the grace to have respect for everyone I come across, in Jesus' name, amen.

NOTES

God had given very clear instructions to King Saul through Samuel: "go to war and COMPLETELY Destroy the Amalekites and EVERYTHING they own." But Saul, after their victory, spared king Agag and everything that was good and precious in his sight. When Samuel came to rebuke the king, Saul lied and said: "The LORD bless you! I have carried out the LORD's instructions." That's when Samuel objected and told Saul that he had disobeyed God because he did not carry out the Lord's instructions exactly as was given.

When God gives us a command, He expects us to execute the command exactly as it was given with no addition or subtraction from it. We cannot get God's blessings if we only obey Him partially. In God's sight, partial obedience is no obedience.

1 Samuel 15:9-16

But Saul and the army spared Agag and the best of the sheep and cattle, the fat calves and lambs-- everything that was good. These they were unwilling to destroy completely, but everything that was despised and weak they totally destroyed. When Samuel reached him, Saul said, "The LORD bless you! I have carried out the LORD's instructions." But Samuel said, "What then is this bleating of sheep in my ears? What is this lowing of cattle that I hear?" Saul answered, "The soldiers brought them from the Amalekites; they spared the best of the sheep and cattle to sacrifice to the LORD your God, but we totally destroyed the rest." "Stop!" Samuel said to Saul. "Let me tell you what the LORD said to me last night." "Tell me," Saul replied.

PRAYER

Gracious Father, I receive grace to fully obey Your instructions and carry out Your commands exactly as You gave me, in Jesus' name, amen.

NOTES ....

GOD'S POWER IS NOT FOR SHOW...

Jesus was at a wedding with His mother Mary. When Mary realized that the wine had finished, she came to Jesus and said, "They have no wine." Mary, being the mother of Jesus must have seen her Son perform a miracle while they were are at home. So what she was telling Jesus was, Display some of that your power to these people or show them what you do. But Jesus told her that was not the time for Him to do what she was asking.

The power of God in you is not for entertainment: it is to be used only when God says so. Never use God's power just to show off or to intimidate or embarrass people; God's power is solely for His purposes.

John 2:3-5

When the wine was gone, Jesus' mother said to him, "They have no more wine." "Dear woman, why do you involve me?" Jesus replied. "My time has not yet come." His mother said to the servants, "Do whatever he tells you."

PRAYER

Heavenly Father, help us not to use Your power and gifts in us for the wrong reasons, but to glorify Your name, in Jesus' name, amen.

NOTES ....

....
....
....
....
....
....
....
....
....

She had every reason to abort the mysterious pregnancy but she chose to yield to God. She had waited all her life for that right husband. She kept herself pure and resisted temptations and that's why she was still a virgin. And when she finally got the man of her dreams, God stepped in to disrupt her life. How would Joseph take a pregnancy he knows nothing about? How would her family stand the shame?

Mary could easily have chosen to secretly do away with the baby, but she did not. This was an unusual display of faithfulness and dependence on God. Let these actions from Mary challenge us today to endure through any situation in life and God will always be there to give us the strength. Do not abort that baby you are carrying which may be a physical baby or a dream in the inside of you.

Luke 1:26-35

"How will this be," Mary asked the angel, "since I am a virgin?" The angel answered, "The Holy Spirit will come upon you, and the power of the Most High will overshadow you. So the holy one to be born will be called the Son of God

.

Matthew 1:19

Because Joseph her husband was a righteous man and did not want to expose her to public disgrace, he had in mind to divorce her quietly.

PRAYER

Lord I receive the strength to carry on with my dream and vision until it comes to manifestation. Grant grace to anyone going through though challenges at this time in Jesus name, amen.

NOTES ....

....

....

....

....

....

....

....

....

....

WEEK 26 | WISDOM NUGGET

THROUGH YOU AND NOT JUST FOR YOU

God wants to move you to a point where He can stop doing things for you and start doing things through you. At this point you have grown from a child to a son of God. And God desires that we all grow into becoming His sons and daughters and not remain babies. This explains why you go through some situations in life so they can make you strong and grow you from a baby Christian into a son or daughter.

PRAYER

- ✓ Our heavenly Father, I ask that You help me grow into that level of being Your son and daughter and not remain a baby Christian all my life, in Jesus' name.

NOTES

....
....
....
....
....
....
....
....
....
....
....

As the children of Israel left Egypt heading to the Promised Land, God had a plan for them to live as one and enjoy milk and honey in the land. They actually started off in the land living together as one people until sin came in. Solomon married so many wives who brought in their many gods and the nation went into idolatry. That's when God said, "'See, I am going to tear the kingdom..." And He did that, leaving Israel with two nations: the Southern kingdom called Judah and the Northern kingdom or Israel.

God does divide nations when He sees that His purpose is not being accomplished as He intended. God SEPARATES a people when He sees that the thoughts and actions of one group of people is continually evil. This should be a call to the Leaders of nations and families to fear God and submit to Him without which the security and longevity of that nation or family is not guaranteed.

1 Kings11:31-33

Then he said to Jeroboam, "Take ten pieces for yourself, for this is what the LORD, the God of Israel, says: 'See, I am going to tear the kingdom out of Solomon's hand and give you ten tribes. But for the sake of my servant David and the city of Jerusalem, which I have chosen out of all the tribes of Israel, he will have one tribe. I will do this because they have forsaken me and worshiped Ashtoreth the goddess of the Sidonians, Chemosh the god of the Moabites, and Molech the god of the Ammonites, and have not walked in my ways, nor done what is right in my eyes, nor kept my statutes and laws as David, Solomon's father, did.

PRAYER

Heavenly Father, create in us hearts that fear You and yield to Your Word. Let sin and reproach be taken far away from us, in Jesus' name, amen.

NOTES

Jesus is just from performing so many miracles and decides to go get some rest on a mountain side. As He looks up, He sees a great crowd coming toward Him. The first thing that comes to His mind is: "HOW CAN I FEED THESE PEOPLE?" Jesus did not think of how much offering He can get from them or how He can exploit them in one way or the other. He immediately looked for a way He could satisfy their needs.

When you see people following and submitting to you, what comes to your mind. Do you sought ways to satisfy the hunger in their soul or you look for ways to exploit them. The truth is, if you feed the people, they will in turn FEED YOU even without you asking.

John 6:3, 5, 11

Then Jesus went up on a mountainside and sat down with his disciples. When Jesus looked up and saw a great crowd coming toward him, he said to Philip, "Where shall we buy bread for these people to eat?" Jesus then took the loaves, gave thanks, and distributed to those who were seated as much as they wanted. He did the same with the fish.

PRAYER

Compassionate Father, give me a heart of compassion for the people I come across and to always look out for their good and not my selfish interests, in Jesus' name, amen.

NOTES ....

....

....

....

....

....

....

....

....

....

The Shunamite woman has lost her son and runs to find Elisha to help her. Close to Elisha's house, the servant Gehazi runs towards the woman to ask if everything was ok. In response, the woman told Gehazi, "ALL IS WELL." The woman understood that her solution was not with Gehazi; her solution was with Elisha. So it is needless wasting her time telling Gehazi a problem he cannot solve. So she ran towards Elisha and told him her son was dead and eventually the man of God followed her and resurrected the son.

It is not wise to tell everyone who comes your way about what you are going through. Some people will love to know what you are going through not because they can offer any help, but just because they want to have something to talk about. So choose who you tell your story The bottom line is: if they can't fix it then they shouldn't hear it.

2 Kings 4:26-27

Run to meet her and ask her, 'Are you all right? Is your husband all right? Is your child all right?'" "ALL IS WELL," she said. When she reached the man of God at the ..But the child's mother said, "As surely as the LORD lives and as you live, I will not leave you." So he got up and followed her.

PRAYER

Heavenly Father, give me the wisdom to share my challenges only with those who can help fix the problem, in Jesus' name. Lord, I commit every challenge I am going through into Your hands and I trust You for an answer, in Jesus' name, amen.

NOTES ....

....

....

....

....

....

....

....

....

....

A lot of people have misunderstood the voice of God which came to them and this has even led to some people thinking God 'lied' to them. David and his brothers could have easily thought that way too. The LORD sent Prophet Samuel to anoint David as king over Israel. He got there and in the presence of the whole family, poured oil on David and said today I anoint you king over Israel. Samuel left but David returned to the field to continue as a shepherd. This continued for more than one decade. The Prophecy was given when David was seventeen but he only became king at age of thirty. Jesus told the people tear down this temple and I will rebuild it in three days. They thought it was the physical temple but He was referring to His body.

When God gives you a Word, be sure to go back to Him to get understanding into that Word. The first hearing brings information while the second hearing brings understanding.

1 Samuel 16:1, 13.

The LORD said to Samuel, "How long will you mourn for Saul, since I have rejected him as king over Israel? Fill your horn with oil and be on your way; I am sending you to Jesse of Bethlehem. I have chosen one of his sons to be king." So Samuel took the horn of oil and anointed him in the presence of his brothers, and from that day on the Spirit of the LORD came upon David in power. Samuel then went to Ramah.

2 Samuel 5:4

David was thirty years old when he became king, and he reigned forty years.

Psalm 62:11

Once God has spoken; twice have I heard this: that power belongs to God.

PRAYER

Father, help me to understand Your mind when You speak to me. Let me not rush into action or take hasty decisions without fully understanding You.

NOTES ....

....

....

....

....

....

Judah has lost his son and his widowed daughter-inlaw (Tamar), by their culture was supposed to be taken over by another son of Judah to make kids and a name for the deceased. But Judah chased the girl away. She decided to trap Judah down as she disguised into a prostitute. Judah finds her and goes into her not knowing it's his daughter in-law. When Judah heard that Tamar was pregnant, he ordered that she be brought down to him so they could BURN HER ALIVE. It was then Tamar revealed Judah as the father of the child. When this happened, Judah's response was: "She is more righteous than I, since I wouldn't give her to my son Shelah."

Before we point accusing fingers at others who fell in sin, stop and think about the things we have done in secret. In most cases, we will realize we are like Judah: worse than the one we are trying to crucify.

Genesis 38:15, 16, 24, 26

When Judah saw her, he thought she was a prostitute, for she had covered her face. Not realizing that she was his daughter-in-law, he went over to her by the roadside and said, "Come now, let me sleep with you." "And what will you give me to sleep with you?" she asked. ...About three months later Judah was told, "Your daughter-in-law Tamar is guilty of prostitution, and as a result she is now pregnant." Judah said, "Bring her out and have her burned to death!" ...Judah recognized them and said, "She is more righteous than I, since I wouldn't give her to my son Shelah." And he did not sleep with her again.

PRAYER

Merciful Father, help me not to be judgmental; but let me reflect on my life daily and see how much I need Your grace. Lord, strengthen everyone who is struggling with sin and show us a way out, in Jesus' name, amen.

NOTES

God has sent a young prophet on a mission and warned him NOT TO EAT anything until he returns. The prophet goes on to deliver the message and on his way back, he met an OLD PROPHET who gave him another message urging him to eat. After the young prophet heard that the old man was also a prophet, he decided to submit and went down to eat. Then the LORD spoke and told the young Prophet that he had disobeyed Him and was going to die. And it happened just as the LORD spoke: the young prophet was killed.

It is ok to submit to mentors and coaches: but when their instructions CONFLICT with what God told you, run for your life. Anyone who upholds the words of men more than the Word of God, will certainly not arrive his destination. Therefore while you submit to men, keep an eye on God's Word because God DOES NOT Approve Blind Submission.

1 Kings 13:18-22

The old prophet answered, "I too am a prophet, as you are. And an angel said to me by the word of the LORD: 'Bring him back with you to your house so that he may eat bread and drink water.'" (But he was lying to him.) So the man of God returned with him and ate and drank in his house. You came back and ate bread and drank water in the place where he told you not to eat or drink. Therefore your body will not be buried in the tomb of your fathers.'"

PRAYER

Lord, help me to keep my eyes on You and Your Word. Please take away every spirit of deception in Your church today, in Jesus' name, amen.

NOTES ....

....

....

....

....

....

....

....

....

....

WEEK 27 | WISDOM NUGGET

NOT A GOOD ROUTE

Those who refuse to stay humble, something ends up make them humble. You don't want to go that route. "Now I, Nebuchadnezzar, praise and exalt and glorify the King of heaven, because everything he does is right and all his ways are just. And those who walk in pride he is able to humble.' (Daniel 4:37).

PRAYER

✓ Father, I pray that You grant me the grace to stay humble and not try to exalt myself at any point, in Jesus' name. Amen.

NOTES

....
....
....
....
....
....
....
....
....
....
....
....
....
....

Ahab the king has been seeking an opportunity to execute Elijah. When he finally met Elijah, he called him "troubler of Israel." But was a Elijah really a troubler of Isreal? To answer that question, let's find out what Elijah had done. Elijah had come out to confront Ahab and warned him to repent and stop worshipping idols without which there will be no rain for three years in the land. This to Ahab was wickedness and he regarded Elijah as one who troubles the nation.

Sometimes people will hate you and call you wicked simply because you spoke against what everyone else has allowed. When you walk according to God's pattern, the world will call you wicked. But you must LET GOD and NOT THE WORLD to DEFINE WHAT IS WICKEDNESS.

1 Kings 18:16-18

So Obadiah went to meet Ahab and told him, and Ahab went to meet Elijah. When he saw Elijah, he said to him, "Is that you, you troubler of Israel?" "I have not made trouble for Israel," Elijah replied. "But you and your father's family have. You have abandoned the LORD's commands and have followed the Baals.

PRAYER

Father, I receive the grace to keep my eyes on You and to keep doing what is right in Your eyes even if the world calls it wickedness, in Jesus' name, amen.

NOTES ....

....

....

....

....

....

....

....

....

....

Jesus has just asked a question about His identity and ONLY PETER could answer. Jesus commends Peter, calling him the Rock on which the church shall be built and whatsoever he (Peter) stops on earth will be stopped in heaven. According to Peter, these words have now DISTINGUISHED and made him superior to his peers. Moments after that, Jesus began to tell His disciples (Peter inclusive) how He must suffer and die. Then the same Peter (who now thinks he is boss), TAKES JESUS BY THE SIDE AND BEGAN TO REBUKE HIM telling Him that He would not die. That's when Jesus turned and REBUKED Peter SHARPLY saying, "Get thee behind me Satan" ...for your thoughts are carnal.

Promoting a new believer who has not gained spiritual maturity does not make them grow in the Lord; it makes them stagnant because they will think they already know it all. Like the early church, the first priority for a new convert is to grow them in the Word through teaching and not appointing them into positions. Paul says it clearly when he told Timothy not to appoint a new convert as an elder lest they become PROUD (1Tim.3:6).

Matthew 16:22-23

Peter took him aside and began to rebuke him. "Never, Lord!" he said. "This shall never happen to you!" Jesus turned and said to Peter, "Get behind me, Satan! You are a stumbling block to me; you do not have in mind the things of God, but the things of men."

1 Timothy 3:6

An elder must not be a new believer, because he might become proud, and the devil would cause him to fall.

PRAYER

Lord, help us to know the right people to appoint into positions of responsibility, in Jesus' name, amen.

NOTES

Most people think that God only speaks to a few special persons who have attained some special level of spirituality. While I agree that we may hear God's voice in different dimensions, God speaks to ALL OF US ON A DAILY BASIS. He does this through THE VOICE OF YOUR CONSCIENCE. That quiet voice inside of you that keeps ringing in your mind rebuking or encouraging you to do right is called God's Voice. Sometimes we hear people say, "Something told me to go and apologize but I did not listen." That was God's voice speaking to you. But when you keep ignoring that voice, you end with a SEARED CONSCIENCE which is a mind that no longer reacts to the voice of God.

God desires to speak with us daily. But we often are too busy or distracted to pay attention to what He is saying. Others have simply developed a conscience that no longer fears God or reacts to His voice.

1 Timothy 4:2

Such teachings come through hypocritical liars, whose consciences have been seared as with a hot iron

PRAYER

Lord help me to always pay attention to Your voice as You speak to me daily in Jesus name, amen.

NOTES

Many people can start organizations or establishments but very few can sustain those institutions. Most establishments including Churches often fail the moment the founder dies. This is especially true for Churches and Ministries. But how is it that the establishment Jesus started never failed even after His death? The answer lies in His leadership style. After He had taght His followers for some time, He started Disengaging Himself Progressively from time to time by allowing His disciples to do the things He could have done. He trained them to take over from Him by sending them out to preach and to heal the sick. When He eventually left, there was no Vacuum.

I fear for you if you are the only one who knows the secret of making that business work. If you cannot Start Introducing Your followers into what you do, then be rest assured the day you are gone, that work will be gone. And may I remind you that we all will be gone someday.

Luke 10:1, 3, 17

After this the Lord appointed seventy-two others and sent them two by two ahead of him to every town and place where he was about to go. Go! I am sending you out like lambs among wolves.... The seventy-two returned with joy and said, "Lord, even the demons submit to us in your name."

PRAYER

Heavenly Father, help me to be a good leader by training the people under me to do with excellence the things I do, in Jesus name, amen.

NOTES ....

....

....

....

....

....

....

....

....

....

If everyone was asked to give a reason for doing what they did, we will all have very good excuses for our sinful acts. An unfaithful partner may say he was tempted beyond measure, while a thief may say he had to do that just to have the next meal. A liar may say he lied because that was the only way to save his marriage, job or even his life. But Hebrews 12:4 tells us that all our excuses for sin are NULL AND VOID. If you think you were pushed to the wall, know that others were pushed into open graves and buried alive yet they did not quit on God. If you claim that you did it for survival, know that others went for months without food and water but did not die. The day you received Christ, He gave you an unusual kind of power to resist sin. Nothing including death can make your faith in God break if you put that power to work.

Hebrews 12:4

In your struggle against sin, you have not yet resisted to the point of shedding your blood.

PRAYER

Father, I thank You for the power to resist the devil and all appearance of sin. I have overcome sin and all the power of the enemy cannot bring me down, in Jesus name, amen.

NOTES

Paul's message to Timothy was very clear: *"For the time will come when men will not put up with sound doctrine. Instead, to suit their own desires, they will gather around them a great number of teachers to say what their itching ears want to hear."* (2 Tim. 4.3). If you notice in that verse, IT IS THE MEN WHO WILL GATHER or CALL THEMSELVES A Pastor/Teacher not the other way round. Men hate the truth and so will do anything to get someone who can tell them lies just to please them. If you were called by God you must always make sure you are doing exactly what He called you to do.

Don't be moved by anyone who has a large following or is more popular; most of them are no longer speaking for God. Their ego and selfishness has taken over them and God does not even recognize them as His servants. We are in the days when men will not listen to sound doctrine. But keep on teaching the truth and your reward shall come from the Lord. And for the believer who has abandoned sound doctrine and is now chasing motivational speaking and deception, it is time to return to God before it is too late.

2 Timothy 4:3-5

For the time will come when men will not put up with sound doctrine. Instead, to suit their own desires, they will gather around them a great number of teachers to say what their itching ears want to hear. They will turn their ears away from the truth and turn aside to myths. But you, keep your head in all situations, endure hardship, do the work of an evangelist, discharge all the duties of your ministry.

PRAYER

Lord, help us to cling to sound doctrine. Deliver Your church from every false teaching, in Jesus' name, amen.

NOTES ....

....

....

....

....

....

....

....

....

....

WEEK 28 | WISDOM NUGGET

TIMES HAVE CHANGED

Few years ago ministers were shouting "repent for the kingdom of God is at hand." But today they are shouting, "Can I prophesy?" The church needs to return to the main message Jesus sent us to preach which is: "Repent for the kingdom of God is at hand." (Matthew 3:2).

PRAYER

✓ Dear Father, help me to always inquire of You before I take any step in life, in Jesus' name.

NOTES

....
....
....
....
....
....
....
....
....
....
....
....
....
....
....

A young man by name Demas came to Apostle Paul and probably desired to go with him everywhere for ministry. Paul gladly took him along. He thought to himself, wow, this is a faithful servant he can depend on and can carry him anywhere. That worked for some time as they traveled from coast to coast preaching Christ. But on a particular mission field, Demas was nowhere to be found. At a time when Paul needed him the most because Paul's other helpers had been sent to other assignments. It was at this time that Demas abandoned Paul. Something that was of more importance to him took him away and he abandoned the work of God.

If you want to walk with God and do the things of God, you must have undivided attention. The moment you are in between two decisions, you will end up abandoning the ways of God for the things of this world. In case you have abandoned the things of God or about to, you can make up your mind today not to take the way of Demas.

2 Timothy 4:9-11

Do your best to come to me quickly, for Demas, because he loved this world, has deserted me and has gone to Thessalonica. Crescens has gone to Galatia, and Titus to Dalmatia. Only Luke is with me. Get Mark and bring him with you, because he is helpful to me in my ministry.

PRAYER

Father, I refuse to go after the things of this world. I will walk with You and do only what You have called me to do in Jesus' name, amen.

NOTES

A man had two sons and the younger son came to him and asked for HIS OWN SHARE of the inheritance. The fact that it was HIS OWN SHARE means he was entitled to get it. It only required a little patience on his part and his Dad will hand it to him in due time. But he insisted and his father gave him his possessions. It turned out to be an OVERSIZED Load on his head which brought about his break down. The blessing was not the problem. The problem came because he has not learned how to handle the blessing.

God knows You need that promotion, that marriage or that job but He also knows you are not yet ready to handle the challenges that may come with the breakthrough; so He keeps you waiting until you learn all what you must know. Like the father of the prodigal son, the last thing God will want to give any of His children is an OVERSIZED Breakthrough That Ends Up Breaking Them Down.

Luke 15:12-14

The younger one said to his father, 'Father, give me my share of the estate.' So he divided his property between them. "Not long after that, the younger son got together all he had, set off for a distant country and there squandered his wealth in wild living. After he had spent everything, there was a severe famine in that whole country, and he began to be in need.

PRAYER

Lord, may I not get the kind of breakthrough that will take me away from You. Glue my heart to You in such a way that no matter what I have or who I become, I will not abandon Your ways, in Jesus' name, amen. Lord bring back to You every prodigal child of Yours who is lost out there, in Jesus' name.

NOTES ....

....
....
....
....
....
....
....
....
....

The all-powerful Lord and Savior Jesus Christ came to His hometown to preach and bring down the Kingdom. But unlike people in other places, those in His hometown did not receive Him as One sent from God. They knew His parents, when He was born and they watched Him grow up. They were VERY FAMILIAR with Him and did not see Him to have any kind of power. The choice of words used by Mark is critical. He says, "He (Jesus) COULD NOT DO ANY MIRACLES" ...and "He was AMAZED AT THEIR LACK OF UNBELIEF…"

Familiarity is a deadly tool that the Devil can use to stop your miracle. Their familiarity was so bad it AMAZED Jesus. He finally had to walk away to other places. May we not become too familiar with the things of God or His servants to a point where we miss our blessings.

Mark 6:4-6

Jesus said to them, "Only in his hometown, among his relatives and in his own house is a prophet without honor." He could not do any miracles there, except lay his hands on a few sick people and heal them. And he was amazed at their lack of faith. Then Jesus went around teaching from village to village.

PRAYER

Lord, I pray not to become too familiar with Your ways or Your servants, up to a point where I miss what You want to do for me, in Jesus' name, amen.

NOTES

It is amazing how we can cling to God when we are in trouble. We give God all our time, we pray more, praise more and promise Him our entire lives. This was the case with the ten men with leprosy. Their desire was, "God heal us and we shall give you all the thanks." But after Jesus showed up and healed them, ONLY ONE returned to Give Him Thanks.

Whenever God blesses us with something, we must remember to always come back and appreciate Him for what He has done. It is a good thing to give thanks to the One who gives us all good things. Give thanks to the Lord for all things.

Luke 17:17-19

Jesus asked, "Were not all ten cleansed? Where are the other nine? Was no one found to return and give praise to God except this foreigner?" Then he said to him, "Rise and go; your faith has made you well."

PRAYER

Lord, I thank You for all that You have done in my life and in the lives of others. Without You we will not be who we are and for this I say thank You Lord, in Jesus' name, amen.

NOTES ....

....

....

....

....

....

....

....

....

....

"...If it were not so I would have told you..." Jesus said in John 14:2.

Reading through the Gospels, you will find out Jesus made this statement just Once in His entire ministry on earth. You will agree with me that a man's deepest TRUTH or Secret is rarely spoken out. The above statement is considered an infallible truth from the heart of hearts of Jesus. The choice of words used tells me you can lean on it with your whole life. It gives 100% assurance and drives away every iota of doubt about the reality of heaven.

Beloved, nothing should make you doubt a man who tells you the following words, "If it were not so I would have told you." And these words did not come from any ordinary man, they came from the One who speaks only the Truth and He Himself is Truth. Therefore, never ever doubt the fact that there is a place called heaven. Because if it did not exist, Jesus would have told us.

John 14:1-3

"Do not let your hearts be troubled. Trust in God; trust also in me. In my Father's house are many rooms; if it were not so, I would have told you. I am going there to prepare a place for you. And if I go and prepare a place for you, I will come back and take you to be with me that you also may be where I am.

PRAYER

Dear Lord Jesus, I believe in You and in Your words. I believe there is a place called heaven that You have gone to prepare for us. Lord, help me to always be ready for this place called heaven, in Jesus' name, amen.

NOTES ....

....

....

....

....

....

....

....

....

....

Apostle Paul in his letter to the Corinthians tells them how much he labors for them. Some of the things he tells them need to be said to us in this generation. He tells them he is coming to visit them. But they should not worry to store up gifts for him because he will not want to be a burden to them. Paul was after their establishment in Christ, not after their possessions.

When we labor for people in Christ, our motive should be to get them saved and be ready for heaven and not to get them to church so they can start giving their money and possessions for the work of God. That should not be our objective.

2 Corinthians 12:14, 17, 18

Now I am ready to visit you for the third time, and I will not be a burden to you, because what I want is not your possessions but you. After all, children should not have to save up for their parents, but parents for their children. Did I exploit you through any of the men I sent you? I urged Titus to go to you and I sent our brother with him. Titus did not exploit you, did he? Did we not act in the same spirit and follow the same course?

PRAYER

Father, give us the grace to seek the salvation of men and not their exploitation. Like Paul, may we not be a burden to the people we lead, in Jesus' name, amen.

NOTES ....

WEEK 29 | WISDOM NUGGET

HEAR FROM GOD

A good advice may not be God's advice. Human correctness may not always be God's correctness. So be sure you also hear from God before you take a step. The reason people often find themselves in trouble is often because they failed to inquire of the Lord. "But Jehoshaphat also said to the king of Israel, "First seek the counsel of the LORD" (2 Chronicles 18:4).

PRAYER

✓ Dear Father, help me to always inquire of You before I take any step in life, in Jesus' name.

NOTES

....
....
....
....
....
....
....
....
....
....
....
....
....

As Jesus rounds up His earthly ministry, He showed His disciples the importance of serving one another. Washing the feet of another man was the lowest form of service anyone could offer. And by washing their feet and wiping them, Jesus says they ought to do the same for one another: "If you call me Master and I have served you this way, then you ought to serve one another" Jesus added. In conclusion He says you must put this into practice if you want to be blessed.

It may look foolish in the eyes of others for you to serve your subordinates, but in God's eyes, you are attracting His blessings. Be a servant and don't always desire to be served.

John 13:13-17

"You call me 'Teacher' and 'Lord,' and rightly so, for that is what I am. Now that I, your Lord and Teacher, have washed your feet, you also should wash one another's feet. I have set you an example that you should do as I have done for you. Now that you know these things, you will be blessed if you do them.

PRAYER

Father, I receive the grace to be a servant and not always desire to be served.

NOTES ....

....
....
....
....
....
....
....
....
....

The longer we are in our relationship with God, the more likely we can to get lukewarm if we are merely practicing religion. Christianity is an active relationship with a God who hears and talks to us daily and wants us to engage in new realms of activity with Him. It is not a dead religion like other religions. Our God is alive and active. But when you don't encounter Him for yourself, you will start practicing religion. This was the case with the Pharisees and teachers of the law who thought they were worshiping God but Jesus said their worship was in vain and their teachings are but rules of men and not God's Word. Have we let go of the Ways of God and are now holding on to the traditions of men? God's Word must be the standard for our lives and not a set of rules which contradict what God says.

Mark 7:7-8

They worship me in vain; their teachings are but rules taught by men.' You have let go of the commands of God and are holding on to the traditions of men."

PRAYER

Lord, let Your Word be the standard for my life and not the traditions of men. Lord, let Your church be led by Your Spirit and not man made rules, in Jesus' name, amen.

NOTES ....

....

....

....

....

....

....

....

....

....

Jesus speaks a parable to illustrate a great lesson. He says a man went to his friend at midnight in need of some bread to offer his guest who had just come in. But his friend replied and said he was already in bed and could not come out. Well, the guy outside KEPT ON KNOCKING on the door until the friend inside finally came out to offer his friend as MUCH BREAD as He Wanted: NOT Because they are friends, but because He KEPT KNOCKING.

Have you prayed to God for your healing and it's not forthcoming, please KEEP PRAYING, it will surely come. Have you prayed for the change of that stubborn partner or child and nothing has changed, please keep calling on heaven and your answer will soon come. Sometimes God will answer some prayers not because you deserve it but because He sees your persistence.

Luke 11:5-8

Then he said to them, "Suppose one of you has a friend, and he goes to him at midnight and says, 'Friend, lend me three loaves of bread, because a friend of mine on a journey has come to me, and I have nothing to set before him.' "Then the one inside answers, 'Don't bother me. The door is already locked, and my children are with me in bed. I can't get up and give you anything.' I tell you, even though he will not get up and give him anything because he is his friend, at least because of his persistence he will get up and give him whatever he needs.

PRAYER

Lord, I receive the grace to be persistent in my prayers knowing that You will surely answer me if I don't give up. May You strengthen anyone who is almost giving up on You, in Jesus' name, amen.

NOTES ....

....

....

....

....

....

....

....

....

....

That your parents served God faithfully doesn't automatically make you a saint. Everyone must work out their salvation with fear and trembling. When Samuel grew old, he decided to appoint his sons to take over from him, it turned out that his sons were not like him. The Bible says, "They turned aside after dishonest gain and accepted bribes and perverted justice."

Righteousness is not transferable. So you must teach your kids to know God by themselves. And just because you are a Founder of a church does not automatically make your kids your successors.

1 Samuel 8:1-3

When Samuel grew old, he appointed his sons as judges for Israel. The name of his firstborn was Joel and the name of his second was Abijah, and they served at Beersheba. But his sons did not walk in his ways. They turned aside after dishonest gain and accepted bribes and perverted justice.

PRAYER

Heavenly Father, I commit my kids into your hands and ask that You will draw them closer to You. Let nothing ever take them away from Your presence; let their desire be for You alone, in Jesus' name, amen.

NOTES

TESTIMONIES ARE NOT TO GLORIFY MEN; THEY ARE TO GLORIFY GOD…

Most of the time nowadays we see a repeat of men of God telling people "...make sure you come back and testify when the miracle happens." There is nothing wrong with this if the motive was to glorify God. But in most cases, it is for self-glorification. When they testify, then the world will know that God is using the man of God through whose hands the miracle was done.

The truth is, anyone who has truly been touched by God does not need to be reminded or coerced to testify of what God did for them. Even if you command them like Jesus to tell no one, they will KEEP TALKING ABOUT IT because of the joy that is in their heart. When we pray for people, let our desire be to see them get out of their pain and not to have them go out and tell everyone how anointed we are.

Mark 7:35-36.

At this, the man's ears were opened, his tongue was loosened and he began to speak plainly. Jesus commanded them NOT TO TELL ANYONE. But the more he did so, the more they kept talking about it"..

PRAYER

Father, take away from us every attitude of self-glorification and let our motives be pure as we minister to the people You bring our way, in Jesus name, amen.

NOTES ....

....

....

....

....

....

....

....

....

....

When you come across some scriptures you realize there is nothing new under the sun: nothing happening today that has not happened before. One of the greatest abuses in Christendom today is the abuse of Grace or better still, our freedom from the Law. Many who call themselves 'Grace Preachers' have completely misfired in the way they teach grace. It is true that we have been set free from the Law of Moses and are now living in the freedom of grace which came through Jesus. But being free does not mean we can live a loose life and do whatever we like. We have been freed from the Law and are enslaved to Righteousness. So our freedom in Christ is not freedom to sin but freedom to live in righteousness.

1 Peter 2:16

Live as free men, but do not use your freedom as a cover-up for evil; live as servants of God

.

Romans 6:18

You have been set free from sin and have become slaves to righteousness.

PRAYER

Gracious Father, I thank You for setting me free from the law of sin and death and bringing me into Your grace. Help me to live in the righteousness that Christ purchased for us, in Jesus name, amen.

NOTES ....

....

....

....

....

....

....

....

....

....

WEEK 30 | WISDOM NUGGET

THE HEAD MATTERS

"Anything with two heads is a freak and anything with no head is dead." Good leadership is an absolute necessity for the success of any organization. The greatest tragedy a church can suffer is lack of good leadership.

PRAYER

✓ Lord, I pray that You will give Your church good leaders who understand Your purpose and are passionate for Your work, in Jesus' name. Amen.

NOTES

....
....
....
....
....
....
....
....
....
....
....
....
....
....
....
....

Most people often go to God with one request: Lord give me Your power. The scripture makes us to know that is a very easy thing for God to do. God can gladly give His power to people who do not know Him. But there is something MORE PRECIOUS to God than His power: it is His ways. He will only Reveal His ways to SPECIAL PEOPLE who seek Him and walk with Him.

To the Israelites, God showed them His power, but to Moses He showed His WAYS. His ways reveal His CHARACTER but His power or acts reveal His strength. It is in learning His ways that you become like Him. His ways CAN PRODUCE His Acts but His Acts don't often produce His ways. The ways of God will lead you into heaven but His acts may not. Go for His ways and not His acts.

Psalm 103:7

He made known his ways to Moses, his deeds to the people of Israel:

Romans 11:29

for God's gifts and his call are irrevocable.

PRAYER

Father teach me Your ways so I can become more and more like You in Jesus name, amen.

NOTES

A young demon possessed girl comes across men of God and follows them daily calling on men to listen to them. Everyone who looked at this girl assumed she is speaking under the influence of God's spirit because what she was actually saying was true. But Apostle Paul went a step further to test the spirit which spoke through the girl and he found out it was a demonic spirit. So after many days, Paul decided to cast out the spirit and I bet you, many were shocked.

It will be a great mistake for you to just believe every spirit out there to be the Holy Spirit. Many false prophets have gone out there and we must therefore, TEST EVERY spirit.

1 John 4:1

Dear friends, do not believe every spirit, but test the spirits to see whether they are from God, because many false prophets have gone out into the world

.

Acts 16:17-18

This girl followed Paul and the rest of us, shouting, "These men are servants of the Most High God, who are telling you the way to be saved. "She kept this up for many days. Finally Paul became so troubled that he turned around and said to the spirit, "In the name of Jesus Christ I command you to come out of her!" At that moment the spirit left her.

PRAYER

Lord give us the spirit of discernment to be able to tell which spirit is false. Open our eyes to the deception of the enemy in Jesus name, amen.

NOTES

TRANSFORMATION IS WHAT REALLY MATTERS...

Jesus has just performed so many miracles and people were coming to Him. A woman in the crowd even praised the womb that bore Him. As the crowd kept on increasing, I expected Jesus to be happy that many were coming to Him. But His response was: “This is a wicked generation.” He said this because the people who came did not come for His Word but for a sign.

Before you rejoice over how many members you have, first ask yourself how many will make to heaven when Jesus returns. It is not all about having a great following but about seeing a transformation in the lives of men. Crowds are good as long as those crowds are heading to heaven.

Luke 11:29,32

As the crowds increased, Jesus said, “This is a wicked generation. It asks for a miraculous sign, but none will be given it except the sign of Jonah. The men of Nineveh will stand up at the judgment with this generation and condemn it; for they repented at the preaching of Jonah, and now one greater than Jonah is here.

PRAYER

Father guide our hearts to be always look for the transformation of souls and not just be excited about multitudes coming into our congregations in Jesus name, amen.

NOTES

Apostle Paul is amazed at the sudden turn of events in the life of the Galatians. When they believed in Christ, they started walking by faith and depended on God. But suddenly there was a twist and these same believers now started thinking depending on the Spirit was not enough. So they began to use their minds (the flesh) to determine how to deal with God. Some said they needed to cut their bodies (circumcised) in order to be right with God.

Some of us behave exactly the same. We now think a simple prayer is not enough until we mix it with other things like being anointed with oil or drinking anointed water. It makes no sense for you to have begun in the spirit and you are now in the flesh.

Galatians 3:2-3

I would like to learn just one thing from you: Did you receive the Spirit by observing the law, or by believing what you heard? Are you so foolish? After beginning with the Spirit, are you now trying to attain your goal by human effort?

PRAYER

Lord help me to continue walking with You according to the leading of Your Spirit and not the flesh in Jesus name, amen.

NOTES

Peter, James, and John followed Jesus to the mount of Transfiguration and had an awesome experience. After seeing Moses and Elijah and hearing God's voice, Peter tells his Master he can single handedly build three tents on that mountain for Jesus, Moses, and Elijah. But Jesus knowing fully well that His coming was not to SET UP A MOUNTAIN TOP Ministry, He ignored Peter and they all descended back to the city. Jesus even went on to warn them to tell no one.

Never let anyone push you to start a Church or do something that God is has not called you to do. In all you do, be sure God is the one leading you, else it will end up in failure.

Matthew 17:4,9

Peter said to Jesus, "Lord, it is good for us to be here. If you wish, I will put up three shelters-- one for you, one for Moses and one for Elijah. "As they were coming down the mountain, Jesus instructed them, "Don't tell anyone what you have seen, until the Son of Man has been raised from the dead."

PRAYER

Heavenly Father, help us to only do the things You have called us to. May we not act out of excitement and do what You did not commission to do in Jesus name, amen.

NOTES ....

A man (mostly likely a jew) falls into the hands of thieves and is hurt. He lies on the wayside in need of help. His life was losing blood due to his wounds and his life was at the verge of termination. A Priest came his way but offered him no help. So too, a Levite, when he came to the place and saw him, passed by on the other side. The above two persons were very religious people but did not offer any help to the man. Finally, it was a SAMARITAN who gave this man help. Worthy of note is the fact that Samaritans had no dealings with the Jews and vice versa.

God will sometimes bring us help from an unlikely source; from someone or somewhere you least expect. Therefore when you pray to God for help; keep an open mind.

Luke 10:30-33

In reply Jesus said: "A man was going down from Jerusalem to Jericho, when he fell into the hands of robbers. They stripped him of his clothes, beat him and went away, leaving him half dead. A priest happened to be going down the same road, and when he saw the man, he passed by on the other side. So too, a Levite, when he came to the place and saw him, passed by on the other side. But a Samaritan, as he traveled, came where the man was; and when he saw him, he took pity on him.

PRAYER

Lord I thank You for you will always be my helper. I look up to You and trust that You will always send me help even when those I depend on turn out to fail. Help me to also be of help to others even to people I don't know.

NOTES ....

WEEK 31 | WISDOM NUGGET

BEWARE

Just because a man is popular does not mean he is approved by God. Their popularity does not mean Authenticity. In the book of Acts, we read of some men who rose and had huge followings but before long they vanished. So be careful who you submit to as a father or the kinds of places you choose to make your home church. Discernment is the key to a healthy spiritual life. "Some time ago Theudas appeared, claiming to be somebody, and about four hundred men rallied to him. He was killed, all his followers were dispersed, and it all came to nothing. After him, Judas the Galilean appeared in the days of the census and led a band of people in revolt. He too was killed, and all his followers were scattered" (Acts 5:36-37).

PRAYER

- ✓ Father, I pray that You will open our eyes to know the right places we should belong.
- ✓ Lord, we come against any falsehood in the church these last days, in Jesus' name. Amen.

NOTES

....

....

THIS IS THE ACID TEST FOR TRANSPARENCY...

Everyone can claim transparency but not everyone is indeed guileless. We are not transparent by simply saying I am a transparent person. It has to be seen in our actions. Jesus shows His Disciples how transparent He is by giving them this instruction: "What I tell you in the dark, speak in the daylight; what is whispered in your ear, proclaim from the roofs." In other words, you can quote me anywhere. If you cannot say the same thing you told me about someone in the presence of that person, then your words lack truth. Jesus says, I have no problem with you declaring our private discourse on roofs tops because all what He says is true. We must learn to live a transparent lifestyle.

Matthew 10:27

What I tell you in the dark, speak in the daylight; what is wispered in your ear, proclaim from the roofs.

PRAYER

Father I receive the spirit of truth from You and every word that proceeds from my mouth will be nothing but truth in Jesus name, amen.

NOTES ....

....

....

....

....

....

....

....

....

....

Elijah confronts the prophets of Baal on mount Carmel and tells them the one whose God answers by fire will be the true God. Baal worshipers called on their god all day to no avail. But when it was Elijah's turn, he did not go straight to calling on his God to send down fire on the altar. He made it 'really difficult' for God by POURING ALOT OF WATER on the altar. But in the end, God sent down fire and consumed both the sacrifice and all the water.

When you go to God in prayer, don't try to LOWER YOUR EXPECTATIONS so as to keep it within God's reach or ability. WIDEN your request for our God has all it takes and even more than you can ask or imagine. Even when you have no idea how it will happen, believe God by FAITH and you will see Him at work.

1 Kings 18:33-38

He arranged the wood, cut the bull into pieces and laid it on the wood. Then he said to them, "Fill four large jars with water and pour it on the offering and on the wood." "Do it again," he said, and they did it again. "Do it a third time," he ordered, and they did it the third time. The water ran down around the altar and even filled the trench. Then the fire of the LORD fell and burned up the sacrifice, the wood, the stones and the soil, and also licked up the water in the trench.

PRAYER

Heavenly Father, I believe You are all powerful and can do all things. I chose to believe You for anything no matter how hard it may seem to be and I know that as You did it for Elijah, You will do it for me in Jesus name, amen.

NOTES

A small shepherd boy leaves the jungle and heads to the battlefield to give his brothers food. Just at that instant, Goliath comes out to mock the army of God. God sends David to take him down and that is exactly what happened. And from that one day, the shepherd boy became a PALACE BOY. His friends changed, his meals changed, his clothes changed, and everything about him changed on that one day. All of humanity was heading to a DEAD END; on a highway to destruction BUT on ONE DAY, JESUS the Christ was born and that changed the destiny of all men who believe in Him. Whatsoever you may be going through in life, IT TAKES JUST ONE DAY for God to Turn that story around. Hold unto God and never give up.

Luke 2:11

TODAY in the town of David a Savior has been born to you; he is Christ the Lord.

1 Samuel 17:57

As soon as David returned from killing the Philistine, Abner took him and brought him before Saul, with David still holding the Philistine's head.

1 Samuel 18:2

From THAT DAY Saul kept David with him and did not let him return to his father's house.

PRAYER

Lord, give me the grace to depend on You and not give up. I believe that no matter how long my challenges may have lasted, it will take You just a word and it will be ok. I believe today is my day to see You take me to another level, in Jesus' name, amen.

NOTES ....

....

....

....

....

....

....

....

....

....

James writes a simple message to the brethren encouraging them to be men of action and not just 'talkers.' He completely discourages the 'religious' attitude of sounding very spiritual but having no actions to complement their spirituality. Don't just talk Christianity, SHOW Christianity is his message. Don't send a hungry brother away hungry, telling him "it is well," or "God will provide," when God has placed you in a position to provide. God is not moved by our empty Christian talk; rather He wants our Actions to complement our words. Sometimes we send people back to God whom God has sent to us because He knows we have what they need.

James 2:15-16

Suppose a brother or sister is without clothes and daily food. If one of you says to him, "Go, I wish you well; keep warm and well fed," but does nothing about his physical needs, what good is it?

PRAYER

Merciful Father, give me a heart of compassion for one another. Let me not send someone away in need when I have what it takes to meet that need.

NOTES ....

It came a time in the ministry of Apostle Paul when men began to criticize him. To some, he was not qualified to become and Apostle and to others, he was ignoring certain obligations like circumcision. After Paul had tried to respond to them, he ended up with this conclusion: “I have been crucified with Christ and I no longer live, but Christ lives in me.” It is only when we live our lives as ‘dead men walking’ that we can really experience peace that is beyond understanding.

Galatians 2:20

I have been crucified with Christ and I no longer live, but Christ lives in me. The life I live in the body, I live by faith in the Son of God, who loved me and gave himself for me.

PRAYER

Heavenly Father, let Christ be fully formed in me in such a way the that men will not see me but will see Christ living in me, in Jesus' name, amen.

NOTES ....

....

....

....

....

....

....

....

....

....

At some point in the ministry of Jesus, He made statements that baffled His followers. What He said was so weird that it made Him lose more than half of His congregants. How could they stay with a Pastor who says they must eat his flesh and drink his blood? But even though so many left Him that day, He did not reverse or withdraw the statement. This is because, what the people understood was NOT WHAT HE INTENDED. The same thing happened when he told the Pharisees "before Abraham was (born), I am!" They picked up stones to stone Him because they said Jesus was not even up to fifty years old and He said He was before Abraham.

It is needless trying to explain yourself over and over to some people who OUTRIGHTLY MISUNDERSTAND you and come up with a different meaning to what you said. As long as your INTENTIONS WERE GOOD, it will become evident some time later.

John 6:54

Whoever eats my flesh and drinks my blood has eternal life, and I will raise him up at the last day

.

John 8:56-59

Your father Abraham rejoiced at the thought of seeing my day; he saw it and was glad." "You are not yet fifty years old," the Jews said to him, "and you have seen Abraham!" "I tell you the truth," Jesus answered, "before Abraham was born, I am!" At this, they picked up stones to stone him, but Jesus hid himself, slipping away from the temple grounds.

PRAYER

Lord, give us understanding to the things You speak. Lord, also help me to understand what people say based on their intended meaning and not just the words used, in Jesus' name, amen.

NOTES ....

....

....

....

....

....

....

....

....

....

WEEK 32 | WISDOM NUGGET

QUOTE FROM REV. GODLOVE

"Any anointing that cannot sit down and be teachable is soft target to the devil." (Rev. Nkwelle Godlove). Scripture declares that even Jesus learned obedience by the things He went through. So if Jesus who was God had to learn, then no man is too anointed that he cannot be taught.

PRAYER

✓ Lord, help me no matter how anointed I become to remain teachable, in Jesus' name.

NOTES

....
....
....
....
....
....
....
....
....
....
....
....
....
....
....
....

A situation arose in Corinth among the brethren. Some said they belong to Paul and others said Appollos. Believe me, Paul could have used this incident to his advantage. It could have been a moment for him to draw huge followers to himself. Rather he rebuked them and told them Christ is not divided and that no man died to save them except Christ. There is no need for all the division in the body of Christ today if we can only understand that we are all members of one body irrespective of our different denominations. Let our focus be Christ and wherever Christ is preached by whoever, we should support it.

1 Corinthians 1:11-15

My brothers, some from Chloe's household have informed me that there are quarrels among you. What I mean is this: One of you says, "I follow Paul"; another, "I follow Apollos"; another, "I follow Cephas"; still another, "I follow Christ." Is Christ divided? Was Paul crucified for you? Were you baptized into the name of Paul? I am thankful that I did not baptize any of you except Crispus and Gaius, so no one can say that you were baptized into my name.

PRAYER

Father, help Your church to be united. Send away every form of division and cause us to know that Christ is one and not divided, in Jesus name, amen.

NOTES ....

....

....

....

....

....

....

....

....

....

If you have not been faithful with another man's business, God will not give you a business of your own. God will want to know your level of trust before He can entrust into your hands what you are asking for. The only way you can prove your trustworthiness is by serving others faithfully. Unfortunately, most people do not want to serve anybody or they are very unfaithful when serving others and only look forward to starting their own business or ministry. Jesus says in *Luke:16.12, "And if you have not been trustworthy with someone else's property, who will give you property of your own?"* If you are not PRODUCTIVE working for someone, you will NEVER be productive being your own boss.

Luke 16:10, 12

"Whoever can be trusted with very little can also be trusted with much, and whoever is dishonest with very little will also be dishonest with much... And if you have not been trustworthy with someone else's property, who will give you property of your own?

PRAYER

Lord, help me to be a faithful servant in all that I do. Build in me an attitude of trust.

NOTES ....

After Peter and John healed a lame man by the temple gate, the man latter found them in the temple and held on to them. Everyone ran to see Peter and John (the miracle workers). The Bible says, "and they were astonished." As the Crowd stared at them, it was a good time for them to boast and make for themselves a name. Instead, Peter immediately REDIRECTED the attention of the onlookers to Jesus Christ: "Do not stare at us that way because we have no power to do this. Rather it is God who has glorified His Son Jesus whom you killed" Peter said. He PROJECTED ONLY the name of Jesus and dared not share in His glory. We too must do the same and not take God's glory.

Acts 3:7, 11, 13

Taking him by the right hand, he helped him up, and instantly the man's feet and ankles became strong. While the beggar held on to Peter and John, all the people were astonished and came running to them in the place called Solomon's Colonnade. When Peter saw this, he said to them: "Men of Israel, why does this surprise you? Why do you stare at us as if by our own power or godliness we had made this man walk? The God of Abraham, Isaac and Jacob, the God of our fathers, has glorified his servant Jesus. You handed him over to be killed, and you disowned him before Pilate, though he had decided to let him go.

PRAYER

Lord, guide our hearts and help us to always project You whenever You do something through us, in Jesus' name, amen.

NOTES ....

....

....

....

....

....

....

....

....

....

Everywhere Apostle Paul and his team went to share the Word of God, their audience listened to them as Servants of God and took everything they said as God's instructions. That's ok to do until you meet those who claim to be God's mouthpiece yet they teach another gospel. The Bereans DISTINGUISHED themselves in that, they did not just swallow everything Paul told them. They received Paul's message but then went on to EXAMINE IT to see if IT IS IN LINE WITH GOD'S WORD. Paul commended them for this.

In these last days when many wolves have gone out there in sheep clothing, it is very important that you examine every teaching out there to see if it ties with all scripture.

Acts 17:11

Now the Bereans were of more noble character than the Thessalonians, for they received the message with great eagerness and examined the Scriptures every day to see if what Paul said was true.

PRAYER

Lord, give me a hunger for Your Word so that I can always distinguish falsehood from the truth.

NOTES ....

....

....

....

....

....

....

....

....

....

The SECRET OF MOSES in dealing with the Israelites was to always go back to God and ask for help whenever it became too difficult for him to lead the people. Beloved, as a leader in any form that you are, the People under you are a Task for you. If handling that task is too difficult, always go back to the One who gave you those people and ask for help. Take them to the Lord in prayer. He will change their heart for you and your task will become easy. Never think that pouring your frustration to the people will ever make it less difficult. There are moments you just need to take a retreat with the Lord, away from the people. When you return, there will be a difference.

Exodus 17:4

Then Moses cried out to the LORD, "What am I to do with these people? They are almost ready to stone me."

Exodus 14:15

Then the LORD said to Moses, "Why are you crying out to me? Tell the Israelites to move on.

Numbers 11:2

When the people cried out to Moses, he prayed to the LORD and the fire died down.

PRAYER

Lord, give me the strength and wisdom to lead the people and the task You have given me. Let me not become frustrated but give me Your grace to carry through, in Jesus' name, amen.

NOTES ....

....

....

....

....

....

....

....

....

....

As Jesus sent out His disciples to preach, He gave the FIRM instructions especially in the area of food. He told them to eat whatever was given them. He further told them not to move from house to house but remain in one place: "Eat whatever is set before you" Jesus said.

Food is one of those things that can take much of our attention. Food has even led to the downfall of many. Jesus was trying to avoid what is now very common with today preachers who come for a program and want the best meals to be prepared for them. Instead of concentrating on the Word of God and assignment they came for, they spend time trying to eat the best meals. Jesus says when you go to preach, eat whatever you are served.

Luke 10:5,7-8

"When you enter a house, first say, 'Peace to this house.' Stay in that house, eating and drinking whatever they give you, for the worker deserves his wages. Do not move around from house to house. "When you enter a town and are welcomed, eat what is set before you.

PRAYER

Father, help us to always focus on the assignment You have given us and not on what to eat and what to wear.

NOTES ....

....

....

....

....

....

....

....

....

....

WEEK 33 | WISDOM NUGGET

THINK ABOUT OTHERS

It's easy to say we don't need a bridge when you're already on the other side. Let compassion lead your every action.

PRAYER

✓ Lord, I pray that my every action will be led by compassion for others.

✓ Lord, please take away selfishness from my heart and help me put others ahead of my personal desires, in Jesus' name. Amen.

NOTES

....
....
....
....
....
....
....
....
....
....
....
....
....
....
....

I've often heard people make statements like, if he claims to have the healing gift, why then is he himself sick? If he says God is using him to change lives why has he not changed his own family? If he prays for people and they receive breakthroughs then why is he himself struggling. Even the Pharisees told Jesus, "Physician, first heal yourself." Apostle Paul struggled with this concept for a long time in his ministry. As a mighty healer, he never expected that he could be sick. But it happened that he fell ill and after praying three times for healing and getting no answer, he finally came to terms with the fact that, when God does not take a problem away He gives abundant grace to carry through. God uses our weakness to remind us that He is sovereign and He alone decides what is best for us. He also uses it to create in us total dependence on Him.

2 Corinthians 12:7-9

To keep me from becoming conceited because of these surpassingly great revelations, there was given me a thorn in my flesh, a messenger of Satan, to torment me. Three times I pleaded with the Lord to take it away from me. But he said to me, "My grace is sufficient for you, for my power is made perfect in weakness." Therefore I will boast all the more gladly about my weaknesses, so that Christ's power may rest on me.

PRAYER

Gracious Father, I receive abundant grace from You to overcome every challenge in my challenge, in Jesus' name, amen.

NOTES

In as much as God's Word is to be shared to all right to the ends of the earth, there are moments God will Restrict you from Preaching to some people. This was the case with Apostle as they were Stopped twice from preaching in certain cities.

Sometimes God can Restrict you from Preaching to some people He knows the hearts of the people will not yield to the Word or that there are a more open groups of persons somewhere else that He'd rather send you to. Therefore, as you give the Word out to people, be open to the leading of the Spirit.

Acts 16:6-8

Paul and his companions traveled throughout the region of Phrygia and Galatia, having been kept by the Holy Spirit from preaching the word in the province of Asia. When they came to the border of Mysia, they tried to enter Bithynia, but the Spirit of Jesus would not allow them to. So they passed by Mysia and went down to Troas.

PRAYER

Lord, I open up myself to be led by Your Spirit even when it comes to sharing the gospel.

NOTES ....

....

....

....

....

....

....

....

....

....

Elisha desired a DOUBLE PORTION from his mentor Elijah. But there was a price tag attached to it: "If only you will see me when I am taken up.. then it will be yours." This was a simple instruction but required COMPLETE Obedience. It required that "even if Elijah went to the restroom, Elisha had to create a peep hole just because he didn't know when or where he might be taken."(Dr. Cindy Trim). Elisha resisted the temptations and discouragement at Gilgal, Bethel, Jericho, and at the Jordan. In the end, Elisha got a double portion of Elijah's anointing because he fully obeyed. Had Elisha not fully obeyed the instructions, he would not have received the reward.

2 Kings 2:9-13

When they had crossed, Elijah said to Elisha, "Tell me, what can I do for you before I am taken from you?" "Let me inherit a double portion of your spirit," Elisha replied. "You have asked a difficult thing," Elijah said, "yet if you see me when I am taken from you, it will be yours-- otherwise not." As they were walking along and talking together, suddenly a chariot of fire and horses of fire appeared and separated the two of them, and Elijah went up to heaven in a whirlwind. Elisha saw this and cried out, "My father! My father! The chariots and horsemen of Israel!" And Elisha saw him no more. Then he took hold of his own clothes and tore them apart. He picked up the cloak that had fallen from Elijah and went back and stood on the bank of the Jordan.

PRAYER

Lord, help me to fully obey Your Word and instructions to me so I can get Your reward.

NOTES ....

....

....

....

....

....

....

....

....

....

Adam and his wife Eve have been deceived by the serpent (Satan) to DISOBEY God by eating the forbidden fruit. God shows up and is VERY UNPLEASED with their action. The man blames the woman who in turn blamed the serpent. Despite their excuses, it did not change the fact that they had disobeyed. When it was time for God to release punishment to all three for their sin, God started with the Serpent. He cursed the Serpent by saying: cursed are you. But when it came to the man and the woman, God did not curse them; hallelujah. To the Woman God said: "I will greatly increase YOUR PAINS in childbearing..." and to ADAM God said: "Cursed is THE GROUND because of you... " All three were guilty of THE SAME CRIME. But to the serpent, God placed a CURSE upon him and did not curse the man and the woman. This was the first act of God's mercy for humanity in demonstration. And we must remain thankful to Him for not cursing us.

Genesis 3:13-17

Then the LORD God said to the woman, "What is this you have done?" The woman said, "The serpent deceived me, and I ate." So the LORD God said to the serpent, "Because you have done this, "Cursed are you above all the livestock and all the wild animals! You will crawl on your belly and you will eat dust all the days of your life. To the woman he said, "I will greatly increase your pains in childbearing; with pain you will give birth to children. Your desire will be for your husband, and he will rule over you." To Adam he said, "Because you listened to your wife and ate from the tree about which I commanded you, 'You must not eat of it,' "Cursed is the ground because of you; through painful toil you will eat of it all the days of your life.

PRAYER

Merciful Father, I thank You for showing me unusual mercy and kindness. I am forever grateful to You for always showing mercy to us.

NOTES ....

....

....

....

....

....

....

....

....

Haman has been promoted by the King and everyone is to bow before him when he passes by. But Modecai being a Jew would not do that because Jews only bow to YAHWEH. Upon noticing that, Haman decides he is going to kill Modecai. BUT when he goes to get execution approval from the King, he changed the story from being a ONE MAN OFFENSE and made it to be the OFFENSE OF ALL the Jews. He finally gets permission to go and kill all the Jews living in the land even though he had a problem with just one man: Modecai. This means thousands of INNOCENT lives were to perish had God not intervened.

Sometimes we suffer from things that have nothing to do with us. It may just be an aggression that has been transferred. You try so hard to find why everyone hates you and won't talk to you but you can't find any reason. You could just be a victim of transferred aggression. But just as Haman's plans backfired, those who transfer aggression will always end up in their own mess.

Esther 3:5-9

When Haman saw that Mordecai would not kneel down or pay him honor, he was enraged. Yet having learned who Mordecai's people were, he scorned the idea of killing only Mordecai. Instead Haman looked for a way to destroy all Mordecai's people, the Jews, throughout the whole kingdom of Xerxes. Then Haman said to King Xerxes, "There is a certain people dispersed and scattered among the peoples in all the provinces of your kingdom whose customs are different from those of all other people and who do not obey the king's laws; it is not in the king's best interest to tolerate them. If it pleases the king, let a decree be issued to destroy them, and I will put ten thousand talents of silver into the royal treasury for the men who carry out this business."

PRAYER

Lord, save me from being a victim of transferred aggression. I will not suffer for the issues of another person. Lord, vindicate me from any plot as You vindicated the Jews from the plot of Haman, in Jesus' name, amen.

NOTES ....

....
....
....
....
....
....

As Jesus comes walking on water to meet the disciples in the boat, Peter requested Jesus to permit him to step out and walk on water too. At the permission of Jesus Peter started walking on water towards Jesus until a storm arose and Peter got distracted and became scared. That is when he took his eyes off the Master and began to sink.

The only way we can achieve our goals in life is by fixing our attention on Jesus. We must not let the things happening around us frighten us or discourage us.

Matt 14:28-31.

Peter said to Him, "Lord, if it is You, command me to come to You on the water." And He said, "Come!" And Peter got out of the boat, and walked on the water and came toward Jesus. But seeing the wind, he became frightened, and beginning to sink, he cried out, "Lord, save me!" Immediately Jesus stretched out His hand and took hold of him, and said to him, "You of little faith, why did you doubt?"

PRAYER

Lord, help me to keep my focus on Your Word and not be affected by what is happening around me, in Jesus' name, amen.

NOTES ....

WEEK 34 | WISDOM NUGGET

DISCERN

The greatest asset of a believer is his/her ability to discern when God has stopped speaking through a vessel and the vessel is now speaking on his own. This way you will save both yourself and the vessel.

PRAYER

✓ Lord, grant me the spirit of discernment so I can be able to tell when you are speaking from when you are not.

NOTES

....
....
....
....
....
....
....
....
....
....
....
....
....
....
....
....
....

When it comes to following Christ, there is NO MIDDLE GROUND. You're either for God or you're Against. You can't be godly on Sunday and 'Worldly' on Monday and think you're a believer. Jesus says, you have to make a clear choice as to where you belong. It will be a waste of your time to try to give God eighty percent of your life and then give the world twenty percent and think you're a Believer. God wants a hundred percent of our hearts. He will not share His glory with anything else in our lives. Yield to Him fully or you might as well go ahead and FULLY live for the world and lose eternity with God. He who is not with Christ is against Him.

Luke 11:23

"He who is not with me is against me, and he who does not gather with me, scatters.

PRAYER

Father, help me to fully yield to You, in Jesus name, amen.

NOTES ....

....

....

....

....

....

....

....

....

....

As the Lord enters Jerusalem, the crowds including the disciples sang praises, blessing the Lord for Christ Jesus. Then the Pharisees asked Jesus to rebuke them. In order words, make them stop. In response, Jesus tells them, "If they keep quiet, the stones will cry out." This simply means the accomplishment of God's purpose is not hinged upon ONE PERSON. God can use anything or any man to accomplish His purposes. Never think that God's purposes will crash because you backed out. So, in all we do for God, let's do it joyfully because God would have still accomplished that thing even without us.

Luke 19:38-40

"Blessed is the king who comes in the name of the Lord!" "Peace in heaven and glory in the highest!" Some of the Pharisees in the crowd said to Jesus, "Teacher, rebuke your disciples!" "I tell you," he replied, "if they keep quiet, the stones will cry out."

PRAYER

Lord, I thank You for the privilege to serve and be called Your child and to work for You. Lord, may I never take this for granted, in Jesus' name, amen.

NOTES ....

....

....

....

....

....

....

....

....

....

Reading Judges 21:25 (In those days Israel had no king; everyone did as he saw fit.), it will suggest that the reason everyone is doing what seems right in their own eyes is because there is NO KING. In order words, when we have a king, everything will be fine. Well, that turned out to be so wrong because when they finally had a king, all did not go well. By this time, it was not only the people who sinned, even their king did. A physical king or leader will never bring a solution until you FIRST learn to recognize the Invisible King of kings. If everyone's reason for doing what is wrong is their claim that there is no one to tell them what is right, you should remember that you have the Spirit of God in you telling you right from wrong. Yield to Him and do not do what everyone else does.

Judges:21.25

In those days Israel had no king; everyone did as he saw fit.

PRAYER

Holy Spirit, guide me into all truth and to always do what is right even when everyone else is going the wrong way, in Jesus' name, amen.

NOTES

In Jesus' parable of the seed, He talks of the seed that sprang up so quickly. This seed was the first to shoot out of the ground, it had the first leaves, it was growing like wildfire but it did not last long before the heat of the sun killed it. Jesus adds that, the reason this seed sprang up so fast was because it was on shallow ground. The seed that is on good soil may take long to grow but it will stand the test of time. God wants us to go deep in our knowledge of Him such that when the storms and challenges of life come our way, we will withstand them.

Matthew 13:3-8

Then he told them many things in parables, saying: "A farmer went out to sow his seed. Some fell on rocky places, where it did not have much soil. IT SPRANG UP QUICKLY, because the soil was shallow. But when the sun came up, the plants were scorched, and they withered because they had no root. Still other seed fell on good soil, where it produced a crop-- a hundred, sixty or thirty times what was sown.

PRAYER

Lord help me to go deeper in You by studying Your word and having fellowship with You in Jesus name, amen.

NOTES ....

....

....

....

....

....

....

....

....

David has fallen with Bathsheba and tries to hide it but it only made matters worse for him. He killed Urriah in the process and this increased the guilt he was already struggling with. At the end of the day, God sent Prophet Nathan to him who rebuked him of his sins and showed him the way out. *(2 Samuel Chapter 11and 12*).

God knows our weaknesses and being a loving Father, He expects us to turn to Him for forgiveness immediately we fall into sin. But we often try to cover our sin which only makes it worse for us and pushes us further into sin. We should not make the mistake of David. Let us turn to God for forgiveness every time we sin and He will forgive us and strengthen us not to sin again.

Proverbs 28:13.

Whoever conceals their sins does not prosper, but the one who confesses and renounces them finds mercy.

PRAYER

Father, I come to You this day asking for Your forgiveness for my sins. Lord, give me a heart that fears You and energize me to live above sin, in Jesus name, amen.

NOTES ....

....

....

....

....

....

....

....

....

....

As God addresses King Saul for his disobedience, the Prophet Samuel uses some very strong words that if we look deeper into them, it will sound a bell in our hearts. Saul's sin was portrayed in two ways: Disobedience which God calls Rebellion and Pride which God calls Arrogance. God says to Saul, when you DISOBEY Me, you are not different from the one who practices WITCHCRAFT. And when you are PROUD, you fall into the category of those who practice IDOLATRY. May we examine ourselves today and repent where we need to because God does not take disobedience lightly.

1 Samuel 15:22-23

But Samuel replied: "Does the LORD delight in burnt offerings and sacrifices as much as in obeying the voice of the LORD? To obey is better than sacrifice, and to heed is better than the fat of rams. For rebellion is like the sin of divination, and arrogance like the evil of idolatry. Because you have rejected the word of the LORD, he has rejected you as king."

PRAYER

Lord, take away every spirit of disobedience away from me and help me to always obey Your voice in Jesus' name, amen.

NOTES ....

....
....
....
....
....
....
....
....
....

WEEK 35 | WISDOM NUGGET

WHY THEY FIGHT YOU

They fight you because they fear you. They fear you not because of WHO you are but because of WHAT you carry. When you understand this, you'd act like Jesus in front of your haters: "...but He answered them NOT A WORD" (Matthew 27:14).

PRAYER

✓ Lord, grant me the grace to stay focused on you even in the midst of opposition and hate, in Jesus' name.

NOTES

....
....
....
....
....
....
....
....
....
....
....
....
....
....
....
....

There's a difference between those who follow you because they love you and those who do so because of what they can get. And the sad thing is, the difference is not written on their faces. You can only tell by the passage of time or through the spirit of discernment. So watch out who you call your friend because not all of them are truly friends. Some will abandon you when you need them most. But one of these days, God will so shake your boat so that the things which are shakable can fall off and the things which are permanent can abide.

John 6:26.

Jesus answered, "Very truly I tell you, you are looking for me, not because you saw the signs I performed but because you ate the loaves and had your fill.

PRAYER

Lord, help me to see men beyond their words so I can carefully select my friends. I receive the spirit of discernment, in Jesus name, amen.

NOTES ....

....

....

....

....

....

....

....

....

....

God gave firm instructions to Moses saying: “The fire on the Altar must NEVER GO OUT. You must keep it Burning Day and Night.” That was the only way the altar could remain a sacred place and a lighted place. The altar in the Old Testament was a place where God met with His people. Today our bodies are the temple of God and your life is the altar on which God displays His glory. The secret to a victorious Christian life is to constantly BURN FOR GOD. Any believer who is cold or lukewarm will not go far in their walk with God. Even nature teaches us that flies and other insects don’t go anywhere close to fire. If your life has to be free of all kinds of impurities, then the fire of God must constantly burn in you. Create time daily to wait on the Lord and to study His Word . This is how you rekindle the fire of God in you.

Leviticus 6:12.

The fire on the altar must be kept burning; it must not go out. Every morning the priest is to add firewood and arrange the burnt offering on the fire and burn the fat of the fellowship offerings on it.

PRAYER

Lord, help me to constantly burn for You every day of my life. Let Your fire in me never go out, in Jesus' name, amen.

NOTES

Samson is anointed by God and set apart to carry out a special assignment for God. Upon God's instructions, his hair had never been shaved and he had never been defiled by wine or strong drink. God used him so many times to destroy the Philistines. Nobody could overpower him not even an entire army. At some point in the life of Samson, he began to take the anointing upon him for granted and ended up with Delilah who shaved his hair and the Lord left him. The Philistines came after him and Samson got up to fight them but he did not know the Lord had left him.

The worst thing that can happen to a believer is for the Spirit of God to depart from you. You become very vulnerable and end up as a prey in the hands of the enemy who is always seeking an opportunity to destroy you. You must guard your relationship with God and cherish His protection over your life. Avoid anything that will cause the Spirit of God to leave you.

Judges 16:20.

Then she called, "Samson, the Philistines are upon you!" He awoke from his sleep and thought, "I'll go out as before and shake myself free." But he did not know that the LORD had left him.

PRAYER

Precious Holy Spirit, may You never leave me at any point in my life. Help me not to do the things that against Your will, in Jesus' name, amen.

NOTES ....

....

....

....

....

....

....

....

....

....

Unauthorized to come into the king's presence, Esther says, "If I perish I perish" as she ventures in to make her request. Her entire race was at the verge of being exterminated. She could have sat there crying and weeping, but she took the risk of going in to see the king against all odds. She went in and came back alive and her people were saved.

Only risk takers can change the world. If you dare into what you believe, you will achieve what you dream for. As long as you know the Spirit of God is leading you into that direction, take a step by faith and damn the consequences and I guarantee you that God will not let you down.

Esther 4:16.

"Go, gather together all the Jews who are in Susa, and fast for me. Do not eat or drink for three days, night or day. I and my attendants will fast as you do. When this is done, I will go to the king, even though it is against the law. And if I perish, I perish."

PRAYER

Merciful Father, give me the courage and boldness to advance to venture into my dreams. Take away every spirit of fear from me and stand with me, in Jesus' name, amen.

NOTES ....

....

....

....

....

....

....

....

....

....

LOYALTY IS MORE THAN COMMITMENT...

The greatest virtue Jesus had in His team was people who were loyal to Him. Loyalty is stronger than commitment. You can commit yourself but not be loyal. But you can't be loyal and not be committed. If you have followers who are loyal, you can go to bed and know all is under control. It was loyalty that made Peter cut off the ear of a one of the soldiers who came to arrest Jesus. It was loyalty that caused Mary to go to the tomb of a 'dead man' with spices to anoint His body. Loyalty to a person goes beyond the life of that person; you still have great respect and honor for them though they are not alive. Every leader must pray for God to send you people who are loyal. As a head of a household, you must also pray for your kids to be loyal to you.

Mark 16:1.

When the Sabbath was over, Mary Magdalene, Mary the mother of James, and Salome bought spices so that they might go to anoint Jesus' body.

John 18:10.

Then Simon Peter, who had a sword, drew it and struck the high priest's servant, cutting off his right ear. (The servant's name was Malchus.)

PRAYER

Father, help me to be loyal to You and to the people You have called me to assist. Lord, release the spirit of loyalty upon my kids that they will uphold the name of their family and not bring shame to us, in Jesus' name, amen.

NOTES

"And lead us not into temptation, but deliver us from evil. For if you forgive others their trespasses, your heavenly Father will also forgive you," (Matt. 6:13-14). In this section of the Lord's prayer, the spotlight is placed on our great helplessness and our great need for regeneration. Lest we think that we can master our condition on our own, the Lord teaches us to submit this battle against sin to the Father. And lest we think that mercy is for us alone, the Lord again shows that a tree produces fruit in keeping with its nature.

Where do you need to give the battle against sin to the LORD today? Where do you need to show the mercy that you've been shown today?

Matthew 6:13-14.

"And lead us not into temptation, but deliver us from evil. For if you forgive others their trespasses, your heavenly Father will also forgive you,"

PRAYER

Merciful Father, I thank You for forgiving me my trespasses and I also pray that You help me forgive those who sin against me, in Jesus' name, amen.

NOTES ....

....

....

....

....

....

....

....

....

....

WEEK 36 | WISDOM NUGGET

CHANGE COMES WITH A PRICE

Every "first generation" of CHANGE is the PRICE-Paying Generation. Some of the things you're doing today to make ends meet, your kids will never have to do those same things. And unless YOU DECIDE TODAY to end that circle of failure, poverty, illiteracy etc., your kids will live to fight the same fight another day.

PRAYER

✓ *Lord, I receive grace to end every ugly circle in my family. I declare that it ends with me and the people after me will not have to suffer the same things, in Jesus' name. Amen.*

NOTES

....
....
....
....
....
....
....
....
....
....
....
....
....

In the account below, we find Jesus in a house overflowing with the poor, sick, needy, and broken. The disciples long held misunderstanding of what their Messiah would be gets the best of them again. Their priority is to get Him out of such an improper, inconvenient place for the king of Israel. Little do they know, there's nowhere else He would rather be. In His correction of their misconception, He grants value immeasurable to the poor, sick, needy, broken children of God... He grants this value to you. Irrespective of your socio-economic status, Jesus will rather be with you than the wealthy who do not obey His Word.

Mark 3:33-35

And he answered them, "Who are my mother and my brothers?" And looking about at those who sat around him, he said, "Here are my mother and my brothers! For whoever does the will of God, he is my brother and sister and mother."

PRAYER

Loving Father, I thank You for choosing to be with the lowly and poor and not discriminate like the world that will only pay attention to their families and the wealthy.

NOTES

Jesus Christ, is the centerpiece of time and eternity. The Father has subjected all things to the Son. The Son is prophet, priest, and king to His people. Here we see the line in the sand. Apart from Jesus, there is no way to the Father. In a world that champions relativism and individualized spiritual experiences, Jesus stands alone as Lord and Judge. This may seem difficult but the same God who gives breath to the Christian likewise gives breath to the non-Christian and their rejection of Him will not be excused when He judges. In simple terms: Jesus is God. Believe in Him and be saved.

John 5:22-23.

"For the Father judges no one, but has given all judgment to the Son, that all may honor the Son, just as they honor the Father. Whoever does not honor the Son does not honor the Father who sent him."

PRAYER

Lord Jesus, I believe You are sent from God and God the Father has put all things into Your hands. I receive the grace to honor You and to live for You every day of my life, in Jesus' name, amen.

NOTES

We are time bound creatures who know not how to measure anything without applying the disappointment of finality to it. We've all heard the saying, "All good things must cometo an end," but Christ gives us victory by freeing us from this finality. In Christ, eternal life does not simply mean Heaven when we die, it means we will never die. We will lay these bodies down, but that is only a moving from an imperfect house to a perfect one. Believer, you are not short on time today. Thanks be to Christ, your days will have no end. The only requirement to this is that you keep His Word.

John 8:51.

"Truly, truly, I say to you, if anyone keeps my word, he will never see death."

PRAYER

Heavenly Father, thank You for giving me eternal life in Christ Jesus. I receive the power to keep Your Word by obeying You, in Jesus' name, amen.

NOTES ....

....

....

....

....

....

....

....

....

....

The scandal of the Gospel is that it is only meant for the unworthy. Truly we are all unworthy, but not all can see it. When Christ calls a man, He calls a lost man to be found. He did not come for the well but the sick that His name might be praised for endless ages by those who cried in their heart, "Wash me Savior, or I die," and then, "Amazing grace how sweet the sound that saved a wretch like me." What a Savior! He seeks us, even while we are running headlong into our destruction. He never stops coming after us and He will go to any length to track us down and bring us home to Himself.

Luke 19:10.

"For the Son of Man came to seek and to save the lost."

PRAYER

Loving Father, I thank You for coming to seek and save a lost sinner like me. I am forever grateful to You Lord. Lord, I pray that You will also find many who are still lost out there in their sins, in Jesus name, amen.

NOTES ....

....

....

....

....

....

....

....

....

....

"And he said to his disciples, "Temptations to sin are sure to come, but woe to the one through whom they come! It would be better for him if a millstone were hung around his neck and he were cast into the sea than that he should cause one of these little ones to sin." (Luke 17:1-2). Such a stern warning is given here that we must be careful not to excuse ourselves from it. Many things will indeed come into the Christian's life to try their faith, Christ has said so. However we must be careful that the trials, temptations, and stumblings of God's children never come by our hand. The extent that Christ cares about this can be seen in the graphic judgment He pronounces on the offender here. We are to intentionally and actively seek the strengthening of the faith of our brothers and sisters and not be responsible in any way for their downfall.

PRAYER

Lord, help me to be a source of encouragement to the people around me and not to be a stumbling block, in Jesus' name, amen.

NOTES

"And Jesus, looking at him, loved him, and said to him, "You lack one thing: go, sell all that you have and give to the poor, and you will have treasure in heaven; and come, follow me." (Mark 10:21). There is a form of godliness that we must make every effort to root out of our hearts. Often hard to detect, this self-help Gospel is shown to us here. This man was a "good guy" who had been blessed with material blessings. Wanting to seal the deal, he approaches Jesus for His approval. Jesus, however, will not be added onto a man's works any more than He will be added onto his good fortune. 'All Me' or 'all nothing' is the blow that Jesus strikes into the man's heart and tragically the man leaves with the latter, though pockets full. Jesus is asking the same question to you and me today: will you take all of Jesus or like this wealthy young man, you will rather go with all of the world? For what shall it profit a man if he gains the whole world and lose his soul (Mark 8:36).

PRAYER

Father, help me to always chose to be with You rather than go after worldly riches which will perish. Take hold of my heart so that my every desire will be for You, in Jesus' name, amen.

NOTES ....

....

....

....

....

....

....

....

....

....

WEEK 37 | WISDOM NUGGET

HIS PRESENCE IS YOUR DWELLING PLACE

For the believer, the presence of God is not a place you visit: it is your Dwelling place. Desire His presence more than anything else.

PRAYER

- ✓ Lord, create in me a hunger for Your presence, in Jesus' name.
- ✓ Let me desire to live in Your presence daily, I pray.

NOTES

....
....
....
....
....
....
....
....
....
....
....
....
....
....
....
....

"But I say to you who hear, Love your enemies, do good to those who hate you" Luke 6:27. Christ reverses the curse. People created to bear the glorious image of God are reborn in Christ to display the beauty of God. The command Christ gives us here has little to do with creating a more coexistent society and much to do with being the image bearers He created us to be. Loving your enemies and blessing those who curse you is a reflection of the character of God on display through you. This then is a privilege for us, not a burden. It may be a difficult task to carry out but a willing heart will always find grace to put that into practice.

PRAYER

Loving Father, please give me the grace to love my enemies and to show kindness to those who hate me, in Jesus' name, amen.

NOTES ....

....
....
....
....
....
....
....
....
....

"And behold, I am coming soon. Blessed is the one who keeps the words of the prophecy of this book." (Revelation 22:7). Our lives in Christ are lived in the constant tension of "already, not yet." We have been saved and will be saved. We have been changed and will be changed. And here, Christ and His Kingdom have come and will come. We are to be a people marked by longing anticipation of the fulfillment of promises. We are to long for the day when all will be made right, all will be made new, when our faith shall be sight. That day, is always imminent, when our wondrous King comes to us face to face. Our duty as we anticipate His coming should be to keep His Word.

PRAYER

Lord, I live in anticipation of the day You will come back to take us home. Help me to obey Your Word as I live my days here on earth, in Jesus' name, amen.

NOTES

"You did not choose me, but I chose you and appointed you that you should go and bear fruit and that your fruit should abide, so that whatever you ask the Father in my name, he may give it to you." (John 15:16). The choosing, appointing, fruit bearing, and petitioning are all interconnected. These are the sources and the marks of one abiding in Christ. Because of His choosing and appointing, we bear fruit. Because of our fruit bearing, our wills become progressively aligned with His, and those things which He desires for us become the very things we desire of Him. What spiritual fruit have I seen God produce in my life? Is it enduring? What spiritual fruit am I asking the Father for in Jesus name today?

We must remember that God expects us to carry out the functions for which He chose and appointed us to do. We are here on mission and if we carry it out well, then we will get whatsoever we ask from the Father.

PRAYER

Heavenly Father, I thank You for choosing and appointing me to carry out Your work. I receive the grace to do this work effectively, in Jesus' name.

NOTES

“Not that anyone has seen the Father except he who is from God; he has seen the Father. Truly, truly, I say to you, whoever believes has eternal life.” (John 6:46-47). Who has seen God? Who will see God? Scripture tells us that only He who is from God (Jesus) has seen God. Jesus says to us that whoever believes has eternal life. So what is it to believe? Is it simply a one- time confession of faith or does it require more? To believe is to continue to believe and trust in Jesus. Through belief and relationship with Christ, we too shall see the Father and commune with him eternally. This is not of our own accord but that of our Savior, Jesus Christ. I therefore encourage you to keep believing in Jesus and trust His Word and in the end, you shall see God.

PRAYER

Lord Jesus, I believe You came from God and You have seen God. I believe in You and I pray You help me to keep believing in You till the end in Jesus name, amen.

NOTES

"When they deliver you over, do not be anxious how you are to speak or what you are to say, for what you are to say will be given to you in that hour. For it is not you who speak, but the Spirit of your Father speaking through you." (Matthew10:19-20). How often do you sit in silence when the opportunity arises to share the Gospel? For most of us, it occurs daily. How do we combat this? Scripture tells us to not be anxious about what we will say because the Holy Spirit will speak through us. However, this does not excuse us from arming ourselves with the Gospel. By learning God's Word, we invite the Spirit to work through us as we grow closer to Christ. Then we can rely on the Spirit to move through us in sharing the grace and mercy of Christ.

This scripture also refers to moments when your faith will be tested in the form of persecution. Jesus says when you get arrested and tried for the sake of the gospel, do not worry about what to say for the Holy Spirit will be right there with you to tell you what to say.

PRAYER

Father, I thank You because You will never forsake nor abandon me. You will always be with me even in moments when my faith is being tested. You will always give me the right words to speak in every situation, in Jesus name, amen.

NOTES ....

....

....

....

....

....

....

....

....

....

"You shall worship the Lord your God and him only shall you serve" (Matthew 4:10). When and why do spiritual attacks come? Our enemy is tactically sound in his process. Most spiritual attacks come at times of spiritual highs or the lowest of lows. These are the times that Satan seeks to extinguish a powerful enemy or deliver a fatal blow to a suffering believer. He presents different options to you just to make you abandon the Lord Your God. He believes he can get you since you are desperate and vulnerable. How do we protect ourselves from these attacks? In the same way Jesus set the example. When Satan tempts Jesus with the world he shields himself with God's Word and drives the enemy away. You too may be strong against attack by guarding and arming yourself with the Gospel and focusing on God rather than the circumstances of this world.

PRAYER

Lord, I determine in my heart to worship and serve You alone and no other god no matter what I am going through and I know You will not let me down, in Jesus' name, amen.

NOTES

WEEK 38 | WISDOM NUGGET

ALONENESS TAUGHT YOU SOMETHING

Don't feel bitter or hate those who left you during difficult times. They taught you how to survive by yourself.

PRAYER

✓ Father, I thank You for the moments in my life when everyone left me. I bless Your name for the lessons You taught me in my difficult times. Thank You Father, in Jesus' name, Amen.

NOTES

....
....
....
....
....
....
....
....
....
....
....
....
....
....
....
....
....

WHY HE SENT THEM OUT IN PAIRS...

"And he called the twelve and began to send them out two by two, and gave them authority over the unclean spirits" (Mark 6:7). When Jesus sent His disciples, why did He send them in pairs rather than as individuals? After walking with Him, was each not equipped to minister on his own? This is but one example of how the Gospel is to be shared. We all need the guidance and support of other believers. We are called but we are not called alone. So be sent, but be sent with a community of believers. Are you walking alone or do you have the support of other believers? Do not be alienated but be a part of the body so that you will be encouraged and cared for as you share the good news of Jesus.

PRAYER

Lord, help us to work together and help one another in the advancement of Your Kingdom, in Jesus' name. Father, take away every spirit of division from Your church, in Jesus' name, amen.

NOTES

"Give us this day our daily bread, and forgive us our debts, as we also have forgiven our debtors. And lead us not into temptation, but deliver us from evil." (Matthew 6:11-13). For many believers, prayer is difficult. We often feel inadequate in our words and many struggle to pray around others. Throughout scripture, Jesus teaches us through His example. Jesus compares this simple prayer to that of the Pharisees who often prayed long, articulate prayers for no reason other than impressing others with their knowledge. Prayer should not be difficult if we pray the right way.

What is our daily bread? The daily bread given from God is not only the food we consume which allows us to survive but also the strength and guidance that only He can provide as we become more and more like Christ. We can learn from the prayer of Jesus that prayer is a very simple thing. It is just communicating with the Father, thanking Him for everyday or requesting what you need.

PRAYER

Father, I thank You for this day that You have given me and I thank You for my family for everything You are doing for us, in Jesus' name, amen.

NOTES

“And he said to them, “Pay attention to what you hear: with the measure you use, it will be measured to you, and still more will be added to you. For to the one who has, more will be given, and from the one who has not, even what he has will be taken away.” (Mark 4:24-25).

Those who are in Christ have been given ears to hear His Word. Through scripture, the nature of God is revealed to us. This understanding is not immediately given, but through prayer and study of the Word we learn more each day about who God is and our faith is strengthened. For those who seek God, more understanding and faith is granted. To those who neglect time in the Word, less is revealed. How well do you know the true nature of God? Do you see Him rightly, and how are you to know without knowing the message that He has revealed?

PRAYER

Lord, help me to seek You daily in prayer and studying Your Word. And as I know You Lord, may You keep adding to my knowledge of who You are, in Jesus' name, amen.

NOTES

"Jesus said to him, "No one who puts his hand to the plow and looks back is fit for the kingdom of God." (Luke 9:62.) I will give my life to Jesus once I'm married. Once my debts are paid, I will be an obedient steward and give generously of my finances.

So many times, we resist the commands of Jesus and compartmentalize the gospel. We want everything from Jesus but we only give what is left over or easy. We are willing to follow Jesus until it costs us something. How do you combat the urges to withhold your best from Jesus? Jesus makes it clear that the time to follow Him is now and that we should follow Him completely regardless of the cost. We must let go of earthly comfort and security and trust Jesus. No excuse is good enough for you not to give your best to Jesus. You have put your hand on the plow and there is no looking back.

PRAYER

Lord, help me to yield fully to Your leading and to give You the best of me whenever You make a request from me. Take away every attitude of back-looking, in Jesus' name.

NOTES

"*And calling to him a child, he put him in the midst of them and said, "Truly, I say to you, unless you turn and become like children, you will never enter the kingdom of heaven.* (Matthew 18:2-4).

Whoever humbles himself like this child is the greatest in the kingdom of heaven. "Faith in Christ requires that we relinquish control, and humbly accept that it is Christ in us, and not our own power that not only saves us, but also provides for us daily. Much like a child trusts in his parents to lead and provide, so should we be with Jesus. How often, do you lean on your own power to resist sin only to find yourself painfully stumbling? How many times do you find yourself trying to do it all alone.? Our only righteousness is that of Christ in us, and it is only found through seeking deep relationship with Him.

PRAYER

Lord, help me to be childlike in my walk with You. Let me obey and submit to You as a child submits to the parents, in Jesus' name, amen.

NOTES ....

....

....

....

....

....

....

....

....

....

"It is the Spirit who gives life; the flesh is no help at all. The words that I have spoken to you are spirit and life." (John 6:63).

Who will choose to follow God? Not one. We are incapable of choosing the things of God. Left to our own understanding, we will inevitably perish and spend eternity separated from God. With love, mercy, and compassion, God has sent His Spirit to us through the power of the Gospel. The flesh, which is no help to us, cannot follow or choose God without the understanding and desire granted by the Holy Spirit. Even those who are in Christ must continue to pray and spend time with God through His Word. Where are you in your walk with Christ? Are you walking with Him or keeping Him at a distance until you need Him? We all need Christ. We need Him every moment of every day.

PRAYER

Holy Spirit, I thank You for giving me life in Christ and I submit my whole life to You and ask that You lead me in the right way in Jesus, amen.

NOTES

....

....

....

....

....

....

....

....

....

....

WEEK 39 | WISDOM NUGGET

FAITH: AN INVISIBLE FORCE

Faith is like Wifi even though you don't see it; it has the ability to connect you to your inheritance. Scripture declares that without faith it is impossible to please God. In all that you desire, desire to have faith and faith comes by hearing God's word. Grow your faith by growing your word knowledge.

PRAYER

- ✓ Lord, I pray that as I feed on Your Word, let faith grow in me, in Jesus' name.
- ✓ I connect to my godly inheritance through faith, in Jesus' name.

NOTES

....
....
....
....
....
....
....
....
....
....
....
....

“And he said to them, “I saw Satan fall like lightning from heaven. Behold, I have given you authority to tread on serpents and scorpions, and over all the power of the enemy, and nothing shall hurt you. Nevertheless, do not rejoice in this, that the spirits are subject to you, but rejoice that your names are written in heaven.” (Luke 10:18-20).

Who will mourn at the end of their days? All who are separated from God will mourn. They will be eternally separated from His presence. After seeing His glory all those devoid of Him will thirst for His presence forever. Scripture tells us that this will be more unbearable for those who heard the gospel but rejected Christ.

Do you have a relationship with Christ or have you simply been near the Kingdom, keeping Christ at arm’s length? For us in communion with Christ, we anticipate our glorious reunion and an eternity of walking with the Savior. As followers of Christ we must bring the Kingdom near to those who have not seen, for it is through the Gospel that God speaks and saves.

PRAYER

Lord, I thank You for giving me power over the enemy. Lord, I also thank You for making me a candidate of heaven by writing my name in the book of life.

NOTES

Read Matthew 20:1-16. This passage talks about workers who were hired to work on a field. They all came at different times during the day and the last group only worked for an hour. At the end, the land owner paid all of them equally even though the first group had worked a full shift.

Do you think the early workers are rightly upset? Apply what you have learned about the landowner to God. We see two characteristics up front. He is faithful and He gives graciously. God doesn't show favoritism. Whether you are a new believer or you were saved at an early age, God loves us equally. And because of Jesus, we can approach the throne of grace. Anything the Father gives us is purely because He is generous, not because we deserve it. Do you appreciate provision more than the Provider? In what ways can you learn to be more humble?

PRAYER

Father, I thank You for loving us equally. Thank You for Your generosity, in Jesus name, amen.

NOTES

"At that time Jesus declared, "I thank you, Father, Lord of heaven and earth, that you have hidden these things from the wise and understanding and revealed them to little children; yes, Father, for such was your gracious will." (Matthew 11:25-26).

Jesus admires the way His Father operates. He humbles the arrogant, and gives wisdom to the least likely. Later in the book of Matthew, Jesus tells the disciples to become like children. What is so interesting about children is that they are passionate and get excited about little things we adults tend to ignore. Children aren't cynical. They are hopeful. Does your hope in God mirror that of a child? Do you get excited when you think of God's promises? Do you study the Father the way a child would?

PRAYER

I thank You Father for the privilege to be among those You have chosen to reveal Your truths to. I am forever grateful to You for this, in Jesus' name, amen.

NOTES

"On that day many will say to me, 'Lord, Lord, did we not prophesy in your name, and cast out demons in your name, and do many mighty works in your name?' And then will I declare to them, 'I never knew you; depart from me, you workers of lawlessness." (Matthew 7:22-23).

The best way to get to know someone is to spend time with them. God has revealed Himself to us through His Son. Scripture says that there will be many who know of God, but will be surprised when they are cast away from His presence because they don't KNOW God. So, how do we spend time with God? We read His Word, we spend time in prayer, and we fellowship with other believers.

PRAYER

Lord help me to be ready for You when You return in Jesus name. May I not spend all these years walking with You at the end I drift away and miss heaven in Jesus name, amen.

NOTES

““Jesus said, “For judgment I came into this world, that those who do not see may see, and those who see may become blind.” (John 9:39).

There are times I find myself wondering whether or not I would notice a certain thing happening had I not been saved. Scripture tells us that when we turn to the Lord, the veil is removed (1 Corinthians 3:16). A veil is used to cover someone’s face. Jesus removes that veil when we come to Him. Now that we can see, we are a lot more aware of sin. Now, imagine seeing the world through Jesus’ eyes. How has your life changed since Christ has restored your sight? Are you compassionate towards “the blind”?

PRAYER

Lord, I thank You for opening my eyes to see spiritual things through Your spirit. Thank You for taking away the scales off my eyes, in Jesus’ name, amen.

NOTES ....

....

....

....

....

....

....

....

....

....

““Jesus answered them, “Do not grumble among yourselves.” (John 6:43).

Jesus came to perform the will of the Father. People get irritated because they want to come to Jesus on their terms, not His. If God knew that He was going to send His Son to save the world, don’t you think He would do it in such a way that would yield the most fruit? Jesus mentions a few verses later that the bread He is offering is His flesh. Jesus offered Himself on the cross for us, and in so doing, He offered us life through His death. Do you savor the bread of life that Jesus offers?

PRAYER

Lord, open my eyes to fully grasp the revelation in Your words even when it does not make sense to my hearing, in Jesus' name, amen.

NOTES

WEEK 40 | WISDOM NUGGET

DON'T FEED ON POISON

They say don't bite the finger that feeds you. But I say it depends on what you're being fed with. It is insanity to keep feeding on what is poisonous. Break out of that bondage and set yourself free. Most people are unable to break out of ungodly relationships simply because of what they're getting. But the truth is, those things are only destroying you.

PRAYER

- ✓ Lord, I receive grace to break out of every ungodly relationship, in Jesus' name.
- ✓ Lord, I take off my eyes from those very things that destroy my walk with You, in Jesus' name. Amen.

NOTES

....

....

....

....

....

....

....

....

....

....

"Truly, truly, I say to you, you will weep and lament, but the world will rejoice. You will be sorrowful, but your sorrow will turn into joy." (John 16:20).

"So also you have sorrow now, but I will see you again, and your hearts will rejoice, and none will take your joy from you. In that day you will ask nothing of me. Truly, truly, I say to you, whatever you ask of the Father in my name, he will give it to you." (John 16:22-23).

One of the most beautiful verses in scripture is John 16:23. Do you know why "you will not ask for anything in that day"? Because every need will be fulfilled. We ask things right now because we need them. Scripture shows us that Jesus is our need and we will rejoice when He returns and nobody will be able to take that joy from us. He tells us that we will have difficulties in this life, but the life to come is far better! This should change the way we think about this life and hope for the next!

PRAYER

Lord, I receive the grace to grow through the trials of this life and not give up. By Your comfort I will hold unto You and You will turn my sorrow into joy, in Jesus' name, amen.

NOTES

“For false christs and false prophets will arise and perform signs and wonders, to lead astray, if possible, the elect.” (Mark 13:22).

Jesus says that in the last days there will be false prophets who can perform signs and miracles and that we shouldn’t trust them. We see that today don’t we? People claim outlandish things, then we find that they are only trying to prey on naive people for a quick dollar. So what is something we can do to prepare ourselves against false prophets - the same people that will be deceptive enough to fool even the elect? Read the Bible! See if what they say matches what scripture says. You’ll find that scripture tells us many times to avoid such people.

PRAYER

Lord, may I not be deceived by the false prophets in these last days. Open my eyes and give me discernment to know right from wrong, in Jesus’ name, amen.

NOTES

The culture in Jesus' day was much different than ours. The groom would go to his father and tell him that he is engaged. The father would give the son some land and the son would build a home for his wife. Once the father decided that the place was suitable for his daughter-in-law, he would tell the son to go get his bride. During this time the bride had to constantly wait for her betrothed to come take her home. Jesus promises that He will return once He has prepared a place for His bride. We must wait for Him!

John 14:1-4.

"Let not your hearts be troubled. Believe in God; believe also in me. In my Father's house are many rooms. If it were not so, would I have told you that I go to prepare a place for you? And if I go and prepare a place for you, I will come again and will take you to myself, that where I am you may be also. And you know the way to where I am going."

PRAYER

Lord, I receive Your comfort in my heart today and I refuse to be anxious about the unknown. I believe in Your Word.

NOTES

Scripture says that you are blessed when people hate you for His sake. There is a difference between the beatitudes and the woe's in scripture. Notice that those who are blessed are those who place their faith in Christ, and those who depend on material things will be in despair. I love what the CSB says in verse 23. "Take note - your reward is great in heaven.." If you have to, write it down and then rejoice. Know in your heart that your dependency on Christ is already awarded.

Luke 6:22.

"Blessed are you when people hate you and when they exclude you and revile you and spurn your name as evil, on account of the Son of Man!"

PRAYER

Lord, I receive Your blessings and comfort in the midst of persecution. Help us not to faint when men hate and exclude us because of our faith in You.

NOTES ....

My wife and I went to Cumberland Caverns a few years ago. Halfway through the cave they turned off all the lights. Total darkness. Then they turned on one light above and it lights up the whole area. Now think about the times in Jesus' day. It's been roughly 400 years since God has spoken to His people and they have slipped back into sin. Then comes God in human flesh. A great Light amidst darkness with a message,"Turn from evil, heaven is close." Light reveals what darkness hides. And because of Jesus, we don't have to hide from God.

Matthew 4:17.
"From that time Jesus began to preach, saying, "Repent, for the kingdom of heaven is at hand."

PRAYER

Lord, grant Your saving power to every lost soul out there so they can come to the knowledge of Your saving grace, in Jesus' name, amen.

NOTES ....

....
....
....
....
....
....
....
....
....

What is a thorn in your flesh? We all have them. Some thorns pierce deeper than others. Paul the Apostle had one. Paul's thorn is never identified by name but, just like ours, it was painful and at times debilitating. Whether he faced physical pain, mental anguish, or emotional turmoil, Paul learned to use it to humble himself and rely completely on God's power and not his own.

Do not be discouraged by the thorns you face in life but rather use them to grow deeper in your relationship with God. Allow your character to reflect God's promise so that others will see Him, know Him, and trust Him too.

2 Corinthians 12:7-9.

"So to keep me from becoming conceited because of the surpassing greatness of the revelations, a thorn was given me in the flesh, a messenger of Satan to harass me, to keep me from becoming conceited. Three times I pleaded with the Lord about this, that it should leave me. But he said to me, "My grace is sufficient for you, for my power is made perfect in weakness." Therefore I will boast all the more gladly of my weaknesses, so that the power of Christ may rest upon me."

PRAYER

Lord, I know that You are working in every situation in my life whether good or bad and Your grace is sufficient to see me through, in Jesus' name, amen.

NOTES ....
....
....
....
....
....
....
....
....
....

WEEK 41 | WISDOM NUGGET

BE CAREFUL WITH OPPORTUNITIES

Never enter a door God did not open. Some things you call Breakthrough can bring about your BREAKDOWN. Always go to God in prayer and ask His opinion before you make a move. You will surely hear a still gentle voice in your heart telling you what to do.

PRAYER

✓ Lord, help me to always ask Your opinion about every opportunity before I make a move, in Jesus' name.

NOTES

....
....
....
....
....
....
....
....
....
....
....
....
....
....
....

Do you recognize God's hand in changing your life? If so, are you emboldened to share your personal story with others? In today's verse, Jesus has just miraculously healed a man possessed by thousands of demons! The man is so grateful he wants to come with Jesus but instead Jesus tels him to go tell others what God has done for him.

We may see ourselves as much "cleaner" than this man, or a homeless person begging on the street, or an addict stealing to fuel his habit. The truth is, we are all equally "dirty." Our salvation is no less miraculous than that of the demon possessed man. Be grateful for His gift and obey the command Jesus gives to courageously tell others what God has done for you.

Luke8:39.

"Return home and tell how much God has done for you." So the man went away and toldall over town how much Jesus had done for him."

PRAYER

Father, help us to tell others about Your wondrous works in our lives. May we not conceal and hold back the things You have done for us.

NOTES ....

....

....

....

....

....

....

....

....

....

Read Matthew 4:4. Do you remember who Jesus answered here? He answered Satan during an attack when the enemy thought Jesus was tired, hungry, and vulnerable to attack. What do you hunger for? If your hunger is not for God and His truth then you will be defeated. The devil knows our weaknesses and will try to exploit them. Whether that weakness is physical needs and desires, or possessions and power, or pride, the enemy is probing. Learn from Jesus' example of being strong in our time of weakness. Fight temptation with God's Word, trust in His providence, and relinquish your pride for His power!

Matthew 4:4.

"Jesus answered, "It is written: 'Man shall not live on bread alone, but on every word that comes from the mouth of God."

PRAYER

Lord, help create in me a hunger for Your Word so that with it I can withstand every temptation from the devil, in Jesus' name, amen.

NOTES ....

"And Jesus came and said to them, "All authority in heaven and on earth has been given to me. Go therefore and make disciples of all nations, baptizing them in the name of the Father and of the Son and of the Holy Spirit, teaching them to observe all that I have commanded you. And behold, I am with you always, to the end of the age." (Matthew 28:18-20).

Are you naturally a rebel or a rule follower? This question matters when considering how we react to Jesus' last words to His followers. If you are a rebel, your reaction may be to question by what authority this command is given. The answer to you is clear. God gave Jesus ALL authority – EVERYWHERE. If you are a rule follower this command may seem so overwhelming that you cannot grasp how to accomplish it. Ever since this command was given, churches have struggled with both of these natural inclinations. Jesus knows our weakness to question authority, doubt His power, and become discouraged. That is why He promised to be with us always as we toil to accomplish this Great Commission. When we endeavor to make disciples of others we do so motivated not by our own ability but by our relationship with the living God. Be transformed by your relationship with Christ and show His incomparable glory to others.

PRAYER

Lord, I acknowledge that You have all authority in heaven and on earth. I therefore submit myself to You and walk in Your authority, in Jesus' name.

NOTES ....

....

....

....

....

....

....

....

....

....

"All those the Father gives me will come to me, and whoever comes to me I will never drive away. For I have come down from heaven not to do my will but to do the will of Him who sent me. And this is the will of Him who sent me, that I shall lose none of all those He has given me, but raise them up at the last day. For my Father's will is that everyone who looks to the Son and believes in Him shall have eternal life, and I will raise them up at the last day." (John 6:37-40).

Are you in sync? That question is commonplace in our society, sports, workplaces, and relationships. We want to know that we and those we rely on are on the same page – working toward the same goal. While on earth, Jesus was in perfect sync with the Father by being obedient to His will rather than human desires. Hence, God was "well pleased." Our walk with Christ should be the same. When we give ourselves to Jesus, we can be confident in His protection and be secured in God's promise of eternal life. Of course being in sync requires a lot of practice, communication, commitment, dedication, and support from a loving community. Trust and rely on your perfect partner whose sacrifice has restored our relationship with the Father. Be in sync with Him and He will never leave you or forsake you.

PRAYER

Lord, help me to be in line with Your Word and not what pleases me but what pleases You in Jesus name, amen.

NOTES ....

....

....

....

....

....

....

....

....

....

"*Every tree that does not bear good fruit is cut down and thrown into the fire.*" (Matthew 7:19).

Have you ever tasted fruit that looked beautiful from the outside but tasted terrible? Often people, and for that matter churches, can be similarly disappointing. Don't expend your energy to look good outside but be empty in your character, actions, and behavior. God knows your heart. Your fruit reveals your depth of relationship with the Savior. Don't be satisfied that God has blessed you with gifts or talents. Those gifts require commitment and discipline to practice for the glory of His kingdom. This verse is a stark reminder of the responsibility that comes with being a follower of Christ. God would rather destroy a tree that does not bear fruit than have it spread its disease to the rest of the orchard.

PRAYER

Lord, help me to have a productive Christian life and influence many to know and believe in You, in Jesus' name, amen.

NOTES ....

....

....

....

....

....

....

....

....

....

“Make a tree good and its fruit will be good, or make a tree bad and its fruit will be bad, for a tree is recognized by its fruit.” (Matthew 12:33).

Are you living your life with consistency? Or, do you try to cut your life into parts and store it in different compartments. God wants our character to be revealed in our conduct. In other words, our “being” and “doing” should be a reflection of each other. The Pharisees saw Jesus' good works but doubted who He was. Their lack of belief was fueled by their inconsistent character. They pursued power and placement for personal benefit. When faced with Christ's divine goodness they attacked Him because He revealed the evil in their hearts. Those who have joined with evil will attack us too when we join our character and conduct with Christ's. Expect it and find strength in His promise and truth.

PRAYER

Father, let my life produce good fruit and not bad fruit. Let people look at me and see Christ Jesus.

NOTES

WEEK 42 | WISDOM NUGGET

QUOTE FROM BISHOP NOEL JONES

"If you do not have the future in mind as you live in the present, then the future will not include you when it becomes the present." (Bishop Noel Jones).

PRAYER

✓ *Father, help me to live today with tomorrow in sight. Let my decisions and actions today not destroy the future You have for me, in Jesus' name.*

NOTES

“Jesus replied: “ ‘Love the Lord your God with all your heart and with all your soul and with all your mind.’ This is the first and greatest commandment.” (Matthew 22:37-38).

Have you ever felt strangled by rules and regulations? Sometimes whole organizations, even economies, can be suffocated by an exorbitant amount of rules and regulations. This was the case at the time Jesus came to live among us. The Pharisees had created over 600 laws to follow. Many may have been well intentioned, but naturally followers concentrated on what NOT to do rather than what they were called TO do. This seems stunningly simple but somehow we try to make this relationship complicated. How do you approach your walk with Christ? Stop living your life constricted by your perception of things “good” Christians must avoid. Rather, live your life in the freedom, joy, and purpose that only Christ provides.

PRAYER

Lord, help me to live a Christ-like life, loving as You loved. Form me to become more and more like You.

NOTES ....

....

....

....

....

....

....

....

....

....

"*Do you think that I have come to give peace on earth? No, I tell you, but rather division. For from now on in one house there will be five divided, three against two and two against three. They will be divided, father against son and son against father, mother against daughter and daughter against mother, mother-in-law against her daughter-in-law and daughter-in-law against mother-in-law.*" (Luke 12:51-53).

Do you "go along to get along?" This is often drilled into us at a young age to ensure we don't offend others or are pleasant in work and social situations. The problem in applying this same axiom to our spiritual life is that it often entails sacrificing loyalty and commitment to our faith for a perceived middle ground. The truth is, the depth of our relationship with Christ should know no compromise. Discipleship is not easy. Neither was Jesus' sacrifice for us. Separating ourselves from evil desires, sinful behaviors, and destructive relationships is necessary to fully follow Christ. We can not pick and choose what we like and don't like when we decide to follow Jesus. Are you willing to "not get along" in order to gain eternal life?

PRAYER

Lord, I receive the grace to cling to You no matter how hard following You becomes, in Jesus' name, amen.

NOTES ....

....

....

....

....

....

....

....

....

....

Are you a natural skeptic? It appears Thomas may have been. We often see Thomas' doubt as a weakness or a lack of faith. Instead, let's observe Thomas from the perspective of his actions rather than his questions. Thomas' loyalty to Jesus never faltered. He lived his life before and after Jesus' resurrection as a devoted follower. Many of us doubted before we believed. God blesses us with a natural curiosity which is often displayed as skepticism. How you act on your curiosity is the key. Do you look for answers to your questions? Or, do you allow your doubt to manifest as stubbornness, rigidness, or arrogance? It has been said that a faith never tested is a faith that can't be trusted. Allow your curiosity, doubt, and skepticism to motivate you to find answers in God's Word and the Holy Spirit's counsel. Your faith will grow stronger in it.

John 20:27.

"Then he said to Thomas, "Put your finger here; see my hands. Reach out your hand and put it into my side. Stop doubting and believe."

PRAYER

Lord, help me to believe Your Word even if I don't get a full understanding of it because I know that Your ways are always true.

NOTES

John 3:16 is the most memorized verse in the Bible. So let's look at verse 17. Imagine, the unsinkable ship is sinking. The freezing waters are full of desperate passengers. The few lifeboats are themselves sinking. Out of the darkness comes a swiftly moving boat. From the boat, a figure leans forward, his hands outstretched to the dying passengers. As they grasp his hand, he pulls them to safety within the boat. The rescued then rush to the sides to alert those still in the water. "Look up!", they call. "Reach up! Take the hand of Jesus! It's the only way to be saved!" We are the church – the rescued. And whether the world believes it or not, Jesus is the only way to be saved.

John 3:16-17.

"For God so loved the world, that he gave his only Son, that whoever believes in him should not perish but have eternal life. For God did not send his son into the world to condemn the world, but in order that the world might be saved through him."

PRAYER

Lord, open the eyes of many who are still blind to come to Your saving knowledge and found rescue in You for You are the only way.

NOTES ....

....

....

....

....

....

....

....

....

....

In verse 28 of john 20, Jesus says that eternal security is in "my hand." Then in verse 29 He says that eternal security is in "the Father's hand." A contradiction? Not at all because "I and the Father are one." This is the bedrock of our faith as Christians. As C. S. Lewis pointed out, Jesus is not just a good man or an inspired teacher of morality who was of "one mind" with God. Jesus is fully God! "Once saved, eternally saved," is the "Good" in the Good News of the Gospel.

John 20:27-30.

"My sheep hear my voice, and I know them, and they follow me. I give them eternal life, and they will never perish, and no one will snatch them out of my hand. My Father, who has given them to me, is greater than all, and no one is able to snatch them out of the Father's hand. I and the Father are one."

PRAYER

Lord, I totally surrender my life into Your hands because in You I will never perish. Help me to continue to obey Your voice.

NOTES

One of the distinctive features of Luke's Gospel is the pattern it demonstrates: the Holy Spirit moves and then people and events are set in motion. In the synagogue of Nazareth Jesus reads a portion of Isaiah, chapter 61 concerning the Messiah as Suffering Servant and it begins with "The Spirit of the Lord . . ." as He announces the beginning of His own ministry of salvation. It's important to know the Word. It's important to keep the disciplines. But apart from the power, wisdom, and love of God's Holy Spirit, our actions would be in vain. Let the Spirit guide you.

Luke 4:18-19.

"The Spirit of the Lord is upon me, because he has anointed me to proclaim good news to the poor. He has sent me to proclaim liberty to the captives and recovering of sight to the blind, to set at liberty those who are oppressed, to proclaim the year of the Lord's favor."

PRAYER

Holy Spirit, guide and direct me and lead me into all truth. I totally depend on You.

NOTES

WEEK 43 | WISDOM NUGGET

CHANGE IS WHAT IS NEEDED

It's okay to apologize. But it gets to a point where "I'm sorry," becomes irritating because what the offended really needs is a CHANGE of attitude and NOT mere APOLOGIES.

PRAYER

✓ Lord, help me to genuinely repent of my actions that offend You and others. I receive grace to change in Jesus' name.

NOTES

....
....
....
....
....
....
....
....
....
....
....
....
....
....
....
....

This statement of Jesus in John 10:32 can only be understood in the context of the surrounding verses – particularly verse 30 where Jesus says, "I and the Father are one." The first of the Ten Commandments is "You shall have no other gods before me." This has been the stumbling block for humanity since the beginning when the serpent tempted Adam and Eve with " …you will be like God…" In this passage in John, the Jews picked up stones against Jesus not because He healed the sick, fed the hungry, opened blind eyes, and raised the dead, but because He demonstrated that He, and not the human effort of their law keeping, is the way of salvation. Even though many still struggle with the fact that Jesus is God, it does not change the Word of God.

John 10:32.

"Jesus answered them, "I have shown you many good works from the Father; for which of them are you going to stone me?"

PRAYER

Lord, open the eyes of Your people to see You as God and not be deceived by false religion.

NOTES

The remarkable statements made in John 5;24-25 by Jesus encapsulate the message of this whole chapter that Jesus the Son, has authority equal to God the Father. This is shown in two essential areas – judgment and eternal life – and the keys to both are hearing the truth and believing the truth. Jesus is talking primarily about passing from spiritual death to spiritual life that leads to eternal life BOTH spiritually and physically. In order to demonstrate that authority we have four examples in scripture: raising the widow's son (Luke 7:2); raising Jairus' daughter (Mark 5:22); raising Lazarus (John 11); and, of course, His own resurrection. We too can believe and live.

John 5:24-25.

"Truly, truly, I say to you, whoever hears my word and believes him who sent me has eternal life. He does not come into judgment, but has passed from death to life. Truly, truly, I say to you, an hour is coming, and is now here, when the dead will hear the voice of the Son of God, and those who hear will live."

PRAYER

Lord, may You open the ears of many who have not believed in You to hear Your voice and live.

NOTES ....

....

....

....

....

....

....

....

....

....

It is so important to read scripture in context. Jesus cursed a fig tree and it withered and died. But Jesus wants to be sure that the disciples are not just impressed with spiritual power only. Power in prayer must be based on two components – faith and forgiveness. The faith is not some quasi-magical invocation of the words, "In Jesus Name!" but faith in the finished work of Jesus in purchasing our forgiveness by His death on the Cross. And if our faith does not include a recognition that Christ died for that person we can't forgive just as surely as He died for us, then our faith is lacking and our prayers will be without power.

Mark 11:25.

"And whenever you stand praying, forgive, if you have anything against anyone, so that your Father also who is in heaven may forgive you your trespasses."

PRAYER

Lord, help me to always forgive those who sin against me and not hold anyone in my heart whenever I come to You in prayer.

NOTES

Luke 20:16 is Jesus' final encouragement to the 72 disciples He sends out to preach the Gospel. He wants them – and us – to clearly understand that the Good News of salvation through faith in Christ is the Word and will of God. We need to put aside our own egos or desire to be liked and simply be instruments in His hand. If we have died to ourselves we should not worry about being offended by rejection (you can't offend dead people). The only valid emotions should be sadness for those who reject the truth and joy for those who accept eternal life.

Luke 20:16.

"The one who hears you hears me, and the one who rejects you rejects me, and the one who rejects me rejects him who sent me."

PRAYER

Lord, help me to share Your Word so that men may hear You through me, in Jesus' name, amen.

NOTES ....

....

....

....

....

....

....

....

....

....

The words of Jesus in Matthew 19:27-30 come in response to Peter's question but are clearly relevant to us in this nation that is drowning in material stuff to the exclusion of God. The rich young man turned away from Christ because "he had great possessions." We must daily, almost moment by moment, refocus our hearts and minds away from the bright and shiny distractions of this life and towards the eternal rewards of life in Christ.

Matthew 19:27-30.

"Then Peter said in reply, "See, we have left everything and followed you. What then will we have?" Jesus said to them, "Truly, I say to you, in the new world, when the Son of Man will sit on his glorious throne, you who have followed me will also sit on twelve thrones, judging the twelve tribes of Israel. And everyone who has left houses or brothers or sisters or father or mother or children or lands, for my name's sake, will receive a hundredfold and will inherit eternal life. But many who are first will be last, and the last first."

PRAYER

Lord, I thank You for choosing me to follow You and I thank You for the great reward You have for me when You return, in Jesus' name, amen.

NOTES

....

....

....

....

....

....

....

....

....

....

"Why do you call me Lord, Lord, and not do what I tell you?" This statement of Jesus comes near the end of Luke's version of the Sermon on the Mount (Matthew 5-7). Jesus has laid down some of the radical moral demands for being His disciple. The mark of a true disciple is not how many Jesus bumper stickers we have on our cars or how many "churchy" words we have in our vocabulary. Rather, it's how closely we walk with the Lord in obedience to His Word – letting His words ring in our mind and His heartbeat in our chest.

Luke 6:46.

"Why do you call me Lord, Lord, and not do what I tell you?"

PRAYER

Lord, help me to put Your words in practice and not just be a talker of Your Word in Jesus name, amen.

NOTES ....

....

....

....

....

....

....

....

....

....

WEEK 44 | WISDOM NUGGET

COME AS YOU ARE BUT...

It's Ok to COME AS YOU ARE. I just have a problem when you want to stay the way you came. When Jesus called His disciples, He simply told them, "...follow me...," meaning come as you are. But as soon as they started following, He said that He'd make them fishers of men: signifying a change of what you use to be/do. And this includes the way you dress and the way you talk, because the garments you wore to 'fish, fish' are not the same you'd wear, to 'Fish men.'

PRAYER

- ✓ Lord, I pray I will come to You and yield to the transformation You want to do in me.
- ✓ Lord I pray that the church will become a place where people come and get transformed into who You want them to be. Lord, I pray that the church will not become like the world, but it will be a transformation center, in Jesus' name.

NOTES

....

....

....

....

....

This is the 7th and last "Blessed" in the Book of Revelation reads: "Blessed are those who wash their robes, so that they may have the right to the tree of life and that they may enter the city by the gates." The reference to washing our robes refers back to 7:14 of this book and indicates a willingness to identify with Jesus in His death. Entry into the New Jerusalem is reserved for those disciples willing to be obedient unto death. That is a standard that can only be achieved by the indwelling power of God's Holy Spirit. That Spirit must be nourished daily by both taking in and living out the Word of God.

Revelation 22: 14.

"Blessed are those who wash their robes, so that they may have the right to the tree of life and that they may enter the city by the gates."

PRAYER

Lord, help me to feed on Your Word daily and to spend time in prayers with You because this way I keep myseflt ready for You at all times.

NOTES ....

....

....

....

....

....

....

....

....

....

Would you consider yourself a "good" person? Are you doing good things to keep up with the "Christian Jones's?" Jesus was approached by a wealthy, young man who had led a largely moral life, and when asked how he can inherit eternal life, Jesus points out that no one is truly "good," except for God. Like this young man, simply living a moral life, being nice to others, serving others, and following the law means nothing eternally without giving your life to God, in Christ. We can never be good enough without God's grace.

Mark 10:18.

"And Jesus said to him, "Why do you call me good? No one is good except God alone."

PRAYER

Father, help me to not rely on my good works to save me but to fully depend on Your grace.

NOTES

The Samaritan woman at the well encountered Jesus, God in the flesh, unexpectedly. She viewed the world through the lens of an Old Testament Israelite, where worshippers travelled to temples and synagogues where God was present. Jesus teaches us here that with His coming, and the coming of the Spirit, we no longer have to seek places where we can worship, but since God is omnipresent, and is with us always, we are free to truly worship Him wherever we are, and He wants us to!

John 4:21-24.

"Jesus said to her, "Woman, believe me, the hour is coming when neither on this mountain nor in Jerusalem will you worship the Father. You worship what you do not know; we worship what we know, for salvation is from the Jews. But the hour is coming, and is now here, when the true worshipers will worship the Father in spirit and truth, for the Father is seeking such people to worship him. God is spirit, and those who worship him must worship in spirit and truth."

PRAYER

Lord, help us to know that You are in our hearts and make us to worship You anywhere we find ourselves because You are there.

NOTES ....

....

....

....

....

....

....

....

....

....

Satan's tactics with Jesus in the wilderness are exactly what he uses with us, when he promises happiness, pleasure, and things if we would only turn from God. The truth is, the only things Satan can offer will separate us from God. Satan tempted Jesus in an attempt to undermine God's plan for redemption. In response, Jesus used scripture (Deuteronomy 8) to warn Satan and remain a sinless Savior, so that one day He would fulfill the scriptures and complete His Father's plan. His righteousness and sacrifice provides a way for us to stand before God, blameless.

Matthew 4:7.

"Jesus said to him, "Again it is written, You shall not put the Lord your God to the test."

PRAYER

Lord, help me study Your Word so as to withstand the temptations of the enemy, in Jesus' name, amen.

NOTES

Do you seek to serve others or do you pursue being served? I think we would all like to say we serve first, but when we look in the mirror, we find we are selfish at the core. Christ is the perfect example: God in the flesh, creator of all things, but gave up everything, for us. He did this knowing we would continue to sin and serve ourselves. If our desire is to be more like Christ, we too must humble ourselves, and look to serve others first.

Matthew 20:28.

"Even as the Son of Man came not to be served but to serve, and to give his life as a ransom for many."

PRAYER

Lord, make me a servant and not desire to be served, in Jesus' name.

NOTES

Life is a journey, and we all choose our own path. Satan is circling trying to draw you away from the path that leads to God. Jesus tells us that following His path is the one that's not so easy. It is easier to be self-serving, following the flesh, but the trade off is an eternity of suffering. Jesus opened the gate for all of us at the cross, and calls us toward Him. Are you willing to fight the good fight today, even when it's tough, for the glories that await us one day with Christ?

Matthew 7:13-14.

"Enter by the narrow gate. For the gate is wide and the way is easy that leads to destruction, and those who enter by it are many. For the gate is narrow and the way is hard that leads to life, and those who find it are few."

PRAYER

Lord, help me not to fall prey to schemes of Satan but to walk in Your truth even if it is the unpopular way.

NOTES

WEEK 45 | WISDOM NUGGET 08/11/2020

IMPACT IS ALL THAT MATTERS

Men will not remember you because of HOW OFTEN you met but because of WHAT IMPACT you left on them. One encounter with Impact is worth more than five years of togetherness with no impact.

PRAYER

✓ Father, help me to leave a positive impact in the lives of those I meet everywhere I go. Let my life be a life of impact.

NOTES

....
....
....
....
....
....
....
....
....
....
....
....
....
....
....
....
....

CUT OFF WHATEVER CAUSES YOU TO SIN...

Do you have any sins you battle against a lot? If you're like me, the answer is "yes." We are all human, and our nature is to be selfish, prideful, dishonest, you fill in the blank. Jesus is teaches that there is nothing of earth, even our own hands and eyes, that is worth keeping if it means we lose our eternity. Keep our goal and the chance to praise God face to face in mind always, and fight against the sins you face daily. Heaven is worth it!

Matthew 18:8-9.

"And if your hand or your foot causes you to sin, cut it off and throw it away. It is better for you to enter life crippled or lame than with two hands or two feet to be thrown into the eternal fire. And if your eye causes you to sin, tear it out and throw it away. It is better for you to enter life with one eye than with two eyes to be thrown into the hell of fire."

PRAYER

Lord, help me to completely do away with anything that tries to interrupt my service and commitment to You, in Jesus' name, amen.

NOTES

These words of Jesus in Matthew 5:10-11 are eye opening! Why would he tell us this? Christ knows that being an outspoken follower of His will always opens us up to persecution and hatred, as humanity is often scared of what it doesn't understand. We don't experience this in the same way as Christ followers in some other parts of the world, but we must always remember that loving Christ, no matter the cost, will bring the ultimate blessing when our time on earth is done.

Matthew 5:10-11.

"Blessed are those who are persecuted for righteousness' sake, for theirs is the kingdom of heaven. Blessed are you when others revile you and persecute you and utter all kinds of evil against you falsely on my account."

PRAYER

Lord, give us the grace to stand for You despite the persecution that may arise because we know You shall reward us at the end.

NOTES ……………………………………………………

……………………………………………………………

……………………………………………………………

……………………………………………………………

……………………………………………………………

……………………………………………………………

……………………………………………………………

……………………………………………………………

……………………………………………………………

……………………………………………………………

HIS DISCIPLES WERE ORDINARY MEN...

Do you ever think the disciples of Jesus were extraordinary people, who had talents and gifts you and I don't have? At the beginning of His ministry, Jesus climbs into Simon's fishing boat while teaching to a crowd. The fishermen's unexpected encounter with Christ changed everything. He told them to fish and blessed them with a huge amount of fish, when before they had caught none. When He calls them to become "fishers of men," they felt unworthy, scared, and unqualified. Were they extraordinary? Not on their own, but with Jesus' help they could do extraordinary things, and so can we.

Luke 5:10-11.

"And so also were James and John, sons of Zebedee, who were partners with Simon. And Jesus said to Simon, "Do not be afraid; from now on you will be catching men." And when they had brought their boats to land, they left everything and followed him."

PRAYER

Father, I thank You that You can choose ordinary men like us to do extraordinary things for Your Kingdom. We remain grateful for this and ask that You continue to empower us.

NOTES ....

....

....

....

....

....

....

....

....

....

JESUS IS STILL CALLING MEN TODAY...

Can you hear Jesus calling you? Matthew had a very direct calling from Jesus, and He didn't hesitate to respond. Tax collectors were mostly hated, considered corrupt, and not religious, and yet Jesus chose him specifically. Jesus' power and authority compelled Matthew to follow and should do the same for us today. No matter how messed up we are, how others view us, or how little we already know Jesus, there is no better time to drop everything and follow Him than now. He is calling you.

Matthew 9:9.

"As Jesus passed on from there, he saw a man called Matthew sitting at the tax booth, and he said to him, "Follow me." And he rose and followed him."

PRAYER

Lord, I respond to Your call upon my life this day to do what You have purposed for me to do.

NOTES

Read Matthew 9:16-17. Jesus is responding to followers of John who asked why His disciples weren't fasting as they and the Pharisees did. The purpose of a fast then was for discipline and mourning. He tells them, before offering this analogy, that there's no reason to fast, just to fulfill tradition, while the Christ is present. Christ is the new way, and we don't have to follow old traditions simply because others are doing it. Jesus is reminding them, and telling us, that He should be our focus, as He is the living God!

Matthew 9:16-17.

"No one puts a piece of unshrunk cloth on an old garment, for the patch tears away from the garment, and a worse tear is made. Neither is new wine put into old wineskins. If it is, the skins burst and the wine is spilled and the skins are destroyed. But new wine is put into fresh wineskins, and so both are preserved."

PRAYER

Lord, help us follow You and not the traditions and rules of men. Let us focus on what You say and not the rules that men have laid down.

NOTES

Read Luke 6:35-36. We're given some commands in these verses; to love, do good, to lend and be merciful. It seems like the Lord is telling us to lend and expect nothing in return but actually we are to do all of these without expecting anything in return. Jesus gave of Himself freely, expecting nothing in return. How often do we do these things expecting nothing in return much less doing them to someone we consider our enemy? We can't on our own but Jesus gives us the perfect example, our heavenly Father.

Luke 6:35-36.

"But love ye your enemies, and do good, and lend, hoping for nothing again; and your reward shall be great, and ye shall be the children of the Highest: for he is kind unto the unthankful and to the evil. Be ye therefore merciful, as your Father also is merciful."

PRAYER

Merciful Father, help me to show mercy to men just as You have shown mercy to me in Jesus' name, amen.

NOTES ....

WEEK 46 | WISDOM NUGGET

PREACH CHRIST NOT SELF

When called up to preach, please preach the Gospel of Jesus Christ and not the gospel of "SELF." There are too many hungry souls who care less about your achievements. They just need a WORD FROM GOD.

PRAYER

- ✓ Father, I pray that Your servants will not abuse Your altar. Lord, that they will use it to dish out Your Word and nothing but Your Word, in Jesus' name.
- ✓ Lord, I come against every spirit of self-exaltation in Your children, in Jesus' name.

NOTES

....
....
....
....
....
....
....
....
....
....
....
....

What is your true motivation for serving or seeking to do the will of God? Is it to gain some prominent position in the church? Is it a prideful act to look good in front of others? Is it to seek out some reassurance that you will go to heaven? Ambition or self glorification can easily blind us to our purpose as children of God. If this could happen to two of the disciples, then we should be extremely careful. Remember, the first will be last and the last will be first in the kingdom of God.

Matthew 20:20-23.

"Then came to Him the mother of Zebedee's children with her sons, worshipping Him, and desiring a certain thing of Him. And He said unto her, What wilt thou? She saith unto Him, Grant that these my two sons may sit, the one on thy right hand, and the other on the left, in thy kingdom. But Jesus answered and said, Ye know not what ye ask. Are ye able to drink of the cup that I shall drink of, and to be baptized with the baptism that I am baptized with? They say unto Him, We are able. And He saith unto them, Ye shall drink indeed of my cup, and be baptized with the baptism that I am baptized with: but to sit on my right hand, and on my left, is not mine to give, but it shall be given to them for whom it is prepared of my Father."

PRAYER

Lord, purify my motives for following You and help me to seek You with a pure heart in Jesus' name, amen.

NOTES ....

....

....

....

....

....

....

....

....

....

Jesus didn't come to this world to judge us but rather to show us the way to eternal life. God the creator and sovereign ruler will judge those who do not receive the message that Jesus brought. Jesus was the announcer, the message bearer, the broadcaster. He said repeatedly that He was here to do the will of the Father. To reject Him and His message is to reject the Father. We will all be judged one day. However, when the Father looks on those that do believe this message, He will not see us but rather see His Son standing in our place. A son that is completely righteous and free from sin. That is the good news!

John 12:47-50.

"If anyone hears my words and does not keep them, I do not judge him; for I did not come to judge the world but to save the world. The one who rejects me and does not receive my words has a judge; the word that I have spoken will judge him on the last day. For I have not spoken on my own authority, but the Father who sent me has himself given me a commandment—what to say and what to speak. And I know that his commandment is eternal life. What I say, therefore, I say as the Father has told me."

PRAYER

Lord Jesus, I thank You for saving me and giving me Your righteousness.

NOTES ....

....

....

....

....

....

....

....

....

....

OUR REPENTANCE MAKES HEAVEN REJOICE...

God wants to have a relationship with us. That is, after all, why He created us. Unfortunately, that relationship was severed when sin entered the picture. This doesn't mean He no longer desires to have that relationship. On the contrary, He very much desires it, which is why He sent Jesus. When we repent and turn away from our sin, we help restore that relationship. This is so pleasing to God that even the angels in heaven share in His joy. What sin do you have that requires repentance? If you're not sure then ask God to show you.

Luke 15:10.

"Just so, I tell you, there is joy before the angels of God over one sinner who repents."

PRAYER

Lord, help me to lead someone to Your saving power today because You delight in the salvation of men.

NOTES

Read John 5:28-29. These two verses show us the simplicity of following Jesus. It is us who make it overly complicated. Jesus shared this message shortly after miraculously feeding the 5,000. Even this group was looking for ways to complicate His message. How often do we seek ways to be more Christ-like? Doing more works, reading more books, trying to be good, the list goes on. Not that these things are bad but they aren't a requirement. This is what makes the Gospel so simple. It only requires our belief in Jesus and the message He brought. Out of that belief comes the sanctification that will eventually conform us to His image but it begins with one simple step. BELIEVE!

John 5:28-29.

"Do not marvel at this, for an hour is coming when all who are in the tombs will hear his voice and come out, those who have done good to the resurrection of life, and those who have done evil to the resurrection of judgment."

PRAYER

Lord, help me to believe in the simplicity of Your Word.

NOTES

Read Matthew 5:27-30. Jesus provides imagery in these verses to convey how seriously we are to war against our sin. We are to battle to the point of removing whatever it is that causes us to stumble. What would this look like in the current world? Perhaps it would be to get rid of the computer or device that causes us to sin. But, it goes deeper than this. True sin manifests from the heart and only the great Physician is able heal this area. Pray for forgiveness, repent, store the Word in your heart, and put on the full armor of God to fight this battle.

Matthew 5:27-30.

"You have heard that it was said, 'You shall not commit adultery.' But I say to you that everyone who looks at a woman with lustful intent has already committed adultery with her in his heart. If your right eye causes you to sin, tear it out and throw it away. For it is better that you lose one of your members than that your whole body be thrown into hell. And if your right hand causes you to sin, cut it off and throw it away. For it is better that you lose one of your members than that your whole body go into hell."

PRAYER

Lord, forgive me of every sin I have sinned in my thoughts and in my actions. Cleanse me and make me whole in Your sight, in Jesus' name, amen.

NOTES

Our faith in Jesus doesn't give us the right to pick and choose what commandments we will follow. We don't know what measure of reward or punishment God will allot for breaking any of the commandments. If we don't submit to ALL of His commands, then we may be guilty of not surrendering completely to His lordship in our lives. Jesus makes it very clear that even what we would consider to be the least of one of the commandments can have eternal consequences if we choose to deliberately disobey and teach others to do the same.

Matthew 5:19.

"Therefore whoever relaxes one of the least of these commandments and teaches others to do the same will be called least in the kingdom of heaven, but whoever does them and teaches them will be called great in the kingdom of heaven."

PRAYER

Lord, give me the spirit of obedience to Your Word as it is and not to pick and choose what suits me.

NOTES ....

....

....

....

....

....

....

....

....

....

WEEK 47 | WISDOM NUGGET

YOU MUST PREPARE

Between the time of your call and the time of your manifestation lies the preparation time. You can't skip this time and expect to succeed. Many who tried have made a shipwreck of their calling and so you must not make the same mistake.

PRAYER

- ✓ Gracious Father, I come to You this day asking that Lord, You will grant me the grace to adequately prepare for the calling You have for me, in Jesus name.
- ✓ Teach me all that I will need to know at this time before I take a step forward.

NOTES

....
....
....
....
....
....
....
....
....
....
....
....

Read luke 22:31-32. These verses illustrate just how deep the forgiveness of Jesus is. Jesus knew that Peter's faith would falter; that he would end up betraying Jesus in one of His greatest hours of need. Even so, Jesus prayed that Peter's faith would not fail completely and that when he had turned again, or repented, that he would go on to strengthen those around him. Oh, that we would show that same level of grace to those that have wronged us. Our forgiveness might just be the catalyst that causes someone else's faith to grow exponentially.

Luke 22:31-32.

"Simon, Simon, behold, Satan demanded to have you, that he might sift you like wheat, but I have prayed for you that your faith may not fail. And when you have turned again, strengthen your brothers."

PRAYER

Merciful Father, help me to give forgiveness even in advance to those who offend and will offend me, in Jesus' name, amen.

NOTES

Read Acts 18:9-11. We are not promised that the Christian life will be easy. In fact, these verses make it clear that spreading the gospel may cause tribulation for us. However, we are called to proclaim the gospel because there are people all around us who need to hear it. This isn't a request but rather a command that was given before Jesus ascended into heaven. Paul had been enduring many trials while spreading the gospel and the Lord reassures him to keep speaking without fear. He doesn't promise that it will be easy. He even points out that attacks will come but they are to be endured because there are people that need to hear the Good News.

Acts 18:9-11.

"And the Lord said to Paul one night in a vision, "Do not be afraid, but go on speaking and do not be silent, for I am with you, and no one will attack you to harm you, for I have many in this city who are my people." And he stayed a year and six months, teaching the word of God among them."

PRAYER

Lord, I thank You because You will never leave me alone even in the most challenging moments. Lord, I pray for Your comfort upon those going through persecution at this point in time.

NOTES

If we truly love Jesus then we will have a desire to live out His commands. He showed us how to do this by serving others. Jesus' life and ministry was marked by constant service to others. What other king in history lowered himself to the status of a slave so that his slaves could be called kings? This is the kind of heart where God longs to dwell and the Holy Spirit will bring constant renewal. Others will know we are disciples of Jesus by the way we love one another. Love should be the constant motivator for all that we do for the Kingdom. If we find that we are having trouble keeping Jesus' commands then we should spend time in prayer examining how much we really love Him.

John 14:23-24.

"Jesus answered him, "If anyone loves me, he will keep my word, and my Father will love him, and we will come to him and make our home with him. Whoever does not love me does not keep my words. And the word that you hear is not mine but the Father's who sent me."

PRAYER

Lord, help me to keep Your Word and act in accordance with Your Word.

NOTES ……………………………………………………

Have you ever wanted to do something for the Lord, a mission trip, teach a class, or even sing in the choir, then for whatever reason it didn't happen? Did it seem as though God closed the door every time you tried? God's plans for you at that time were maybe something you never considered. He may ask you to influence your co-workers, friends, and family. He may ask you to be His missionary right where you are. Are you willing to follow and do whatever He asks of you? We have been bought with a price that He has paid. Isn't it time that we surrender to His will no matter what He asks us to do, even if it's to sit still for now, even if it doesn't conform to our plans? He knows what is best for us and what will draw us closer to Himself. Trust Him and surrender to Him daily. If you do that, you will find yourself right where you are supposed to be.

Mark 5: 19.

"And He did not permit him but said to him, "go home to your friends and tell them how much the Lord has done for you, and how much He has had mercy on you."

PRAYER

Lord, help me to incline my ears to Your words and the leadership or Your Spirit.

NOTES

Have you received devastating news? Perhaps a death in the family, has your wife decided that she no longer wants to be married to you? Or your boss has just told you that the company is downsizing and no longer needs you? Was your immediate reaction despair? If so, listen to your Savior's voice as He whispers "Talitha Cumi" ("Arise Maiden"). He is where hope is found. He is the sustainer of everything. When hope seems a stranger and life seems much too heavy to bear, focus on His voice and have faith in the One from whom all Love springs forth. He will help carry you through. All we have to do is believe in Him, have faith that He is exactly who He claims to be and His grace will be sufficient for whatever news comes our way.

Mark 5:35-36.

"While he was still speaking, there came from the ruler's house some who said, "Your daughter is dead. Why trouble the teacher any further?" But overhearing what they said, Jesus said to the ruler of the synagogue, "Do not fear, only believe."

PRAYER

Lord, I choose to believe You no matter what the circumstance maybe. I know You have the power to change every situation.

NOTES

Read Matthew 11:27. What a statement! Have you ever sat and wondered about God? What is He like? What is His heart and mind like? What does He think about people? Does He really care about us? Jesus answers everyone of those questions and more. He simply says, do you want to know what God is like? Well, then look at me! They are one and the same. A relationship with Jesus is a relationship with the Creator and Sustainer of all things. And what does the Creator of all things think of us? What does He offer us? Jesus answers that too. Read Matthew 11:28-30 and you will hear how the God of the universe describes Himself and what He will do in our lives. He says He will carry our burdens. The God of everything says He will carry your problems. All we have to do is ask. How extraordinary! How blessed we truly are!

Matthew 11:27.

"All things have been handed over to me by my Father, and no one knows the Son except the Father, and no one knows the Father except the Son and anyone to whom the Son chooses to reveal him."

PRAYER

Lord, I thank You for choosing to reveal the Father to me. Thank You for this privilege and I pray that You will call many more into this amazing grace.

NOTES

WEEK 48 | WISDOM NUGGET

GOD REQUIRES DECENCY

Be descent at all times especially when you come to minister unto the Lord. God is expecting you to bless His people and not to seduce them. Unfortunately the reverse is true nowadays in the church. It is a shameful thing to see how Christians disrespect the altar of God by their indecency. God is not pleased with that.

PRAYER

- ✓ Lord, forgive us for the ways we have desecrated Your holy place by our indecency.
- ✓ Father, may You cause the church to return to the place of reverence for You in both our lifestyle and our outfit, in Jesus' name.

NOTES

....

....

....

....

....

....

....

....

....

....

Do you ever feel like things just keep getting worse and worse? Like you're going from the frying pan into the oven? Take courage, God is sovereign and He is walking with you, taking every step alongside you. We may not understand why until we are with Him for eternity, but rest assured everything is for a purpose and, as Tim Keller once said, "If we knew what God knows, we would ask for exactly what He gives." So, trust Him and know the God who made the stars is in control of every aspect of your life.

Acts 23:11.

"The following night the Lord stood by him and said, "Take courage, for as you have testified to the facts about me in Jerusalem, so you must testify also in Rome."

PRAYER

Lord, I thank You for Your good thoughts and plans for me. I stand in confidence knowing that You can never let me down.

NOTES ....

The people at the synagogue were awestruck! They had seen a Man command a demon with a few words and the evil spirit had no choice, but to obey. They had never seen such authority, such authentic power. Let me ask you, when was the last time you were awestruck? Can you think of the last time you stopped in amazement at God's power? He sets every day into motion and sustains it until the next, yet we become blinded by routine. We fail to see the majesty of every day. Each one should be seen as a gift to do His will. So, take time to stop and be awestruck. He upholds everything with a word. What power! What authority! What love!

Mark 1:23-26.

"And immediately there was in their synagogue a man with an unclean spirit. And he cried out, "What have you to do with us, Jesus of Nazareth? Have you come to destroy us? I know who you are—the Holy One of God." But Jesus rebuked him, saying, "Be silent, and come out of him!" And the unclean spirit, convulsing him and crying out with a loud voice, came out of him."

PRAYER

Lord, I lean on You because You have the power to keep my life from any form of danger and destruction. I send Your Word into every stubborn situation and I command it to bow, in Jesus' name, amen.

NOTES

Ignorance of sin is not an excuse for the continuation of sin. None of us are ignorant to the fact that we should seek time with Jesus daily and the more time we spend with Christ the more we are transformed by Him. He purges sin out of our lives and makes us more like Himself. So, we are faced with the same decision today as those Jesus spoke about in the passage we find john 15;22. Are we going to accept Jesus and, because of Him, remain guiltless, becoming more and more like Him daily in every aspect of our lives? Or are we going to reject Him and have no excuse for our sin, becoming more and more like the world daily? Only one of those options offers hope. We all have tried living life the wrong way making the wrong choice. Only a fool would continue on that path. So, which option are you going to choose today?

John 15:22.

"If I had not come and spoken to them, they would not have been guilty of sin, but now they have no excuse for their sin."

PRAYER

Lord, I choose to submit to You and repent of my sins as You point out my weaknesses. I surrender my life to You and ask that You give me power over sin.

NOTES

What? Blessed are those who are depressed? Is that what this means? Heavens, no. Have you thought about what bless or blessed means? It comes from the Greek word "makarios." This word was used to describe the joy of the gods. It described a joy that holds its secret within itself; serene, untouchable, self-contained, and impervious to chance or change. A joy independent of circumstance. This joy is the Christian's, not in the future, but now. Matthew 5:3 is not a prophetic glimpse into the future. Jesus is saying "O' the complete joy for the one who realizes how helpless he is and places all of his faith in Me, for he is a citizen of the Kingdom of Heaven and will experience this Joy for all eternity! What a gift he possesses!" And remember, that eternity begins now and this joy is not something we will receive, it is something we have received already! A depression ridden Christian life should be unthinkable! Focus on Christ and the joy He offers! Face today like you are blessed, set apart, a child of God...because you are!

Matthew 5:3.

"Blessed are the poor in spirit, for theirs is the kingdom of heaven."

PRAYER

Lord, I thank You for the joy that You give me on a daily basis because of Your work of salvation.

NOTES

Isn't it remarkable that Jesus, hours from the cross, stops to pray. He stops to pray for us. Two thousand years later and He is still interceding for us. He makes it clear that there are things in this world opposed to God and His plan for us, but isn't it comforting to know that God stands watching over us every moment of every day protecting us. We stumble and fall in life because we try to do things in our own strength without stopping to pray for ourselves, much less anyone else. We fail to realize that we are helpless without God's help. Let today be the moment that you let go and place everything you are in His hands. He is waiting, hand outstretched, for His children. All we have to do is ask.

John 17:15:17.

"I do not ask that you take them out of the world, but that you keep them from the evil one. They are not of the world, just as I am not of the world. Sanctify them in the truth; your word is truth."

PRAYER

Lord, I thank You for the protection You give me daily as I live in this world.

NOTES ....

....

....

....

....

....

....

....

....

....

Have you ever walked through a vineyard or an orchard while the fruit is beginning to ripen? The aroma and colors of the trees mixed with the sweet smell of the fruit offers beauty to all of the senses. But if you look down on the ground you see a different story. There on the ground you find fruit apart from the vine or tree and it offers no alluring qualities. It is brown, soft and decaying. Yellow jackets and other insects ravage the inside of the fruit as it returns to dust.

Jesus reminds us here that we are no different from the fruit you see in a vineyard or orchard. We are either connected to Him, growing, developing into that which God intended us to be and in doing so we honor our creator. Or we can try life on our own apart from Jesus, which leads to death and decay, even while still physically alive, offering nothing to those around us except for a place next to us on the ground among the yellow-jackets of life. Where are you today? Clinging to the branch and reflecting God's glory or are you among the insects and decay?

John 15:4-5.

"Abide in me, and I in you. As the branch cannot bear fruit by itself, unless it abides in the vine, neither can you, unless you abide in me. I am the vine; you are the branches. Whoever abides in me and I in him, he it is that bears much fruit, for apart from me you can do nothing."

PRAYER

Lord, help me to cling to You alone all the days of my life. Let nothing be able to separate me from You, in Jesus' name, amen.

NOTES ....

WEEK 49 | WISDOM NUGGET

SUSPICION OR DISCERNMENT

Suspicion and Discernment look like identical twins but they're not in any way related. So always give a second look to know which of them is talking to you. The Bible encourages us to test every spirit. It did not tell us to suspect every spirit. Suspicion comes from your mind and may lead you astray, but discernment comes from the spirit and is always right.

PRAYER

- ✓ Lord, I receive the spirit of discernment to be able to tell what is from You, and what is not in Jesus name.
- ✓ Lord, I refuse to yield to the suspicions of my mind but I will be open to listen to the voice of my spirit, in Jesus' name, Amen.

NOTES

....
....
....
....
....
....
....
....
....

Do you want to get into heaven? Here is the "how-to" manual for entrance into heaven. Jesus tells us how. He says that we must be "born again... born of water and the spirit." Water symbolizes cleaning. When we ask Jesus into our lives, the sins of the past are washed away and we are born again as new creatures, we are born of water. But if that were all that happens we would repeat the very same sins and be back in the same place as before. Jesus knows this and that's why we must be born of spirit also. When we hand our lives over to Jesus, He cleanses our sin and He enters His creation and His power (spirit) is now in us. He enables us to be something we never thought we could be and accomplish things for His glory that we never thought we could accomplish. In the process of being born again, we die unto ourselves, Jesus takes residence in our hearts, enabling us to become citizens of the Kingdom, sons and daughters of God for eternity! He has made it so simple and He does all the work. Do you want to get into Heaven? Jesus tells us how. Just ask! So, what are you waiting for? You could be a citizen of the Kingdom today! Already born again? If so, you have a "how-to" manual. Make sure you share it today with someone.

John 3:5-8.

"Jesus answered, "Truly, truly, I say to you, unless one is born of water and the Spirit, he cannot enter the kingdom of God. That which is born of the flesh is flesh, and that which is born of the Spirit is spirit. Do not marvel that I said to you, 'You must be born again.' The wind blows where it wishes, and you hear its sound, but you do not know where it comes from or where it goes. So it is with everyone who is born of the Spirit."

PRAYER

Lord, I come to you today believing that You are the son of God and that You came to die for me and that You rose from the dead and went to heaven and You are coming back to take me home. Thank You for saving me.

NOTES ....

....

....

....

....

....

....

....

....

We get to talk to God. Let that sink in a moment. It gets better. He invites us to pray to Him. What an amazing opportunity for us to draw close to Him. We obviously need Him - three times Jesus encourages us to come to Him for what we need. When we draw close, then what does He do? He promises to respond. Ask your Father for what you need and you will receive it. Seek what God has for you and you will find it. Knock and watch the door swing open wide. Be close to Him. Be comforted by Him. Be encouraged that He will provide all that we need for our good and His glory!

Matthew 7:7-11.

"Ask, and it will be given to you; seek, and you will find; knock, and it will be opened to you. For everyone who asks receives, and the one who seeks finds, and to the one who knocks it will be opened. Or which one of you, if his son asks him for bread, will give him a stone? Or if he asks for a fish, will give him a serpent? If you then, who are evil, know how to give good gifts to your children, how much more will your Father who is in heaven give good things to those who ask him!"

PRAYER

Father, I thank You for the privilege to talk to You and even ask and receive from You the things I ask. Thank You Lord.

NOTES

Many of us find it easy to worry and fear. Jesus' disciples must have experienced the same emotions when faced with the perceived threat of persecution. While speaking to His disciples, Jesus addresses who we should and should not fear. He acknowledges that His followers will battle fear while proclaiming His name. He commands them to not fear man, for man cannot destroy the soul. Instead, fear only a holy God who can destroy both body and soul. And understand that this holy God values you and is attentive to us- to the extent of even knowing the number of hairs on our heads. Have confidence in how our Father loves us and equips us to do His will. Do not fear man. Fear God, and boldly proclaim His truth.

Matthew 10:27-31.

"What I tell you in the dark, say in the light, and what you hear whispered, proclaim on the housetops. And do not fear those who kill the body but cannot kill the soul. Rather fear him who can destroy both soul and body in hell. Are not two sparrows sold for a penny? And not one of them will fall to the ground apart from your Father. But even the hairs of your head are all numbered. Fear not, therefore; you are of more value than many sparrows."

PRAYER

Father, I refuse to fear or worry about the unknown. You have all authority and power and You can always deliver from any situation.

NOTES ....

....

....

....

....

....

....

....

....

....

Falling on His face, the Son of God calls out to His Father for reassurance while exemplifying submission and obedience to the will of the Father. He humbly pleads that the redemption of man might be accomplished in another way, but, above all, He desires the will of God to be accomplished. We see Jesus here as fully God and yet fully human. He didn't want to die, but he wanted God to be glorified more. Jesus set the example we can follow. We can trust God to work for our good and His glory even in circumstances that we had rather not endure. His way trumps our fears.

Matthew 26:39.

"And going a little farther he fell on his face and prayed, saying, "My Father, if it be possible, let this cup pass from me; nevertheless, not as I will, but as you will."

PRAYER

Lord, I submit my will to You and I yield to Your will even when it seems to be a tedious task. You will always give me strength to push through.

NOTES

Jesus called out the Jewish religious leaders of His day for being hypocrites. Their actions were self-motivated and merely external. They sought to discredit Jesus' authority by showing He was breaking the Jewish tradition of the Elders, but at the same time they were far from God themselves. Furthermore, their teachings were from the tradition of men and not from God. Be aware of anything or anyone that puts works-based or empty, tradition-based gospels before you. Not only are human traditions ineffective for cleansing the heart, they lead to disregard for God's Word. God's gospel is the real change agent for cleansing the sinner's heart.

Mark 7:6-8.

"And he said to them, "Well did Isaiah prophesy of you hypocrites, as it is written, "'This people honors me with their lips, but their heart is far from me; in vain do they worship me, teaching as doctrines the commandments of men.' You leave the commandment of God and hold to the tradition of men."

PRAYER

Lord, help me to truly honor You not just with the words that I speak but let my life be a reflection of Christ living in me, in Jesus' name, amen.

NOTES ....

....
....
....
....
....
....
....
....
....

"Repent or Perish." Jesus almost always has compassion on those who suffer. But in this text, He does not intend for His point to be missed. As He was teaching, those present asked Him about two events not recorded elsewhere in scripture. They wanted to know if the Galileans killed by Pilate or those on whom the Tower of Siloam fell were killed because they were worse sinners than others. We often want to point to the sin of others and reason away our own sin. Jesus discredits this thinking. We must remember that all sinners need a savior, and only true repentance brings salvation. Will you turn from your sin and follow Him today? If you are already a follower of Jesus, will you share Him with others so they may know Him too?

Luke 13:2-5.

"And he answered them, "Do you think that these Galileans were worse sinners than all the other Galileans, because they suffered in this way? No, I tell you; but unless you repent, you will all likewise perish. Or those eighteen on whom the tower in Siloam fell and killed them: do you think that they were worse offenders than all the others who lived in Jerusalem? No, I tell you; but unless you repent, you will all likewise perish."

PRAYER

Lord, I repent of my sins today and I ask for Your forgiveness. Lord, help me to share my faith with everyone You bring my way, in Jesus' name, amen.

NOTES

WEEK 50 | WISDOM NUGGET

GOD'S GOT YOUR BACK

True peace begins when you know who is at the wheel. Relax, God's got your back. He knows the end of the year even before the beginning of that year. He is alpha and omega.

PRAYER

✓ Gracious Father, I choose to be at peace and let You have the wheel. I totally commit my life into Your hands O God. Do with me as it so pleases You, Father, in Jesus' name. Amen.

NOTES

....
....
....
....
....
....
....
....
....
....
....
....
....
....
....

When Jesus called Himself the bread of life, He was referring to His death on the cross. As He did often, He was using a physical object to teach a spiritual truth, which was frequently misunderstood. He was merging physical and spiritual truth. While Jesus is not literal bread, He is the spiritual bread that satisfies the spiritual hunger of those who believe in Him. His death on the cross completely satisfies the required payment for sin. Nothing more is needed. No matter the need in your life, be it physical, emotional or spiritual, Jesus has earned the right to be all you need. He overcame death, hell, and the grave when He laid His life down for you and then rose up from the grave victorious. Praise God for His all-sufficient providence. No matter your situation, He is the solution you need.

John 6:48.

"I am the bread of life."

PRAYER

Father, help us to truly desire You and You alone because in You we can find anything else we are looking for.

NOTES

Pastor Erik once said, "We don't do big-dealness around here." Jesus didn't put up with it either. In this passage, The Pharisees were well known for their pompous attitudes. Jesus always pointed out their external, self-motivated actions. They longed for the approval of men, which they often received. They didn't receive the same from God, for their gospel-void accomplishments were an eyesore before Him. Jesus knew who the Pharisees really were, and it was disgraceful. Their fame and fortune was found in the temporary praise of men. Let your big-dealness be found in Jesus; the benefits are eternal.

Luke 16:15.

"And he said to them, "You are those who justify yourselves before men, but God knows your hearts. For what is exalted among men is an abomination in the sight of God."

PRAYER

Lord, I open up my heart before You and I say cleanse me and purify me and make me holy, in Jesus' name, amen.

NOTES ....

....

....

....

....

....

....

....

....

....

Sometimes, it is hard to see God working; to see His Kingdom advancing. Like the Pharisees, we often want to see "signs" and "wonders" or hear a "word" from God before we trust Him and obey His plan. But Jesus said that cosmic signs wouldn't reveal the Kingdom of God. The Pharisees couldn't see their present reality. The Kingdom was already present in the person of Jesus, and it was being manifested in the lives of His followers. Our present reality is that He is still with us and He is still working in and through His people to advance His Kingdom. We can trust God and stand on His revealed Word – no special signs needed.

Luke 17:20-21.

"Being asked by the Pharisees when the kingdom of God would come, he answered them, "The kingdom of God is not coming in ways that can be observed, nor will they say, 'Look, here it is!' or 'There!' for behold, the kingdom of God is in the midst of you."

PRAYER

Lord, help me to see You working in our midst and be a part of the advancement of Your Kingdom, in Jesus' name, amen.

NOTES ....

Fear. Jesus addresses fear multiple times throughout the Bible. The message is often the same- "Don't allow fear to overtake you." Of course, He says this knowing that panic is often our first inclination and safety is our desire. And neither are they qualities of the faithful. We panic in the moment- forgetting who we are in the boat with. We cry out for safety when we should just be crying out to Him. And what does He give in return? He provides "a great calm." Pray for confidence in the One who controls the wind and the waves and brings peace in the middle of your great storms. He controls nature – He can meet your need too.

Mathew 8:25-26.

"And they went and woke him, saying, "Save us, Lord; we are perishing." And he said to them, "Why are you afraid, O you of little faith?" Then he rose and rebuked the winds and the sea, and there was a great calm."

PRAYER

Lord, I believe in Your awesome power to save and to deliver. I refuse to succumb to fear but I will trust in You, in Jesus' name, amen.

NOTES ....

....

....

....

....

....

....

....

....

....

There is a choice to be made: Chosen by God or loved by the world. According to Jesus, you cannot have the admiration of the world and the acceptance of Christ. Knowing this should bring us comfort when we are rejected and despised for the sake of Christ. The world's reaction to us serves as a gauge to where we are in our walk with Christ. If you find yourself seeking the approval and applause of this fallen world, you will easily receive it but the reward is temporary. However, if you intentionally seek to walk with Christ, expect the world to reject you, but know that His love is enough for you and it is eternal. "Choose you this day whom you will serve…"

John 15:19.

"If you were of the world, the world would love you as its own; but because you are not of the world, but I chose you out of the world, therefore the world hates you."

PRAYER

Lord, I thank You that You have chosen me and separated me from this world. I keep my eyes on You when the world hates me and I know that I will get a crown in the end, in Jesus' name, amen.

NOTES ....

....

....

....

....

....

....

....

....

....

As God by His Word commanded light into the darkness in the beginning, we as followers of Christ are to be light into this darkened world. The truth that is shown in us, cuts through the lies the world has swallowed and offers the only hope of reconciliation to a loving, merciful, and perfect God. The light that shines from within us is Christ Himself. He is alive and working in our hearts. Changing us. Healing us. Conforming us to the perfect image of Himself. How can we hide such good news, such beauty and truth? We cant. "A city set on a hill cannot be hidden." Let your light shine brightly and fully. Rejoice that you can offer a picture of hope to this darkened world.

Matthew 5:14-16.

"You are the light of the world. A city set on a hill cannot be hidden. Nor do people light a lamp and put it under a basket, but on a stand, and it gives light to all in the house. In the same way, let your light shine before others, so that they may see your good works and give glory to your Father who is in heaven."

PRAYER

Father, I thank You for making me the light of the world. Let my life be a shining light for the world to look and see Jesus through me, in Jesus' name, amen.

NOTES

WEEK 51 | WISDOM NUGGET

FIRST THINGS FIRST

Jesus said go and make disciples. He never said go and make church members. So when talking to people, "Come to our CHURCH," must not be your goal. But the truth is, when DISCIPLESHIP takes due course, CHURCH MEMBERSHIP is inevitable.

PRAYER

✓ Lord, let my goal for speaking to anyone about You be to see the salvation of their souls. Lord, I pray that we will not be carried away by the need to grow our church membership that we now forget the need for the people to really encounter You.

NOTES

....
....
....
....
....
....
....
....
....
....
....
....
....

So often we set our sights and hearts on earthly desires. The priceless treasure that Christ offers is hidden to carnal man, and is of no profit to him. Only those that are in Christ can truly know the infinite value of the Kingdom of God. Only in rightly seeing His majesty can we take our focus off of worldly ambitions. The treasures of this world will inevitably rust and fall away, but what Christ has purchased with His blood is eternal! What choice will you make? Will you be the wealthy young ruler who refuses to give up his possessions, or will you be the merchant and trade it all for him? Trust in what God has promised, and what Christ has bought. A ton of gold pales in comparison to an eternity with Him.

Matthew 13:44-46.

"The kingdom of heaven is like treasure hidden in a field, which a man found and covered up. Then in his joy he goes and sells all that he has and buys that field. Again, the kingdom of heaven is like a merchant in search of fine pearls, who, on finding one pearl of great value, went and sold all that he had and bought it."

PRAYER

Lord, help me to set my heart on heaven and not keep pursuing earthly things and lose sight of the treasure called heaven.

NOTES

There is a general call to repentance that brings forth many claiming to be followers of Christ. The reality is that, in our church. we are a mixture of those who are truly in Christ and those who are not.

As followers we are to endure with patience and longsuffering in the promise that His sheep will answer the shepherds call. Only those called by God's "effectual" call will be saved from the "fiery furnace".

One group, a heavenly reward of eternity with God. The other, those who gnash their teeth in angry defiance and those who weep in eternal separation from God. Ours is not the job to determine who is Christ's and who is not. God is a perfect judge and we are incapable of rightly considering our own hearts, how then can we see into another's? There will be plenty of brothers and sisters who I would have had no doubt of salvation that will be missing in God's kingdom, and plenty whom I would have easily condemned to hell that will worship Christ for eternity.

Matthew 13: 47-50.

"Again, the kingdom of heaven is like a net that was thrown into the sea and gathered fish of every kind. When it was full, men drew it ashore and sat down and sorted the good into containers but threw away the bad. So it will be at the end of the age. The angels will come out and separate the evil from the righteous and throw them into the fiery furnace. In that place there will be weeping and gnashing of teeth."

PRAYER

Father, may You open the ears of Your people to hear the call You are making for them to come into Your Kingdom so that they can escape the punishment that is coming at the end of time.

NOTES ....

....
....
....
....
....
....
....
....
....

Satan has been blinding mankind and the nations since the fall in the garden. Upon the arrival of Jesus, Satan knew his time was at hand. The first beings to recognize Christ were the demons. They knew who He truly was, even if His followers at the time did not. After the temptation of Christ in the desert, the final act of destroying Satan's hold had begun. God's plan cannot, and will not, be stopped by anyone of His creatures. His plan is perfect, His plan is complete, and His plan is just. Once we are in Christ we now have the power of the Holy Spirit to engage the enemy in the battle against evil. But, be careful to not focus on things accomplished by the Spirit through you in this age. The real joy, the true blessing is spending eternity in complete communion with God. If you are in Christ, and He in you, your name is written in the Lamb's book of life. And nothing can blot that out.

Luke 10:17-20.

"The seventy-two returned with joy, saying, "Lord, even the demons are subject to us in your name!" And he said to them, "I saw Satan fall like lightning from heaven. Behold, I have given you authority to tread on serpents and scorpions, and over all the power of the enemy, and nothing shall hurt you. Nevertheless, do not rejoice in this, that the spirits are subject to you, but rejoice that your names are written in heaven.""

PRAYER

Lord, I walk in power and dominion over the devil and I maintain the consciousness that Satan has fallen.

NOTES

The combined wisdom of the human race still falls impossibly short of comprehending the mind of God and the secrets of heaven. To see God without the hindrance of sin, and experience Him as He truly is in all His glory will be the eternal reward of all of those who are in Christ, and Christ in them. "Who has ascended to heaven and come down?" (Proverbs 30:4) Only Christ has the right to enter heaven, for heaven is His home, and His Kingdom. Jesus was not created at the time of His birth. Christ has existed for eternity as the Son with perfect communion with God the Father and the Holy Spirit. The only way for us, humans, tainted with sin, to enter into His Kingdom was for Him to become fully human and to live a perfect life. To become the perfect sacrifice, and take on the sin of those who were predestined from the foundation of the world to be called adopted children of God. For that perfect lamb to be lifted up, up on a tree and become sin. Upon that man, who was upon that tree, God poured out His wrath and Jesus bore that cup. He bore that wrath for me, a sinner made clean by His precious blood, so I may have eternal life with Him.

John 3:13-15.

"No one has ascended into heaven except he who descended from heaven, the Son of Man. And as Moses lifted up the serpent in the wilderness, so must the Son of Man be lifted up, that whoever believes in him may have eternal life."

PRAYER

Lord Jesus, I thank You for coming to die in my place and reconciling me back to God. I choose to trust You and Your saving power that You will lead me into heaven.

NOTES ....

....

....

....

....

....

....

....

....

....

The finished work of Christ has afforded us the ability to worship God anywhere and everywhere. God is not limited to geographic location, nor to a day of the week. And, importantly, worship is not limited to race, creed, gender or ethnicity. Our worship should exist at all times, and wherever we may be. Those of us in Christ enjoy a communion not limited by time or space, for we have the Holy Spirit In us. He is a part of us, a part that cannot be separated. The Holy Spirit intercedes for us, helping us, growing us, sanctifying us. Worshiping in truth without the spirit is not true worship, as is spirit with no truth. We must do both. How do we worship in truth? By learning the truth from God's Word. How do we worship in spirit? By allowing God's Word to penetrate our hearts, changing us and conforming us to the image of Jesus Christ.

John 4:24.

"God is spirit, and those who worship him must worship in spirit and truth."

PRAYER

Father, I thank You for choosing me to be Your child. I pray that You take away every filthiness from me and make me holy so I can worship You in truth and holiness, in Jesus' name, amen.

NOTES

In our modern culture we think hard work is our key to success. We, as Christians, can tend to apply that same principle to our salvation and Christian walk. It can manifest itself in the form of legalistic practices to try and "earn" grace. If success in life comes from effort and hard work then we can simply carry that over into our religion, right? No. There is no amount of blood, sweat or tears from us to justify our salvation. Our salvation Is a gift, not earned or paid back. We are incapable of such holiness on our own, and there is nothing in us that is at all desirable to God. If our salvation was up to us, to gain or keep, we could not ever have any hope of seeing God. Christ took our sin on the cross, and only because He is holy and perfect are we saved. In exchange for our sin, we received His righteousness. The reformers called it an "alien" righteousness, because it does not belong to us. There was blood, sweat, and tears used to secure our salvation, but it was not ours. The only thing we must do, is to believe and repent. Believe in Him whom He has sent, and that is Jesus Christ.

John 6:28-29.

"Then they said to him, "What must we do, to be doing the works of God?" Jesus answered them, "This is the work of God, that you believe in him whom he has sent."

PRAYER

Heavenly Father, I believe in Your Son, Jesus Christ, that You sent Him to die in my place, to save me from sin and that He is coming back to take me home. Lord, help those who have not believed to also know this truth.

NOTES ....

....

....

....

....

....

....

....

....

....

WEEK 52 | WISDOM NUGGET

GIVE HONOR TO WHO IT IS DUE

God is no respecter of persons but man is. That's why to man God's Word says: "Give to everyone what you owe them: If you owe taxes, pay taxes; if revenue, then revenue; if respect, then respect; if honor, then honor. (Rom 13:7). We must not use this statement to cover up for our arrogance. God expects His children to be very respectful and of a gentle spirit.

PRAYER

- ✓ Merciful Father, we humbly ask for Your mercy in all the instances we have been arrogant, thinking we were acting in accordance with Your Word.
- ✓ Father, from this day on, I will give respect to those who deserve it, in Jesus' name, Amen.

NOTES

....

....

....

....

....

....

....

....

....

Read John 15:9-11. What a promise from our Lord! Fullness of joy, everlasting, and abundant. The same love God has for His Son, Christ has for those of us that abide in Him. How does one abide in Christ? My favorite definition of "abide" is conform. When we conform to Christ, we are being "fashioned" into the image of Him. Being made into Him, and patterning ourselves after Him. The closer a relationship we have with Christ, the more we desire what He desires and the more we cling to Him, the more we let go of the world. We must continually, and intentionally, pursue a more perfect relationship in His perfect love by keeping His commandments. And what were Christ's commandments? Love God with all your heart, all your soul, and all your mind. But don't forget the second part: love your neighbor as you love yourself. Christ, by implication, is telling us that there is no other source of true joy; that everything this world has to offer pales in comparison. Let us continually seek to abide in Him deeper, and deeper and experience the joy that surpasses all human understanding.

John 15:9-11.

"As the Father has loved me, so have I loved you. Abide in my love. If you keep my commandments, you will abide in my love, just as I have kept my Father's commandments and abide in his love. These things I have spoken to you, that my joy may be in you, and that your joy may be full."

PRAYER

Lord, I thank You for loving me unconditionally. I receive grace to obey Your Word and as I do that I know You will give me fullness of joy.

NOTES

Where does our sin come from? Are we made sinful from what we eat or from our environment? Jesus answered this question in Mark 7: 14-15:14 "And He called the people to Him again and said to them, "Hear me, all of you, and understand: There is nothing outside a person that by going into him can defile him, but the things that come out of a person are what defile him."

Our sin comes from inside, it is a manifestation, or an outpouring of our will, of our sinful hearts. If we believe that sin is strictly from our environment, then we cannot be held liable for what we do. Scripture makes it abundantly clear that each and every one of us is responsible for our own sin. As it has been said, "The heart is the heart of the problem." As we see in the following verses, God is telling Peter that the Gospel of Jesus Christ is to be given not only to the Jews, but also to the Gentiles. The Good news of Jesus Christ was never intended to be kept with Jewish people alone. God's plan of salvation was meant to go to all corners of the earth. Remember, sin starts in the heart. When we continually struggle with sin we need to examine our hearts and seek to deepen our relationship with Jesus Christ. The problem will always be on our end, not His.

Acts 10:11-15.

"And saw the heavens opened and something like a great sheet descending, being let down by its four corners upon the earth. In it were all kinds of animals and reptiles and birds of the air. And there came a voice to him: "Rise, Peter; kill and eat." But Peter said, "By no means, Lord; for I have never eaten anything that is common or unclean." And the voice came to him again a second time, "What God has made clean, do not call common.""

PRAYER

Heavenly Father, I thank You for including me in Your plan of Salvation. Lord I pray that Your mercy will also reach out to all who are yet to know You, in Jesus' name, amen.

NOTES ....

....

....

....

....

....

....

....

....

PHOTO *Galery*

About this Book
ABOUT THE AUTHOR
BEWARE OF ANOTHER GOSPEL
50
BEFORE YOU SAY
"YES"
TEMPERAMENTS
EVANG. GILB